AF843200

AI MARKETING ESSENTIALS

AI Marketing Essentials: Concepts and Practice for the Digital Age explores the dynamic intersection of AI technology and marketing, providing theoretical frameworks for understanding its fast-growing potential in the development and implementation of successful marketing strategies.

By guiding the reader through the principles, tools, and techniques of AI in marketing, this comprehensive textbook will help readers understand how they can leverage AI to transform different marketing functions throughout the lifecycle of a product, from initial strategy to product development, pricing, and distribution. This book combines theoretical understanding with insights from industry to reinforce learning, featuring real-life examples and case studies from different industries and countries across the world. In the first section, the book introduces the AI marketing discipline and how it has evolved. It explains the fundamental AI concepts such as machine learning, big data, NLP, and algorithms, which are crucial to understanding how they work.

In further sections, the applications of these technologies are explored and explained in various marketing functions through case studies from multiple industries and concepts from marketing and technology. The application of these functions across retail, products, service, and business-to-business operations is then explored, followed by a critical discussion of the social and ethical dimensions and future directions for the use of AI in marketing.

An accessible guide for understanding the AI marketing space, this book will suit undergraduate and postgraduate students as well as marketing professionals looking to build foundational knowledge in the concepts and impact of AI in marketing.

Jagdish N. Sheth is a renowned scholar and a global thought leader. He has been awarded the Padma Bhushan Award. The award is India's highest civilian award for non-resident Indians (NRI), literature, and education. He has published more than 300 research papers and 30 books across various disciplines and is the Charles H. Kellstadt Professor of Business at Emory University's Goizueta Business School.

Varsha Jain is the professor of marketing at ESSCA School of Management, France, and is co-editor of the Journal of Consumer Behavior and associate editor for Psychology and Marketing. She has received multiple awards and authored over 180 publications, including papers in A* and A journals and books worldwide.

AI MARKETING ESSENTIALS

Concepts and Practice for the Digital Age

Jagdish N. Sheth and Varsha Jain

Routledge
Taylor & Francis Group
LONDON AND NEW YORK

Designed cover image: Shutterstock

First edition published 2026
by Routledge
4 Park Square, Milton Park, Abingdon, Oxon, OX14 4RN

and by Routledge
605 Third Avenue, New York, NY 10158

Routledge is an imprint of the Taylor & Francis Group, an informa business

British Library Cataloguing-in-Publication Data
A catalogue record for this book is available from the British Library

ISBN: 978-1-032-81883-2 (hbk)
ISBN: 978-1-032-81231-1 (pbk)
ISBN: 978-1-003-50186-2 (ebk)

DOI: 10.4324/9781003501862

Typeset in Times New Roman
by SPi Technologies India Pvt Ltd (Straive)

Access the Support Material: www.routledge.com/9781032812311

To our spouses, kids, families, friends, and colleagues, who are strong foundations in our lives.

I especially want to thank my son, Goransh Thakur, and my husband, Bibhuti Thakur, for their consistent help and support and for being the strong pillars in my life.

Varsha Jain

Dedicated to Professor Philip Kotler, who has been my mentor and supporter for more than 50 years.

Jagdish Sheth

CONTENTS

ACKNOWLEDGEMENTS

We sincerely acknowledge the support extended by Prutha Shah (Postdoctoral Fellow, MICA, India), Samarth Jain (Goizueta Business School, Emory University, USA), Parth Salunke (Assistant Professor of Marketing, FLAME University, India), and Kush Mehta (Doctoral Scholar, MICA, India). Their assistance, thoughtful inputs, and research support contributed meaningfully to the development of this book. We are grateful for the time and effort they generously shared throughout this journey.

ABOUT THE AUTHORS

Jagdish N. Sheth is Charles H. Kellstadt Professor of Business in the Goizueta Business School at Emory University. He is globally known for his scholarly contributions in consumer behavior, relationship marketing, competitive strategy, and geopolitical analysis. Professor Sheth has over 50 years of combined experience in teaching and research at the University of Southern California, the University of Illinois at Urbana-Champaign, Columbia University, MIT, and Emory University.

Dr. Sheth is a recipient of the 2020 Padma Bhushan Award for literature and education, one of the highest civilian awards given by the Government of India. He is also a fellow of the Academy of International Business (AIB); fellow of the Association of Consumer Research (ACR); fellow of the American Psychological Association (APA); fellow of the American Marketing Association (AMA); distinguished fellow of the Academy of Marketing Science (AMS); and a distinguished fellow of International Engineering Consortium. Dr. Sheth is the recipient of an honorary doctorate in Science, awarded by the University of Illinois at Urbana-Champaign (2016), and honorary doctorate of Philosophy, awarded by Shiv Nadar University (2017). He is the recipient of all four top awards given by the American Marketing Association (AMA).

Dr. Sheth has been on the board of several companies including Norstan, Pacwest-Telecom, Cryocell International, Shasun Drugs and Chemicals, and WIPRO Limited. Over the 50 years, he has been an advisor to numerous companies including Whirlpool, Motorola, Texas Instruments, Cox Communications, Rockwell International, AT&T, Bellsouth, WIPRO Consumer Care, Aditya Birla Group, L.M. Mittal (Avanta), E&Y, Square D, Ingram Micro, Hughes Corporation, and others. This has included mergers and acquisitions as well as strategic positioning or repositioning of the company.

His Rule of Three book has been the foundation for investment bankers and policymakers with respect to industry consolidation including horizontal mergers and acquisitions. Professor Sheth has authored or co-authored more than 300 papers and several books including *The Global Rule of Three: Competing with Conscious Strategy* (2020), *The Howard-Sheth Theory of Buyer Behavior* (2020), *Genes, Climate and Consumption Culture: Connecting the Dots* (2017), *Breakout Strategies for Emerging Markets* (2016), *The Sustainability Edge* (2016), *The 4 As of Marketing* (2012), *Chindia Rising* (2011),

Self-Destructive Habits of Good Companies (2007), *Firms of Endearment* (2007), *Tectonic Shift* (2006), *The Rule of Three* (2002), *and Clients for Life* (2000). His autobiography, *The Accidental Scholar* (2014), has inspired others in the areas of education and academic entrepreneurship.

Professor Sheth has been an advisor to the Government of Singapore in repositioning the nation for the future. He has also been the policy advisor to the US Government about the future of the telecommunications industry.

Dr. Sheth is the Founder of Center for Telecommunications Management (CTM) at the University of Southern California (USC) which has now become an institute. He is also the Founder and Chairman of India, China, and America (ICA) Institute which analyzes the trilateral relationship and its impact on geopolitics, security, trade, and investment. He and his wife, Madhu Sheth, have established the Sheth Family Foundation to support several charities in India and in the United States. They have also established the Madhuri and Jagdish Sheth Foundation to support scholars and scholarship in the field of marketing. The Sheth Foundation supports the AMA-Sheth Foundation Doctoral Consortium, hosted annually by different universities. It also supports research in emerging fields through AMA, ACR, AMS, and AIB. Finally, Professor Sheth is the Founder and Chairman of the Academy of Indian Marketing (AIM), which supports research and scholarship among Indian scholars in marketing and management.

Prof. Varsha Jain is the Professor of Marketing, ESSCA School of Management, Paris, France. She is the co-editor-in-chief of the *Journal of Consumer Behaviour* (JCB, "A" Journal) and an associate editor at *Psychology and Marketing* ("A" Journal), and co-track chairperson for consumer behavior at the Academy of Marketing Science, USA, the annual conference, 2026. She has authored over 185+ publications, including multiple papers in A* and A journals, such as the *European Journal of Marketing*, the *International Journal of Information Management*, the *Journal of Advertising Research*, and the *Journal of Business Research*.

She has received over 30 international and national awards and gold medals in scholarship. The most recent is the Research Award – Professor, Springer Nature, India, 2025; 2024 Best Paper award for a special session held at Winter AMA 2024 at AMA Annual Conference, USA, 2024; the Best Methodology Paper Award at Newcastle University along with Lanchester University Management School and Brunel University, UK (2023) at Marketing, Strategy, and Policy (MSP) Conference, UK; and Best Paper (Runner-up) award for a special session held at Winter AMA 2023 at AMA Annual Conference, USA.

In her global research career, she is a visiting guest at Emory Business School, Atlanta; Michigan State University; and the University of Washington, USA; and a visiting scholar at Greenwich University, London, and The Medill School, Northwestern University, USA. Her interests are consumer behavior and digital marketing, primarily newer technologies, including Artificial Intelligence (Al), Augmented Reality, Virtual Reality, and Metaverse. She is also the co-editor of numerous special issues on AI, digital, and social media marketing. She has co-authored books with Prof. Jag Sheth related to Consumer Behavior, AI and Services, Customer Services in Digital Context, Customer Relationship Marketing in the Digital Age, Disruption and Innovation in Branding, Qualitative Research in the Digital World, Brand India, and Purpose-Driven Branding with Prof. David Aaker. With these global legends, she is working on more books on AI, marketing, and global digital consumer behavior.

1

INTRODUCTION

Learning Objectives

Having studied this chapter, you are expected to be able to:

1 Explain the evolution of AI and explain its core concepts
2 Understand the benefits of using AI in marketing, including personalization, measurement, creativity, and efficiency.
3 Distinguish between types of AI used in marketing management
4 Identify the key role of AI in Marketing
5 Analyze the role of AI in transforming marketing through automation, enablement, and stakeholder empowerment.

OPENING CASE: REVOLUTIONIZING CUSTOMER EXPERIENCES—WALMART'S AI-DRIVEN MARKETING

Walmart is a well-known retail company that embraces new ways of improving customer experiences through inbound marketing and innovation. Walmart has grown from a small discount store to a global giant. The company's unwavering dedication to new ideas is at the heart of technological advancement and adoption, with artificial intelligence leading the way (Marr, 2024). The marketing plan of Walmart remains strongly embedded in the idea of artificial intelligence, which is currently focused on its agentic AI system, the Sparky, Marty, Associate, and Developer framework, improving personalization, pricing, supply chain efficiency, and customer services. Pricing is now powered by AI-driven dynamic pricing models, and it has helped the company to reach net sales of the enterprise, which were about $648 billion in Financial Year (FY) 2025, showing a 5% rise compared to the recent year. Retailers have always had to be careful with prices, and Walmart is no different. Retailers work hard to keep their prices ahead of their competitors while maximizing profitability. Walmart used

DOI: 10.4324/9781003501862-1

AI-enabled dynamic pricing. To make price changes in real time, these AI systems churn through vast amounts of data, such as prices from competitors, market trends, customer demand, and even weather patterns (Mohan, 2021). In the long run, AI driven With a long-term view, AI-powered dynamic pricing can help retain customers by offering personalized or time-sensitive deals that align with their preferences and purchase behavior. When implemented alongside transparent communication and a sense of fairness, such pricing strategies enhance trust and satisfaction (Jasrotia, 2023. Research has shown that customers are more likely to return when they perceive pricing to be clear and equitable, reinforcing brand loyalty and enabling repeat business. Walmart leverages vast amounts of customer data—such as purchase history, loyalty program participation, and digital interactions—to enable these pricing decisions (Roden et al., 2017). This data not only drives more accurate, real-time pricing but also informs demand forecasting, which helps Walmart optimize its supply chain to ensure that desired products are available when and where customers need them.

Another key marketing lesson from Walmart is its ability to adapt quickly to change. The retail giant continues to demonstrate agility by rapidly innovating through advancements in AI. By analyzing purchase history, browsing habits, and social media interactions, these online platforms offer a seamless, customized experience to each customer based on their needs and preferences (Başev, 2024). Unlocking the power of generative AI, the company used chatbots to provide customer support and went a step ahead by using conversational commerce to negotiate with its suppliers (Van Hoek et al., 2022). The case of Walmart becoming strategic with AI will present an interesting idea about how marketing can be transformed in the digital age, using technology. Through dynamic pricing, hyper-personalization, real-time inventory optimization, and conversational commerce, among many other areas, the company has been able to incorporate AI right throughout its marketing value chain. Such efforts have not only made customers' experience enjoyable but have also made huge business improvements. Walmart, as a retailer that resisted the change of nature of the retail industry but turned to innovation to continue playing a competitive role in the market, is a strong beginning point for discussing the overall contribution of artificial intelligence to contemporary marketing and advertising. Because of the ever-evolving landscape of a digital market, Walmart appears as a bright example of how AI can change many things (Cao, 2021).

Understanding Marketing Management

Marketing is the most direct business activity that aims to recognize, predict, and fulfil customer demands at a profit. Kotler and Armstrong (2018) state that marketing seeks to win new clients by promising to offer greater value and serve returning ones by providing a constant sense of satisfaction. Technology has emerged as a key enabler toward the realization of such goals in the fast-moving and highly dynamic digital economy. Zappo's is an online retailer that uses technology to deliver exceptional customer service through free shipping, easy returns, and personalized support.

The Role of Technology in Modern Marketing

Marketers have had their work revolutionized by technological instruments such as data analytics, customer relationship management technology, artificial intelligence

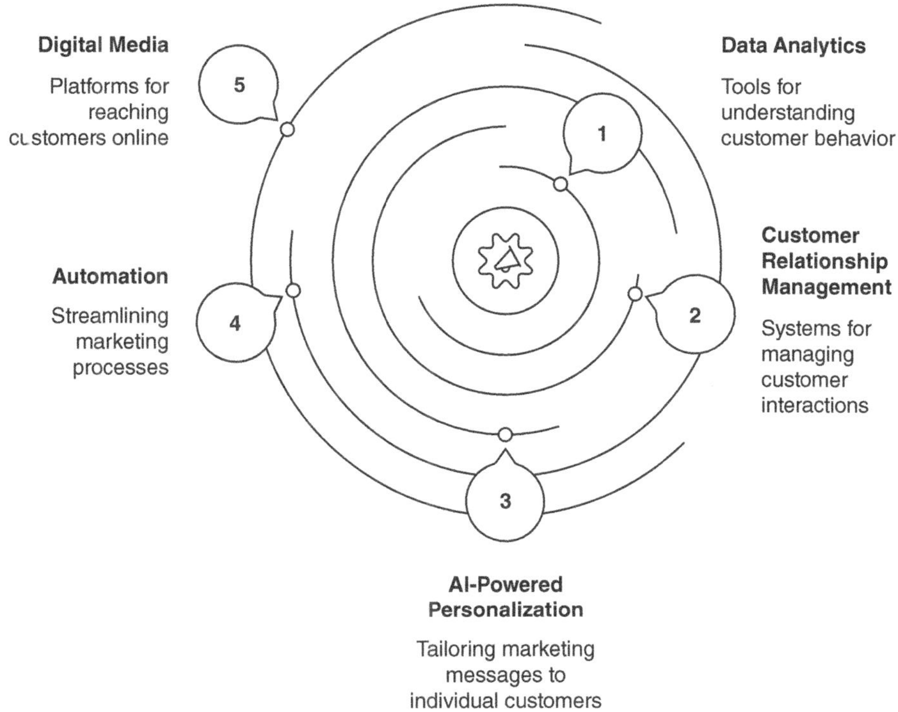

FIGURE 1.1 Evolution of marketing with Tech-AI.

(AI)-powered personalization, and automation (Jain, 2017). Although the conventional wide-scale media, such as the print media, contributed immensely in the past, the emergence of the digital medium has transformed the marketing world. Increasing competition and consumer expectations make it no longer optional anymore to use technology as a platform; actually, it is the platform itself. Domino's showcases this transformation by integrating AI, GPS tracking, and mobile apps to personalize orders and enhance delivery experiences, turning technology into its primary marketing platform (Figure 1.1).

The Shift Toward Data-Driven Strategies

The decision of marketing used to be mostly based on intuition, previous experiences, and generalization of demographics. However, with the advent of digital tools and AI, there has been a major change in this way of working, data-driven strategies, which allow marketers to make more accurate and measurable but also more personalized decisions (McKinsey, 2021). The main aspects of this shift include:

Today, marketers are basing their decisions on data, including consumer behaviors, purchasing trends of consumers, and performance metrics for campaigns, and this helps them to follow the evidence and make offering decisions that they can act on quickly, allowing for greater and more predictable resource allocation.

Granular Consumer describes knowing that marketing decisions can be based on the capabilities of analyzing tracking individual-level data, for example browsing behavior within a website, transaction history with the brand, and social media behavior or engagement to reveal a more specific brand perspective on more nuanced customer insights. Understanding these tactics leads to significantly more engagement and conversion rates (Northbeam, 2024).

Personalization at Scale: Spotify brands that leverages past listening history to produce playlists for its users. One good example is the "Discover Weekly" playlists created originally by using the AI-enabled personalization engines.

Improved Targeting and Segmentation: Data unlocks the opportunity for brands to micro-segment the audience. A beauty retailer, KICKS (Sweden), for example, uses its customer relationship management (CRM) data to personalize messages to its members, like to remind them of their available unused rewards or to surface promotions for products not in their preferred promotional views.

Real-Time Optimization and Agility: Analytics now enables brands to make instantaneous adjustments to campaigns. Google, for instance, uses click measurement of ads and reviews to drive the search results and advertising campaign, as the behavior of users changes the metrics (McKinsey, 2021).

Integration of Data Sources: This report touches on using platforms, i.e. Segment and Tealium, used by Woolworths Supermarket, Australia, as there are many other tools to connect the online data, CRMs, email platforms, and social media to form one single view of the customer, which enables consistent messaging and communications and an easy omnichannel experience.

AI in Marketing

AI is the process by which a machine, especially a computer system, simulates human cognitive functions such as learning (acquiring information and rules for using it), reasoning (using the rules to reach approximate or definite conclusions), and self-correction. AI includes various sub-domains, such as machine learning (ML), natural language processing (NLP), computer vision, robotics, and expert systems (Russell & Norvig, 2020). A personal styling service brand Stich Fix, USA, uses AI and ML to analyze customer preferences.

What Is AI? Its Evolution?

The concept of AI dates to 1956 when Alan Turing, a pioneer in computer science, proposed the Turing Test to assess whether a machine could exhibit human-like intelligence (Guo, 2015). The term "artificial intelligence" was formally introduced in 1955 at the Dartmouth Summer Research Project, where researchers aimed to develop machines that could solve problems and learn from data. AI has changed over the years, and its more recent developments have changed the discipline of marketing because of improved consumer insights, real-time personalization, predictive analytics, automated campaigns, and enhanced customer engagement strategies (Davenport et al., 2019).

AI has its conceptual roots in the 1940s with the advent of digital computers and early work by Alan Turing. However, the term "artificial intelligence" was formally coined in 1956 at the Dartmouth Conference, led by McCarthy and colleagues. This event marked the official beginning of AI as a distinct research field (Russell & Norvig, 2020). After a slowdown in the 1970s, AI research picked up again with the development of expert systems like MYCIN, a Medical Informatics Computer Program that mimicked human

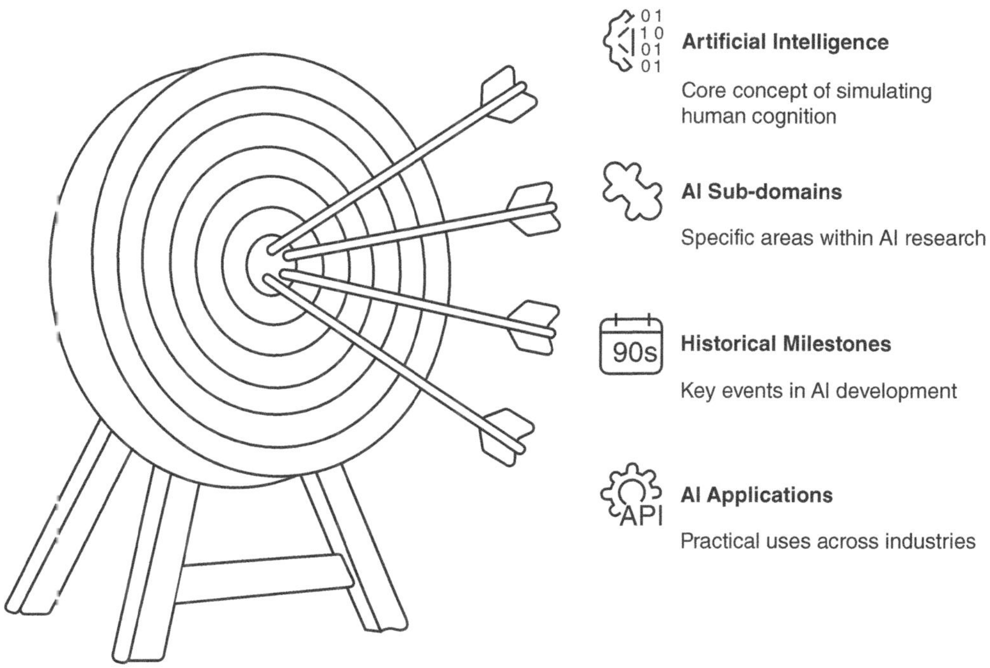

FIGURE 1.2 Marketing growth.

decision-making in specific fields. By the 1980s, AI saw a shift toward ML, where systems could improve performance by learning from data. This marked the beginning of AI's growing commercial use, setting the stage for today's data-driven, intelligent technologies.

In the 21st century, development in AI technology has continued to increase exponentially; for instance, from narrow AI, which can perform essential functions such as text editing, to the most advanced AI like GPT-3 and AlphaGo (Radanliev, 2024). The future of AI is bright, and the most important milestone is that it has become an integral part of human lives and revolutionized sectors across industries. It has recently become a lot more popular among users compared to what was expected at the launch. Also, AI can generate better insights because it has access to user-generated data. For example, data from autonomous cars like Tesla, smart speakers, and virtual assistants like Alexa Echo and Google Assistant (S et al., 2021). Marketers utilize AI systems in many ways and can perform marketing tasks, including creating products, retail, pricing, and advertising, far more effectively. AI for Marketing was first used in the 1990s to build customer relationship management systems (Ozay et al., 2024). These tools employ customer-based analytics, track how people interact with an organization in general, and assist in targeting marketing messages to them. Additional AI technologies entered the marketing infrastructure over time, enabling predictive analytics, an advanced understanding and forecasting of consumer behavior, and greater operational efficiency in inventory management and ad placement areas. The ability of direct human interaction with the employment of chatbots and smart speakers currently drives the practical use case of AI. Additionally, AI generates individualized content, delivers projects, finalizes purchases, and aids individuals. It has the ability to mitigate global issues like poverty and climate change, apart from business-related issues (Figure 1.2).

Digital Transformation and Marketing

Marketing has undergone many phases. It started with the Production Era (late 1800s–1920s), which was all about mass production efficiency based on the premise that supply equals demand. Then the Sales Era (1920s–1950s), where aggressive selling and promoting took the place of customary demand. Now came the Marketing Era (1950s–1990s), which flipped marketing from selling and promoting to understanding the characteristics that compose customer needs and customer wants, and using market research and a marketing mix to better satisfy both needs and wants. Next: the Relationship Era (1990s–2000s) recognized that business processes thrive when they can efficiently create long-term relationships with customers, and they take their social responsibility into account. The transition from the Relationship Era to the Digital Transformation Era (2000s) was a journey, not an event. It started with digitization, the transition to digital information from analogue information (e.g., scanning a brochure to digital form, rather than printing). Then it continued on to digitalization, where technology tools helped improve business processes (for instance, using email marketing, rather than direct mail). Finally, we experienced the manifestation of digital transformation as a strategic evolution from the previous two elements (digitization and digitalization) to rethink how businesses create value for customers utilizing technology. Examples of digital transformation are numerous and changing frequently. Amazon can analyze real-time data to dynamically modify prices, Netflix uses algorithms to personalize content delivery, Starbucks merges its customer-facing mobile app with its loyalty program to provide optimal interaction when customers are in-store, etc. Digital transformation isn't about using technology tools; it's about creating a cultural shift.

Benefits of AI in Marketing

According to Huang & Rust (2020), AI is causing a displacement in marketing as it assists organizations in understanding customer needs and wants by analyzing vast amounts of data. This deeper insight allows for increased personalization, enhanced customer satisfaction, and more targeted communications methods across media. For instance, e-commerce entities such as Amazon track browsing and purchasing habits to present specific recommendations, and Pandora uses AI algorithms to determine and curate music playlists according to a customer's listening tendencies. AI enhances customer acquisition and retention by improving campaign performance, forecasting churn, and providing real-time feedback as chatbots. In marketing operations, AI simplifies content creation, assists in allocating advertising budgets, and includes predictive analytics to improve customer service. Larger firms benefit by building their own AI system, allowing them to control customer data more directly, which maximizes compliance with privacy obligations and facilitates competitive differentiation among customer bases. By just using AI in a given strategy, entities can gain an edge over their competitors, increasing engagement across social media channels, determining what data indicates actionable insight from millions of data points, and even forecasting future market demand with improved accuracy.

Increased Returns

AI can help in increasing the return on investment in marketing activities. It has helped in reducing costs by replacing various roles, such as acting as a virtual assistant and analyzing live data to get insights for decision-making (Dwivedi et al., 2019).

Although the initial cost of AI may be high, its long-term benefits can be substantial and usually outweigh the monetary effects, especially for larger firms. Over time, AI aids in maximizing resource use and increasing efficiency, which allows for better utilization of marketing budgets and significant savings (Lee et al., 2022). Once these savings are reinvested into internal capabilities around AI, firms can gain a competitive advantage and accelerate innovation. AI also allows firms to better understand their customers. This enables firms to have a customized marketing strategy and achieve improved return on investment. For example, H&M utilizes AI-powered chatbots to provide styling suggestions and customer service that enhance their customers' shopping experience while promoting engagement and reducing operational costs (Zahair, 2024).

Enhanced Measurement

The conventional methods for measuring and evaluating the efficiency and productivity of marketing strategies are becoming less effective. A key challenge in traditional approaches is the reliance on data processing, which is not only time-consuming but also prone to errors. This limitation can be addressed by leveraging AI-driven data analytics tools, which enable the rapid and accurate evaluation of large datasets, enhancing decision-making and overall marketing performance (Uddin & Hossan, 2024). These tools have numerous other benefits, like analyzing consumer engagement at each touchpoint and gaining deeper insights using real-time analysis of customer interactions. AI can also assess and determine which customer interactions are most useful for each person, and then managers can use those resources to their full potential. In addition, marketers can improve their decision-making for current and future marketing efforts by gaining clear and actionable understandings. For example, Amazon uses big data of its customer, their shopping history, and cart history to create offers, provide discounts, coupon codes, and discount vouchers (Alrumiah & Hadwan, 2021).

Hyper-personalization

While traditional segmentation methods based on geography, gender, education, and class continue to hold value, especially in culturally diverse markets, advancements in AI have introduced more dynamic and behavior-based segmentation approaches that allow for deeper personalization and predictive targeting (Kumar et al., 2024). With the continuous improvement of marketing dynamics, hyper-personalization is the way forward to delight each customer. AI empowers marketers to create a personalized experience that each consumer resonates with profoundly. AI is helping transform all kinds of information, including browsing behavior, social media, purchase history, and demographic information, into impactful, multidimensional customer profiles. The demographic profile is essential because it provides context, but AI has taken us beyond the multi-dimensional profile to recognize behavioral patterns, purchasing preferences, and real-time needs. This allows for extremely personalized marketing methods, where products, messages, and content are specific to each consumer journey.

Internet AI is also able to produce content in accordance with the preferences of the consumer and give them hyper-personalized, real-time communication. It assists brands to go the extra mile in satisfying the customer and make them experience something memorable to remain loyal and satisfied. Cadbury employed AI deepfakes in India, where it developed personalized promotion content to its distributors and retailers in the festive season. Retailers would need to input their information, and an ad with an Indian film actor, Shah Rukh Khan, will be produced to promote their store to aid in engaging stakeholders and connecting with the customers (Yadav, 2024).

Better Decision-Making

As consumers have more and more choices to engage with their time, they are becoming more reliant on intelligent systems to create efficient decision pathways. AI, for example, can empower consumers to make informed purchase decisions that are relevant, bespoke, and timely. Utilizing large content data sets of consumer behavior can allow a brand to demonstrate options they would have typically approached, using data points like their previous purchases, browsing history, or their social media interactions. For example, Spectrum, an internet service provider, can utilize AI to analyze social media posts where they were not tagged and use those unfiltered posts as insights into user feelings, positioning, and to better their messaging about concerns (Iide, 2025). This type of sentiment and social listening process allows brands to better support consumer decision-making that relates to alleviating hesitation, improving service, and allowing consumers to make more informed and meaningful choices. AI and the opportunity to support decision-making in an environment of transparency are further endorsed by the provision of automation options for comparisons, real-time reviews, and predictive suggestions. The growth of AI and the expansion of opportunities to support consumers' decision-making benefit the buyer's ability to make better, faster choices, while assisting brands in growing their level of responsiveness and relevance in every encounter.

Automate Creativity

The most considerable marketing question is whether AI can be more creative than people. Since this technology is very dependent on previous data, is it capable of generating innovative products like humans? In 2016, 20th Century Fox partnered with IBM Watson to produce a movie trailer of the science-fiction horror Morgan (Morgan - A.I. Trailer | IMDB, n.d.). The AI was fed information on 100 movie trailers and movie scenes of the movie and produced a trailer within 24 hours, whereas it should take between 10 and 30 days on average. Today, there are also different fan-made AI trailers on the internet due to the more sophisticated AI existing now. Generative AI is applied by marketers to generate personalized and unique content for their consumers. Ogilvy Nutella Italy produced Nutella Unica, an individual package of Nutella (The Drum, 2017). Its unique AI algorithm had been trained on dozens of patterns and thousands of color combinations, coming up with more than seven million unique package designs. These jars were sent to the whole country and sold within one month. These are illustrations that even AI is able to design personalized/unique product offers that appeal to consumers.

Some brands are developing brand-generated messages that are adapted into personalized messages that result in improved engagement, bonding with the customers, and affection toward the brand. It is an inexpensive way of advertising and customization, namely toward emerging brands that do not have sufficient resources. AI supports marketing creativity by automating simple tasks, such as email marketing and push notifications, so marketers may turn their focus toward more strategic and creative work (Haleem et al., 2022). AI provides insights to enhance ideation, but creative decisions, like brand voice, emotional appeal, and storytelling, require human judgment. In addition, while AI-generated content may enhance efficiency, marketers must add oversight to ensure this content aligns with brand values and campaign objectives.

Omnichannel Engagement and Customer Service

In a digital-first world, consumers connect with brands through a variety of platforms—apps, websites, stores, and social media. AI empowers omnichannel experiences by unifying customer data, predicting preferences and needs, and ensuring consistent communications on any platform. Brands can use AI-enabled tools like chatbots and customer data platforms to provide customized, real-time support across channels and make engagement processes less expensive and easier to scale. AI enables organizations to automate marketing activities, consolidate consumer data, and effectively integrate and synchronize across various platforms. It has the capacity to accumulate client information regarding a wide range of sources, including customer reviews online, web browsing histories, in-app activities, chatbot messages, and multiple social networks, and it allows marketers to detect different client profiles in a better way and provide them with customized content and services. The brands may also incorporate their chatbots and voice assistants on the platforms using AI technology to create conversations and offer customer support services (Rohit et al., 2024). Such integration and customer service are facilitated by the Starbucks app; they can make orders, pay, and receive rewards. It is also connected with its loyalty program and offers personalized offers and rewards to them according to their purchase history and preferences (How Starbucks Builds Loyalty and Enhances Customer Experience (CX) With Rewards Programs, n.d.) (Figure 1.3).

Types of AI in Marketing Management

There are many ways to categorize AI in marketing, including by its purpose, the problems it solves, or by the technology it uses (Chung et al., 2022). There is no universally accepted framework, as AI is rapidly advancing. A well-established way to classify AI looks at its ability to model human intelligence.

Reactive AI

Reactive AI is the simplest form of AI. Reactive AI can react to an input given to it through a fixed output with no memory and no learning capability over time. Marketing has used

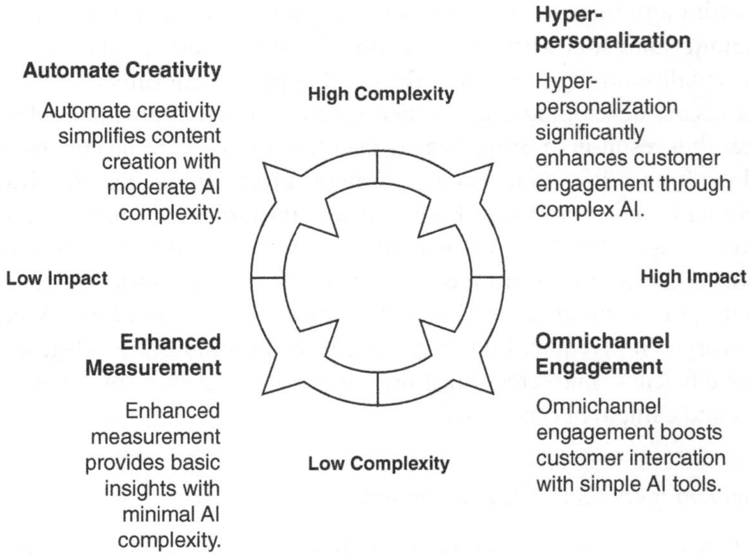

FIGURE 1.3 Benefits of AI in marketing.

reactive AI in rule-based automation (e.g., chatbots that can engage with consumer queries by using preformulated responses for simple questions), and though limited, there are advantages to automating routine consumer queries in terms of improving efficiency.

Reactive machines operate without memory or learning capabilities, but they are still valuable in marketing and customer service due to their predictability and consistency. Since these systems respond in fixed ways to specific inputs, their actions are highly reliable, making them ideal for tasks where accuracy, security, and trust are crucial, such as handling routine customer queries or processing standard transactions.

They find application in such things as the Deep Blue, a computer made by IBM in the 1980s to play chess, which won a match with a world champion, Garry Kasparov (Deep Blue | IBM, n.d.). Deep Blue recognizes chess pieces and also logs their moves on a chessboard. It anticipates the next action, and it chooses the most appropriate action. However, Deep Blue cannot process historical data.

Theory of Mind

Theory of Mind (ToM) represents a more advanced stage of AI where systems aim to understand human emotions, beliefs, and intentions, enabling deeper human-machine interaction (Mao et al., 2024). Unlike reactive or memory-based AI, ToM would allow machines to recognize and respond to users' emotional and cognitive states in real time. While still largely theoretical, this development holds potential for creating empathetic AI tools in marketing, like emotionally responsive virtual assistants or adaptive advertising that reacts to consumer moods.

The idea behind machines and robots is that they should be able to see and learn from humans like young children or infants do. They should also be able to take in information, formulate their thoughts, ask questions, and come to conclusions.

The developments that have made social robots more human-like have seen them being highly desirable in many areas, such as the public services sector, education, aging care, and personal assistance. A good example of this work of the scientists is Sophia, a social humanoid robot. Having a sharp vision, Sophia is able to recognize people, trace faces, and communicate with other individuals. Severe AI methods, including ML, AI, animatronics, which, based on hardware, imitate a feature characteristic of life, and NLP, were integrated into the design of Sophia, the social humanoid robot. Despite the challenges, Sophia is believed to be one of the steps toward superintelligence.

Limited Memory

The limited memory, as it is most commonly applied nowadays, refers to a machine that is able to analyze information. A machine having a small memory can become responsive. Other than that, it also acquires experiential knowledge based on the analysis of past data in terms of inputs or actions. A system cannot learn and become more efficient in making a decision or judgment without training information and observation. Reinforcement and supervised/unsupervised learning are all covered by limited memory. Image recognition can be used as an example of limited memory. Image recognition involves thousands, even millions of images with labels, which are used to train the system to identify and distinguish items as it is being scanned. The system gains experience in as much as it gets more training photos as input. New photos can also be recognized with accuracy with this learning experience increasing. Another example of a limited memory application is the self-driving car; it makes snap decisions and avoids accidents based on the current information (the car's speed, the speed limit, the distance to other cars, etc.).

Limited Memory AI can learn past information and make decisions based on that information; in other words, it is more advanced than a reactive machine, but it also retains information temporarily and normally takes a large amount of data to do so. As an example, a self-driving Tesla car makes its decision based on recent information and learning, but it cannot store an experience in its memory like a human driver would do. Limited Memory AI is capable of learning from historical data and making predictions from that knowledge, meaning it has more sophistication than a reactive machine, but it also stores data for a limited time and usually needs a large data set for it to work. For instance, a self-driving car Tesla makes its decisions using recent data and learning, but unlike a human driver, it cannot retain an experience from its "memory."

Self-Aware AI

Self-aware AI represents a hypothetical future stage where machines might possess consciousness, emotional understanding, and a sense of self. This level goes beyond current AI capabilities and remains purely theoretical, with no working models in existence (Chung et al., 2022). While often discussed in philosophical or speculative AI discourse, it is not yet a focus of practical AI development.

The development of self-aware AI will significantly impact marketing professionals, particularly in consumer relations. The self-aware robots will be able to engage with customers in a manner that ensures relationships, sharing of emotions, and empathetic behavior, which enhance customer pleasure and experience. Robots at this stage are to actively

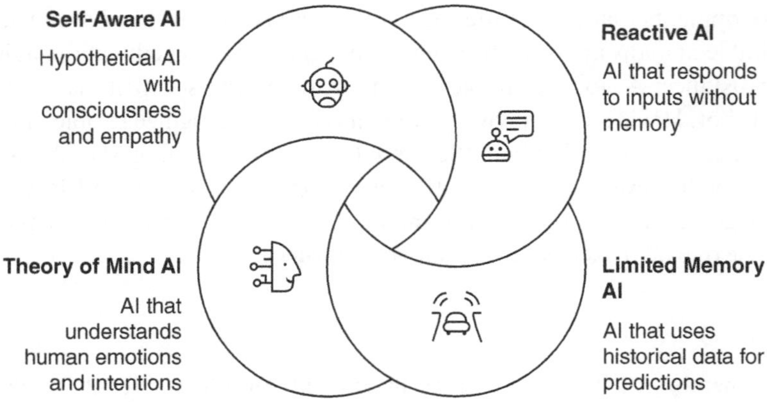

FIGURE 1.4 Types of AI in marketing management.

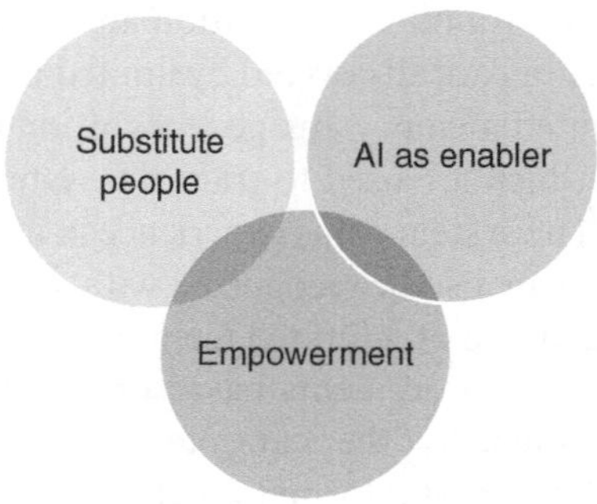

FIGURE 1.5 AI's Role in transforming marketing.

participate in exemplary and vibrant interactions with people, where they can build relationships in social settings and assist human beings in their work (Figure 1.4).

AI's Role in Transforming Marketing

With the continued disruption caused by AI in marketing, it is crucial to define its role. Understanding AI's roles, responsibilities, and positioning in the marketing environment is vital, even though the previous section emphasized the various benefits of implementing AI. To help readers understand the effects of AI on companies and customers, this section lays out the three primary roles of AI in marketing (Figure 1.5).

Substitute People—Automation and Efficiency

Automation of processes is a crucial benefit of using AI. It has a significant effect on marketing functions. Marketers have to deal with repetitive, tedious tasks while looking to earn as much money as possible for their marketing team. Further, there is always a shortage of qualified professionals in service sectors, including transportation, education, healthcare, and customer support.

AI provides solutions by automating various processes in an orderly manner and allows robots to take over the tasks that humans are not performing with complete dedication for multiple reasons. Because of this, the accuracy and efficiency of these operations are enhanced, and the possibility of a shortage of human resources is reduced.

Transportation companies like Uber and Lyft use AI algorithms to help drivers be more productive by finding the best routes and assigning jobs correctly. These algorithms can look at a lot of data in real-time, like location, traffic trends, and customer demand, to find drivers and passengers. Because of this, AI cuts down on the need for human dispatchers, makes dealing with customers and workers more efficient, and helps the business make the most money possible.

The use of AI for automation significantly affects many fields, including customer service. A decade ago, thinking people could talk to machines to solve problems was hard. AI chatbots and virtual assistants have changed how customers ask businesses for help. The chat and voice algorithms were made easy for anyone to use and handle a wide range of customer questions and issues. It is in their power to react appropriately and provide immediate help when needed. People no longer have to wait long to get their pressure cooker fixed or make a service request. AI bots not only free up customer service reps from answering the same questions repeatedly, but they also save time in situations where real people are needed, making this marketing job more effective.

As a result, businesses can be more productive and effective by replacing tedious tasks that humans used to do with tasks that computers can do. The gadget can work continuously without losing effectiveness because it doesn't tire workers and frees them to work on more complex tasks requiring human judgment and analytical thought, saving time and money. However, finding the right mix between AI and human involvement is very important. It is essential to check and change the algorithm regularly to ensure it meets customer needs and has no bugs or biases that could hurt customers.

AI as an Enabler—Speed, Accuracy, and Innovation

AI has transformed the marketing space in some significant ways, mainly by speeding up certain aspects of the services and allowing for greater accuracy and cost-efficiency. Marketers can spend less time on tactical coordination and execution tasks and more time on strategic and creative decisions. For example, AI can analyze large volumes of data in real time, allowing for rapid and data-based decision-making, far greater than what is possible under human analysis. The same applies to digital advertising, where AI can analyze customer data, identify target audiences, and show insights from historical performance, with the overall effect of increasing the efficiency and profitability of the advertising effort. The ability of AI to automate many functions in the marketing process assists marketers in rapidly changing when customer needs and preferences change, using less human effort and reducing bias.

AI has also ignited a wave of innovation in marketing practice. With the introduction of AI capabilities, not only is the analysis of data different from before, but the way that content is created and delivered has also changed. For instance, generative AI accelerates the creation of FAQs, website content, and personalized documents for customers, while recommendation engines, on the other hand, customize messages immediately based on customer responses. In fact, the level of technology using avatars to acting as AI brand endorsers to virtual assistants is redefining the way customers interact with businesses. For instance, Alexa is integrating all of these types of technologies as customers access businesses on its platform via browsing, purchasing, and using a voice assistant to access business support. This demonstrates a greater level of frictionless, personalized service enabled by AI.

Empowerment: Consumer and Supplier

When AI is employed in marketing functions, the vision is to benefit businesses and empower other stakeholders. The examples discussed above, such as using AI to optimize ride-sharing or customer support, do not just cut costs but also enhance customer experience (CX) and returns for drivers. Thus, while incorporating AI in marketing, businesses should aim to unleash their capabilities to empower and benefit customers and suppliers alike.

AI plays a critical role in assisting consumers with informed purchase decisions by analyzing user preferences and recommending relevant products. Through intelligent recommendation systems, AI suggests options that align with individual needs and interests. Additionally, AI-powered chatbots support users in real time, answering queries, registering requests, and guiding them through the decision-making process. Businesses, especially in the service sector, increasingly rely on AI to deliver personalized CXs. By tailoring interactions and offerings, companies aim to meet the unique expectations of each consumer. Platforms like Netflix exemplify this use of AI, employing advanced algorithms to analyze user behavior and personalize content recommendations, thereby enhancing overall user satisfaction and engagement.

AI plays an important role in streamlining corporate operations and managing sourcing with suppliers. It also helps in predicting orders from customers using historical demand patterns, inventory levels, optimizing production scheduling, procurement, and inventory management. It helps assess processes and communicate with suppliers so that they can procure or produce and supply raw materials more effectively. Moreover, AI-enabled software also automates essential functions such as invoice processing, logistical coordination, and relationship management, eliminating human errors and delays. Large organizations, like Walmart and FedEx, use these services to provide hassle-free and streamlined experiences to suppliers and sellers.

CLOSING CASE—DEUTSCHE TELEKOM

The use of AI in business introduces new dimensions, enhances the effectiveness of customer service, and introduces new capabilities (Dwivedi et al., 2019). There are two primary alternatives that firms can make before embracing the use of AI in their businesses. Purchase the AI systems off the shelf, which is a costly alternative, or develop its own AI systems. To develop their AI systems, the companies require a team of developers, support from partners, testing, and product teams. The idea to develop AI-based software, computers, voice control options, and chatbots is expected to enhance the efficiency of the customer service of individual and business customers.

A typical inquiry of a corporate client may require a thousand human actions in multiple software systems, some of which involve the entry of the booking, handling of requests, and beginning of orders. Thus, the organization will save a lot of cash, time, and stress by developing intelligent software to conduct such types of activities!

Chatbots have the potential to enhance customer support effectiveness and efficiency. They work 24/7 and handle daily tasks. According to recent findings, 66% of the chatbot experiences were rated 1 out of 5 in a telecom situation; this is one of the reasons why design, context, and human-bot handoff are crucial to the implementation of these systems (Vlahos, 2023).

Deutsche Telekom is among the top integrated telecommunications companies in the world. It has its headquarters in Bonn, Germany, and it offers fixed-line, mobile, internet, and digital services to millions of people in Europe and other parts of the world. The digital assistants provided by Deutsche Telekom are multiple, and most are easily recognized by the users. The AI systems will be more effective in offloading human agents of menial tasks, and this will leave them with more time to perform the jobs that machines cannot perform (Ag, 2017). Nonetheless, they will not be in a position to substitute real human service representatives whenever dealing with complex matters wholly. In this perspective, automated intelligence machines are being made to deal with specific customer problems. Virtual assistants, such as Tinka, Sophie, and Vanda, will soon be able to learn based on the chat logs and real customer and agent conversations. They are able to use a growing body of knowledge, store their acquired knowledge, and determine the most effective strategies and solutions. They also aspire to hear and touch humans when dealing with customers. Notably, Deutsche Telekom (a telecom company with its headquarters in Germany) established eLIZA, a full-scale AI program, to unify the entire AI solutions of the Deutsche Telekom Group and streamline its work in this direction (Ag, 2023).

You can compare Tinka (one of the virtual workers in Telekom Austria), a chatbot, to a search engine. To date, Tinka has been taught over 1,500 answers, and her answers continue to be updated regularly (Ag, 2023). Tinka is on-call at any hour of the day to assist the Telekom users in Austria—instantaneously without necessarily having to wait. Tinka is shown as an icon on the screen of customers, with a long-haired young lady with a text input field below her. She can answer approximately 80 percent of the questions asked of her. When she cannot answer, she forwards questions to a human colleague.

Although Tinka is already in operation, the developers of Deutsche Telekom are still working together with clients to tailor Tinka to the needs of its clients. Moreover, they have continued to include more sources of information in her overall database. To demonstrate what can now be done by Tinka, one can look at the example of assisting customers in installing Wi-Fi networks based on LTE at home and showing them how to insert SIM cards into their phones. She especially does well in sending clients who have tough questions to other available support channels. She is able to connect clients and customer care agents. She proposes to use email as an alternative in the case when there are no agents available.

In the near future, Tinka will be in a position to call patrons by their names and identify them. She will also be in a position to remember and utilize the previous discussions. Tinka may now view the history of a customer who has already visited the Austrian T-Mobile website, subject to the approval of the client. Consequently, the correspondence to her will become much more focused and concentrated on the problems brought to attention by the clients.

Sophie, a chatbot and service bot on the company site, is supporting the service staff on the site, which is owned by Deutsche Telekom, a subsidiary of Congstar. With regard to the Facebook Messenger application, it is also used as a chatbot.

Sophie has the opportunity to personally meet every customer by name. This functionality is so strong that it poses a challenge to the popular Messenger platform on Facebook, given the many restrictions that Facebook has imposed. It is planned that Sophie will be able to independently manage most consumer requests on the Facebook page belonging to Congstar and refer complex ones to the support team. One should then take more advantage of personalization, like the instance of payments. Sophie is able to constantly improve her client service due to her artificial intelligence, as she will be able to learn from her experiences.

The eLIZA program has a team of Deutsche Telekom Innovation Laboratories (and other areas of innovation) and a design team engaged by T-Mobile Austria and Telekom Deutschland.

Considering the enormous amounts of money that companies like Amazon and Google are allocating to AI, we believe it would be highly reasonable for us to focus on applying AI to customer service, and, in the long-term, on creating a variety of other points of interest, says Jan Hofmann, CEO of eLIZA. We would like to use AI to solve specific problems with clients.

The eLiza program will form the basis of implementing AI-based solutions in the locations of the Group and international boundaries. The knowledge will be given to Tinka, Sophie, and their virtual colleagues in one day through chat logs and real customer care agent-customer interactions. Moreover, the students will have the capability to memorize and apply the best ideas, techniques, and methods that they will obtain through these sources.

Discussion Questions

- Discuss the evolution of AI, various tests, and experiments that led to the current AI technology. Explain the concept of AI.
- Explain the benefits of AI in marketing, its characteristics in the context of social media marketing, and e-commerce.
- Describe the types of AI in marketing management. Draw a comparison of their uses in marketing, choosing an industry of your own.
- Discuss the role of AI in marketing. How it empowers businesses to improve their marketing strategy.
- Discuss how AI can help in cost saving, streamlining strategic effectiveness of marketing strategy, and delight consumer using an example.

Assignment Questions

1. Select a company of your choice and analyze how it uses AI to enhance customer experience. Discuss benefits, risks, and potential improvements.
2. Compare Reactive AI and Limited Memory AI by identifying real-world marketing applications for each. Which do you think creates more value, and why?
3. Research and evaluate a marketing campaign where AI was used for hyper-personalization. Did it improve customer loyalty? Justify your analysis with evidence.
4. Develop a short proposal on how a mid-sized retail brand could implement AI across its marketing value chain (customer insights, personalization, pricing, and customer service).

MINI CASE: SEPHORA

Sephora is one of the world's leading beauty and personal care brands. It is known for its digital-first innovation. Sephora customers often faced the challenge of a choice overload due to the company's thousands of products in its catalog. To fix this challenge, Sephora turned to AI to simplify discovery and personalize experiences as well. It introduced "Sephora Virtual Artist," which is an AI/AR-powered tool that allows customers to try on different products, like lipsticks and eyeshadows, virtually. The AI analyzes the facial features and skin tones to recommend the shades or products that are the best fit for the specific customer. In its customer experience, personalization can also be seen to extend into skin care routines like AI-driven skin diagnostic tools that recommend products, based on selfies and questionnaires. Sephora also uses AI by analyzing purchase history and app behavior data to generate personalized product recommendations. By segmenting customers by their preferences, Sephora can execute targeted campaigns and deliver promotions via app notifications, emails, and in-store kiosks, thus enhancing omnichannel engagement. The AI forecasts demand well in advance to ensure that trending products are in stock as and when demand rises. It helps with stock optimization and ensures that popular SKUs are replenished quickly across their global stores. While AI does have a lot of advantages in areas like Customer Experience, Data-Driven Marketing, and even Operations, it does face a lot of risks and governance challenges. The risk of an algorithmic bias always exists when the AI doesn't correctly match the shade to a diverse skin tone. To combat this, Sephora has invested heavily in inclusive datasets and improved its training model to ensure that AI recommendations are more equitable. The Sephora case study teaches all marketers that AI has a lot of power in bridging the digital and even physical retail space to deliver an immersive, personalized customer experience. Sephora demonstrates the benefits of AI in personalization, decision-making, and omni-channel marketing.

HBR Case Links:

- https://www.hbs.edu/faculty/Pages/item.aspx?num=40694&
- https://hbr.org/2021/07/how-to-design-an-ai-marketing-strategy
- https://hbr.org/2021/05/getting-ai-to-scale

Application of Concept and In-Class Activities

Concept (Kotler Link)	*Application in Practice*	*In-Class Activity/Illustration*
Evolution of AI (marketing history & technology adoption)	Firms leverage AI's progression from early automation to advanced machine learning to reshape marketing strategies.	**Timeline Exercise**: Students create a visual timeline linking different AI milestones to various marketing applications.
Data-driven marketing (marketing research & analytics)	Marketers rely on AI tools for data-driven marketing, such as getting real-time customer insights, predictive analytics, and optimizing their campaigns.	**Data Mapping Activity**: Provide mock customer dataset; groups identify key data points out of the mock data.
Benefits of AI in marketing (value creation & ROI)	AI enhances ROI through hyper-personalization, efficient measurement, creativity, and omnichannel engagement.	**ROI Simulation**: Students calculate potential returns from an AI campaign (e.g., chatbot adoption) and then compare it to a normal customer service agent.
Types of AI (AI in marketing systems)	Reactive, Limited Memory, Theory of Mind, and Self-Aware AI provide different levels of personalization.	**Classification Game**: Students match real-world tools (chatbots, recommendation engines, Generative AI, Agentic AI) to the correct AI type.
AI's role in transforming marketing (automation, enablement & empowerment)	AI substitutes routine tasks, enables innovation, and empowers different stakeholders, like customers and suppliers, with personalization and decision support.	**Debate/Role Play**: One group defends "AI as substitution," another supports "AI as empowerment," discussing opportunities and risks for marketers.

Key Terms

- Artificial intelligence (AI)
- Machine learning (ML)
- Natural language processing (NLP)
- Digital transformation
- Data-driven marketing
- Hyper-personalization
- Omnichannel engagement
- Reactive AI
- Limited memory AI
- Theory of mind AI
- Self-aware AI
- Automation
- Enablement
- Empowerment
- Chatbots

References

Ag, D. T. (2017, April 19). *Machines keep getting smarter – with human help*. Deutsche Telekom. https://www.telekom.com/en/company/digital-responsibility/digital-responsibility-artificial-intelligence/artificial-intelligence/machines-keep-getting-smarter-492102

Ag, D. T. (2023, December 7). *Artificial intelligence at Deutsche Telekom*. Deutsche Telekom. https://www.telekom.com/en/company/digital-responsibility/details/artificial-intelligence-at-deutsche-telekom-1055154

Alrumiah, S. S., & Hadwan, M. (2021). Implementing big data analytics in e-commerce: Vendor and customer view. *IEEE Access*, *9*, 37281–37286. https://doi.org/10.1109/access.2021.3063615

Başev, S. E. (2024). The role of artificial intelligence (AI) in the future of the advertising industry. *International Journal of Education Technology and Scientific Researches*, 2. https://doi.org/10.35826/ijetsar.729

Cao, L. (2021). Artificial intelligence in retail: Applications and value creation logics. *International Journal of Retail & Distribution Management*, *49*(7), 958–976. https://doi.org/10.1108/ijrdm-09-2020-0350

Chung, K., Le, D., Thaichon, P., & Quach, S. (2022). Types of artificial intelligence (AI) in marketing management. In *Routledge eBooks* (pp. 29–40). https://doi.org/10.4324/9781003280392-4

Data-Driven Marketing Is the Future — Here's Why It Matters. (2024). *Northbeam blog*. https://www.northbeam.io/post/data-driven-marketing-is-the-future----heres-why-it-matters

Davenport, T., Guha, A., Grewal, D., & Bressgott, T. (2019). How artificial intelligence will change the future of marketing. *Journal of the Academy of Marketing Science*, *48*(1), 24–42. https://doi.org/10.1007/s11747-019-00696-0

Deep Blue | IBM. (n.d.). https://www.ibm.com/history/deep-blue

Dwivedi, Y. K., Hughes, L., Ismagilova, E., Aarts, G., Coombs, C., Crick, T., Duan, Y., Dwivedi, R., Edwards, J., Eirug, A., Galanos, V., Ilavarasan, P. V., Janssen, M., Jones, P., Kar, A. K., Kizgin, H., Kronemann, B., Lal, B., Lucini, B., … Williams, M. D. (2019). Artificial intelligence (AI): Multidisciplinary perspectives on emerging challenges, opportunities, and agenda for research, practice and policy. *International Journal of Information Management*, *57*, 101994. https://doi.org/10.1016/j.ijinfomgt.2019.08.002

Guo, T. (2015). Alan Turing: Artificial intelligence as human self-knowledge. *Anthropology Today*, *31*(6), 3–7. https://doi.org/10.1111/1467-8322.12209

Haleem, A., Javaid, M., Qadri, M. A., Singh, R. P., & Suman, R. (2022). Artificial intelligence (AI) applications for marketing: A literature-based study. *International Journal of Intelligent Networks*, *3*, 119–132. https://doi.org/10.1016/j.ijin.2022.08.005

How Starbucks builds loyalty and enhances customer experience (CX) with rewards programs. (n.d.). *Renascence journal*. https://www.renascence.io/journal/how-starbucks-builds-loyalty-and-enhances-customer-experience-cx-with-rewards-programs

Huang, M., & Rust, R. T. (2020). A strategic framework for artificial intelligence in marketing. *Journal of the Academy of Marketing Science*, *49*(1), 30–50. https://doi.org/10.1007/s11747-020-00749-9

IIDE. (2025, January 29). In-depth marketing strategy of Spectrum - 2025. *IIDE - The Digital School*. https://iide.co/case-studies/marketing-strategy-of-spectrum/

Jain, E (2017, May). Marketing and technology: Role of technology in modern marketing. *ResearchGate*. https://www.researchgate.net/publication/317308663_Marketing_and_Technology_Role_of_Technology_in_Modern_Marketing

Jasrotia, S. (2023). Artificial intelligence in modern marketing: A critical review. *Journal of Innovation and Emerging Research*, *5*(1), 3131–3138. https://doi.org/10.52783/jier.v5i1.2316

Kotler, P., & Armstrong, G. (2018). *Principles of marketing* (17th ed.). Pearson Higher Education.

Kumar, V., Ashraf, A. R., & Nadeem, W. (2024). AI-powered marketing: What, where, and how? *International Journal of Information Management*, *77*, 102783. https://doi.org/10.1016/j.ijinfomgt.2024.102783

Lee, Y. S., Kim, T., Choi, S., & Kim, W. (2022). When does AI pay off? AI-adoption intensity, complementary investments, and R&D strategy. *Technovation*, *118*, 102590. https://doi.org/10.1016/j.technovation.2022.102590

Mao, Y., Liu, S., Ni, Q., Lin, X., & He, L. (2024). A review on machine theory of mind. *IEEE Transactions on Computational Social Systems*, 11 (6), 1–19. https://doi.org/10.1109/tcss.2024.3416707

Marr, B. (2024, July 2). The amazing ways Walmart is using generative AI. *Forbes*. https://www.forbes.com/sites/bernardmarr/2024/02/15/the-amazing-ways-walmart-is-using-generative-ai/

McKinsey. (2021). *The big reset: Data-driven marketing in the next normal*. https://www.mckinsey.com/capabilities/growth-marketing-and-sales/our-insights/the-big-reset-data-driven-marketing-in-the-next-normal

Mohan, S. (2021). Artificial intelligence in retail. In *Productivity press eBooks* (pp. 193–222). https://doi.org/10.4324/9781351032940-7

Morgan - A.I. Trailer | IMDb. (n.d.). [Video]. *IMDb*. https://www.imdb.com/video/vi2528818713/

Ozay, D., Jahanbakht, M., Shoomal, A., & Wang, S. (2024). Artificial intelligence (AI)-based customer relationship management (CRM): A comprehensive bibliometric and systematic literature review with outlook on future research. *Enterprise Information Systems*, *18*(7). https://doi.org/10.1080/17517575.2024.2351869

Radanliev, P. (2024). Artificial intelligence: Reflecting on the past and looking towards the next paradigm shift. *Journal of Experimental & Theoretical Artificial Intelligence*, 37, 1–18. https://doi.org/10.1080/0952813x.2024.2323042

Roden, S., Nucciarelli, A., Li, F., & Graham, G. (2017). Big data and the transformation of operations models: A framework and a new research agenda. *Production Planning & Control*, *28*(11–12), 929–944.

Rohit, K., Shankar, A., Katiyar, G., Mehrotra, A., & Alzeiby, E. A. (2024). Consumer engagement in chatbots and voicebots: A multiple-experiment approach in online retailing context. *Journal of Retailing and Consumer Services*, *78*, 103728. https://doi.org/10.1016/j.jretconser.2024.103728

Russell, S. J., & Norvig, P. (2020). *Artificial intelligence: A modern approach* (4th ed.). Pearson.

The Drum. (2017, June. *Nutella: advert-top-1 by Ogilvy Italy*. https://www.thedrum.com/creative-works/project/ogilvy-italy-nutella-nutella-unica#:~:text=With%20this%20objective%2C%20Nutella%20Unica,to%20create%20millions%20of%20combinations

Uddin, M. K. S., & Hossan, K. M. R. (2024). A review of implementing AI-powered data warehouse solutions to optimize big data management and utilization. *Academic Journal on Business Administration, Innovation & Sustainability*, *4*(3), 66–78. https://doi.org/10.69593/ajbais.v4i3.92

Van Hoek, R., DeWitt, T., Lacity, M., & Johnson, V. (2022, November 18). How Walmart automated supplier negotiations. *Harvard Business Review*. https://hbr.org/2022/11/how-walmart-automated-supplier-negotiations

Varsha, S.N., Akter, S., Kumar, A., Gochhait, S., & Patagundi, B. (2021). The impact of artificial intelligence on branding. *Journal of Global Information Management*, *29*(4), 221–246. https://doi.org/10.4018/jgim.20210701.oa10

Vlahos, J. (2023, October 5). Creating customer service bots that people don't hate. *Harvard Business Review*. https://hbr.org/2023/10/creating-customer-service-bots-that-people-dont-hate

Yadav, L. (2024, October 29). AI in ads: Boosting brands or breaking trust? *Campaign India*. https://www.campaignindia.in/article/ai-in-ads-boosting-brands-or-breaking-trust/499094#:~:text=In%202021%2C%20Cadbury%20ran%20a,local%2C%20geo%2Dtargeted%20messages

Zahair, A. (2024, May 9). AI-powered customer service: Revolutionizing the support experience. *Corporate Vision Magazine*. https://www.corporatevision-news.com/ai-powered-customer-service-revolutionizing-the-support-experience/

2

HOW AI IS TRANSFORMING MODERN MARKETING

Learning Objectives

Having studied this chapter, you are expected to be able to:

1 Provide an explanation of the exact role of AI in transforming modern marketing practices, from personalization to strategic decision-making.
2 Distinguish between weak AI and strong AI and identify their applications in marketing.
3 Evaluate the practical uses of AI across different marketing functions, ranging from advertising, customer service, sales, and CRM.
4 Assess the strategic benefits and ethical challenges of AI in market intelligence, personalization, and decision-making.
5 Discuss opportunities and risks in applying AI to marketing and elaborate on the path forward.

OPENING CASE: NETFLIX AND AI-POWERED PERSONALIZATION

Netflix is a global streaming service that has transformed the way people consume content. It was founded in 1997 as a digital versatile disc (DVD) rental service and has now expanded to a user base of over 260 million subscribers. Netflix disrupted television not only in how we watch it, but also in the medium that we watch it in. Netflix is not a huge repository of movies and shows; the thing is that there are more than 260 million subscribers all over the world until the middle of 2025. The algorithm that relates to the personalization of the viewing experience to engage customers with is the recommendation engine, which is an AI-based system designed by Netflix not only to recommend what to watch but also to tailor the viewing process in order to make the customer want to watch more (Schrage, 2017). The invisibility of a recommendation engine is the key to customer retention, as it is the system

DOI: 10.4324/9781003501862-2

that defines the viewing experience of the customer to watch more of the content (Schrage, 2017). This technology never proposes what one watches, but formulates the viewing experience. Artificial intelligence, which operates on billions of interactions each day, is the heart of this system. It tracks what you are watching, when you take a break, what you re-watch, and even the nature of titles that you move the mouse over and do not click. It is on this sea of behavioral data that the algorithm understands what you like and personalizes your homepage so that it is personal and yours. Internal reports of Netflix reveal that over 80% of all that is viewed is a consequence of this AI-based suggestions.

It is not just about convenience. The recommendation system is a significant retention tool that Netflix has in its commercial. After getting into the site, the viewer is bound to hang around and subscribe when s/he is suddenly presented with titles of interest. This approach and strategy have helped to reduce the churn and ensure Netflix remains differentiated in a saturated streaming market.

AI also informs the input into what is being created by Netflix. Netflix is making more informed judgments about what content to allocate its resources to by examining tastes locally and the general trends, whether it spreads Korean dramas or the possibilities of virality in true crime. Talking about the one particular example, Squid Game did not fall on its luck as it is highly likely that it was the movie thoroughly appropriate to all the knowledge that the world is seeking to receive more high-production survival thrillers. AI will also help arrive at the decision of what greenlit is and how it can be positioned and marketed.

Besides personalization and content strategy, AI also offers a continuous cross-device user experience. Adaptive streaming technology can also change the quality of the video being viewed according to the capability of the network so that the video is watched without buffering. This is a very critical aspect that helps to provide satisfaction to the viewer, especially in low-bandwidth locations, although the viewer will never see this actually coming into action. The Netflix scenario explains that data is being transformed into knowledge, and knowledge into action, with the help of AI. This does not only help the customer experience but also strategy-making. Netflix began as a business that would deliver contents through DVDs and has expanded into a technology-based media empire. Its success is also indicative of how contemporary business can be built to have a sustainable competitive advantage through scale, or content, and intelligent systems that learn, adapt, and service the users in an improved form each time one clicks the button. The move in the history of Netflix preconditions the further discussion: AI is not only going to be the province of a limited number of companies anymore—it is determining how modern companies work in all industries.

AI in Business Today

As discussed in the opening case, artificial intelligence (AI) can transform raw data into something significant to act upon, which can result in the improvement of customers and even more in business approach. The entertainment is not the only one talking about this transformation—it is also the observation of the general transformation taking place in the industry, where AI is changing the role of modern marketing.

Role of AI in Modern Marketing

AI is not a thing that used to be done in garages or a technology showcased at any trade show; it is now a part of the everyday operations of businesses all over the world. The technology, which was initially viewed as a fresh technology, happened to be an absolute need-based competitive advantage generator. Examples of how AI is marketed include innovating market research, audience segmentation, campaign design, and measurement. AI helps marketers to make batches of decisions that are more evidence-based, much faster, and more predictive, whether predicting product demand, launching new trends, or optimizing media spend. It does not displace creativity or strategy; it refines it since it provides a more perfect insight, is more effective, and can be changed in real time. In this chapter, the author discusses the basis of AI, its development, and how it is transforming marketing as a science, not hypothetically, but practically.

Core Concepts of AI in Marketing

In order to comprehend the impact AI is having on marketing, one must also know the fundamentals of AI. The concepts are used to base the application in personalization, advertising, customer services, and strategic decision-making. On such a fundamental lack of clarity, AI in marketing risks being perceived as a buzzword and not as a concrete toolset.

Weak vs Strong AI

AI has been commonly defined in literature as either weak AI or strong AI. Weak AI is the form of AI that fulfils tasks well within a limited scope. These systems cannot have general reasoning skills, but are good at their programmed actions. The voice assistants such as Siri, the recommendation engines, and the chatbots functioning based on AI in customer service all serve as examples. Specifically, narrow AI usage is already widespread in marketing, where narrow AI can be used to analyze customer data, make preferential predictions, and automate procedures (Figure 2.1).

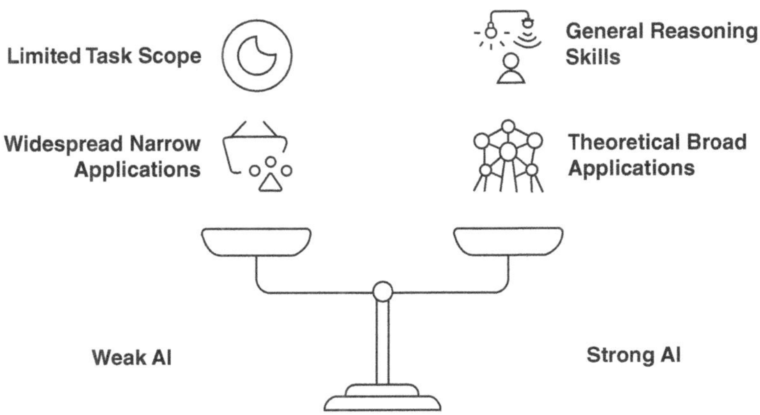

FIGURE 2.1 Comparing AI capabilities and applications.

Strong AI is the as-yet hypothetical concept of a machine with human-level intelligence, that is, an artificial general intelligence (AGI) and its even more advanced descendant, artificial superintelligence (ASI), which would be even more capable in all respects than a human intelligence. At the moment, these types of AI exist simply as research topics and do not contribute to marketing practice.

As concerns marketers, the emphasis is still placed on narrow AI since it brings quantifiable business benefits in the present time—better targeting, ad spending efficiency, and consumer-specific experience. On one hand, strong AI is the topic of prospective discussion, but on the other, it is narrow AI that changes the marketing strategy and implementation in the present.

Artificial intelligence is not a vision of the future anymore: it is an active reality that can significantly change the process of connecting consumers and businesses. In marketing, AI is used to make recommendations for the market, refine ad targeting, forecast market trends, and is used in automating customer interactions. Whether it is augmenting online shopping experiences or ensuring the provision of relevant content across the channel, AI is helping brands to effectively and efficiently engage audiences now more than ever before.

It is both the factories that are automating production lines or even apps that are preemptively reading your subsequent food obsession; the power of AI is everywhere. Machine learning (the technology that underpins fraud prevention) and natural language processing (NLP) (the technology that underlies chatbots) are the engine rooms of this revolution—these technologies work silently in the background to propel the engines of the modern business.

This assumption leads one to the question right away: how did we get here? To understand what effect AI has in marketing nowadays, it is better to briefly dwell upon its history and how decades of researches changed it into a commonly used business tool. Stitch Fix, USA, employs machine learning to analyze customer preferences and predict fashion choices, exemplifying how AI research transitioned into everyday personalization.

A Brief History of AI

As much as the story of AI is not that of technology, but rather that of a journey of an idea, as of theory into practice. The 21st century has seen an unprecedented surge in repurposing research and development in AI, which has been described as an AI renaissance. This revival has been necessitated by the following three factors: exponentially increasing computing power, a vast assembly of data, and sophisticated algorithms that have been perfected and applied to big data sets. When combined, they have helped in the development of breakthroughs in other areas like machine learning and deep learning, which is a ground-breaker in what is up to date in AI.

It has revolutionized nearly all fields, including image recognition and NLP, to self-driving cars. The latest AI development is deep learning. They have already attained almost human capabilities in their ability to recognize objects in pictures as well as the ability to translate languages and even to suggest medical diagnoses, for example, Mayo Clinic (USA). The above-mentioned ChatGPT release last year is a testament to the progress of generative AI capable of writing human-like chatbots, continuing a conversation, and even creating art. It is also disclosed that AI can revolutionize the industries, enhance creativity, and alter the manner in which individuals relate with machines (Figure 2.2).

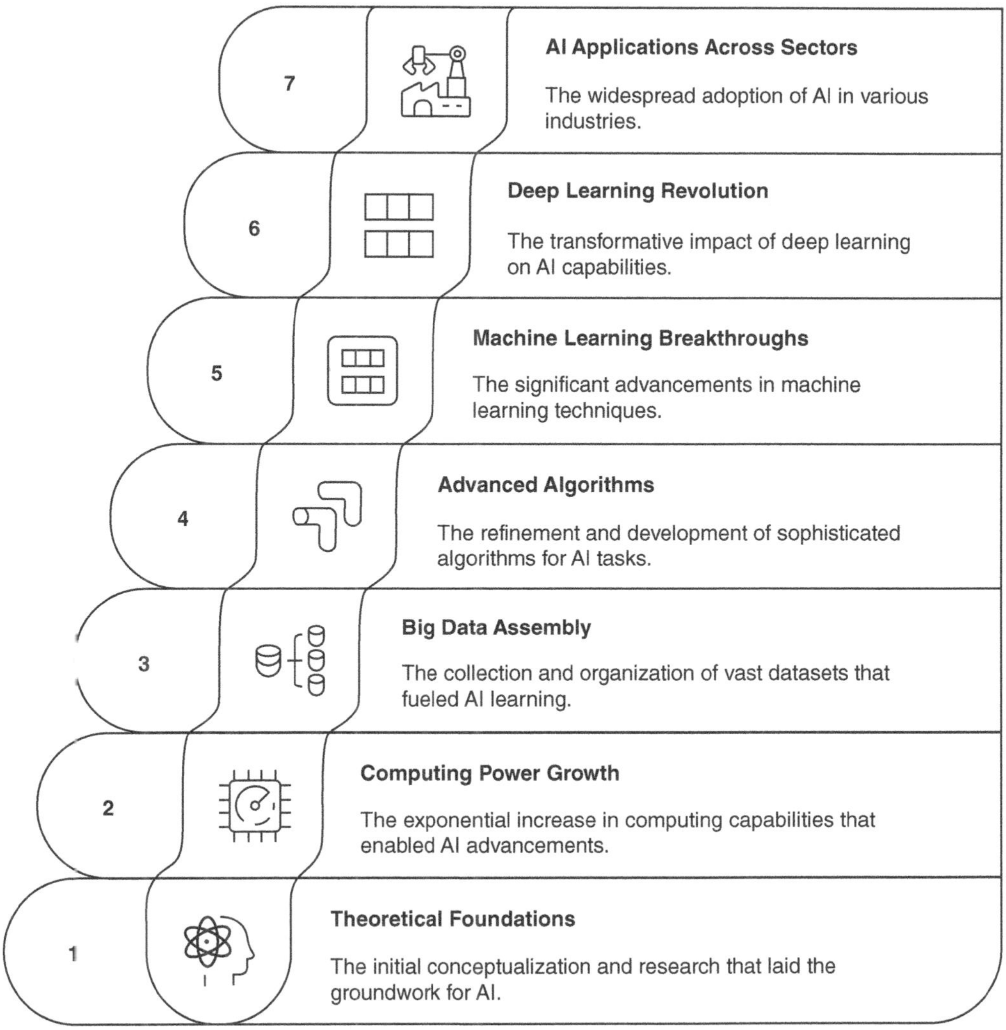

FIGURE 2.2 Journey of AI development.

Nowadays, AI is not just changing the factories and boardrooms, but it's also changing our daily lives, how we date, commute, and even speak to our friends on social media. As this grows, we are walking on a thin line, which raises a lot of questions about ethics and morals.

Next, we won't be talking about machines replacing humans, but how do we coexist? Imagine a farmer using AI to predict the yield of the crop or a doctor finding out the patient's symptoms with the help of AI. These examples show that AI is not only a technological tool but a partner in solving real-world challenges. To understand how this partnership works in marketing, we must first look at the foundation that powers all AI applications: data.

Big Data AI

AI cannot function in isolation—it thrives on data. In marketing, big data acts as the raw material that makes personalization, prediction, and automation possible. Without data, AI is like a powerful engine without fuel. The success of AI in marketing relies on how good and how much data it has access to. This big data is obtained through various touchpoints—visiting the websites, online purchases, the interaction we have with the mobile app, loyalty programs, and the use of social media. Based on the analysis of such large datasets, AI may establish patterns, predict behavior, and personalize campaigns. To give another example, e-commerce stores utilize the history of purchases in order to make product recommendations, whereas streaming video services utilize the history of viewing activities in order to make viewing recommendations. Big data is also more than just numbers, especially in marketing, where big data determines an in-depth map that can plan consumer preferences and behavior, fueling AI-driven modern campaigns.

Ottonomy.IO, a logistics company in the United States, uses AI-powered autonomous delivery robots that predict delivery bottlenecks and reroute in real time. Hospitals now use data analytics the way we use weather satellites to look for disease, identifying the spread of Coronavirus Disease (COVID) before test kits are depleted or revealing rare cancer trends in routine bloodwork. Tools like International Business Machines Corporation (IBM)'s Watson do not just calculate numbers; they provide doctors with findings from millions of cases around the world, transforming a 20-minute consultation into a virtual global and historical medical conference.

In conclusion, without sufficient data, AI is as effective as a Michelin-starred chef without a pantry. Those seemingly "smart" recommendations and lifesaving forecasts are not simple; they are formed from the messiest and most human-like dataset in the world.

Generative AI in Marketing Creativity

After we comprehend the role of data, the next question arises—what can AI do with it? The most promising response is generative AI, which is not about predicting but creating.

Generative AI can be defined as tools that can generate new text, images, audio, or videos based on patterns learned in huge datasets. In contrast to the traditional AI tools that categorize or anticipate, generative AI generates something original, which is especially useful when it comes to creative marketing purposes. Text models, including generative pre-trained transformer (GPT-3) (text generation) and image models like DALLE (image generation), can generate campaign copy, layout ad images, or create branded content in bulk and lightning-fast speed.

This has a number of advantages for marketing. AI-generated copy can be used in other segments of the audience, product descriptions can be customized and written in under one second, and A/B tests can be prototyped and tested in a short period of time. The visual generation tools allow companies to gain access to a vast amount of design ideas without covering costs and time-consuming lengthy production. Recent studies, including that by Jain et al., highlighted that generative AI allows marketers to be more productive and creative, and they will be able to devote more time to the strategic plan and make sure they have a consistent brand voice and quality. In a few words, generative AI is a question of complementing human forces but not replacing them, as a kind of final assistant to a marketer who will not only be faster but also more ingenious. One of its more glaring applications is a direct result of this transition—tailored marketing.

AI in Marketing: Transforming the Industry

AI in marketing is transforming the roles of companies in terms of interactions with consumers, campaign optimization, and expansion. With the help of big data and sophisticated algorithms, AI enables marketers to provide hyper-targeted experiences, automate numerous routines, and decide on future trends even more accurately than before. This part details the various ways AI can be used in the marketing field, including personalized campaigns, predictive analytics, and analyzes the game-changer potential.

AI in Personalized Marketing

Generative AI is the creative engine, and personalization is the steering wheel—to ensure that every sentence of every campaign goes to the right customer at the right time.

As a result, the modern-day buyer demands that brands be preemptive of their needs, and the AI can make that so as it transforms limitless behavioral data into viable insights. Customer segmentation will be hyper-specific, via algorithms that cluster them by their browsing or buying history, or even by some outside metric, such as weather. As another example, Starbucks combines transaction histories, app usage, and local weather to send personalized drink offers in its rewards program—increasing loyalty by 21% (Davenport & Ronanki, 2018). In the same line, Sephora uses Color Intelligence Quotients (IQs) to analyze drop-in pictures to identify foundation options and has increased online sales by 35%.

Nevertheless, personalization is not only observed in product suggestion. The personalization of AI is in every interaction, including personalization of the subject lines on the emails that boost the number of times the emails are opened, to the web pages that vary depending on the user clicking.

AI in Advertising

The next step to advertising is personalization, and AI not only decides how to say something, but also when to say, where to say, and what to say.

Persado is an example of a program that generates advertisement copy to generate an emotional reaction with a minimum of 50% more of higher click-through rates than human-generated test cases (Kumar et al., 2021). These ads are automatically delivered to the intended audience at the appropriate time with programmatic advertising, and Google Smart Bidding is used to optimize campaigns in real time, which saves retail brands about 20–30% in acquisition expenses. Meanwhile, AI is also used in other spheres of marketing in the sense of advertising:

- Customer Support—Chatbots, such as Erica, make the process of support much easier, and it takes less time.
- Product Development AI detects holes in consumer demand for new product launches.
- Customer Relationship Management (CRM) & Sales CRM & Sales predictive analytics are predictive analytics that are used to forecast customer churn and to inform sales practices.

In both scenarios, AI won't displace the marketer but the sharper tools in their hands—to lay the foundation of strategic marketing decisions at scale.

AI in Customer Service

Chatbots are using AI to redefine customer interactions through real-time, scalable assistance. Complex queries, whether it is order tracking or troubleshooting a technical problem, can be supported by advanced NLP to enable chatbots to respond. The chatbot of H&M is like a stylist who inquires about preferences and recommends outfits, whereas the Erica chatbot of Bank of America helps 25 million users with their budgeting and fraud notifications, and most of the questions are answered without a person.

In the healthcare sector, the chatbot used by Walgreens assists users in refilling their prescriptions by 15% of the volume in the call center. Hybrid approaches, in which chatbots refer human agents to serious cases, provide a smooth service. The Domino Dom chatbot, which fulfilled 60% of the orders, is an excellent example of efficiency, reducing the average order time to 10 seconds. Nevertheless, drawbacks still exist—a user can become frustrated due to the inability to read between the lines, and excessive automation may lead to the loss of brand empathy. Sentiment analysis is expected to evolve and identify emotions such as frustration in the future, which will allow interaction more closely with a human being.

Sales and CRM

Predictive analytics will enable marketers to be able to predict trends and plan on resource allocation. AI models predict demand and identify high-value customers, as well as reduce churn by using historical and real-time data. The demand forecasting system within the Carrefour chains, combined with AI, minimizes overstock by a margin of 30 but still makes sure that the product is available during peak seasons. The company has a subscriber growth model that considers content preferences and viewing habits as a guiding factor to its content budget of $17B, which leads to a 90% retention rate.

Predictive analytics tools such as IBM Watson and Salesforce Einstein allow small and medium-sized enterprises (SMEs) to embrace predictive analytics without having to possess that expertise. As an example, Discover Weekly by Spotify is an ML-based service that analyzes the listening behavior and provides users with their own playlists, which generate 16% of interactions. Poorly labeled or unlabeled incomplete information is a challenge, as it affects predictions, and interdisciplinary teams are required to make sense of the outcomes. With the development of AI models, explainable AI (XAI) frameworks are essential to making decisions more transparent to stakeholders (Figure 2.3).

AI for Strategic Marketing

Beyond the single campaigns, the actual power of AI is the ability to influence long-term strategy. The decisions related to strategic marketing, such as market opportunity discovery and brand narratives require to be made based on AI to be more significant. Such tools as Google Trends and Talkwalker research search information, conversations in social media, and images to discover emerging cultural and customer trends before they become merely a mainstream activities. An example would be the AI-based intelligence that Nike already

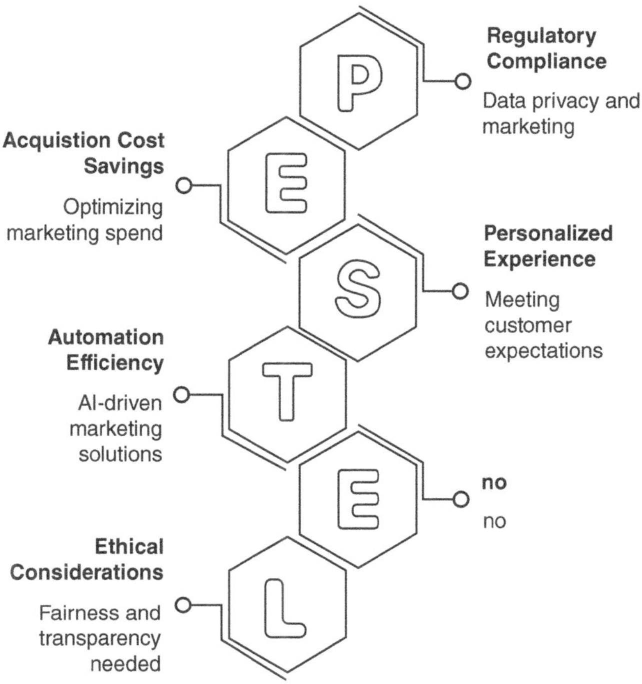

FIGURE 2.3 AI in marketing—transforming industry.

possesses and is becoming increasingly popular in the context of sustainable activeware, which enabled the company to initiate its campaign in the Gen Z segment known as Move to Zero.

AI for Strategic Management: Making Smarter Decisions

AI also enhances market categorization, and brands are able to make customized campaigns, which are much more effective at engaging. As stated in one of the reports by Salesforce in 2023, the engagement rate of companies that utilized AI to target the audience was increased threefold as compared to that of other companies. However, such skills are likely to get disorganized and should be handled exceptionally well to barely achieve discrimination but inclusion. Regardless of the most genuine campaigns, such as Dove and its campaign about the concept of Real Beauty, both machine-based knowledge and human imagination are involved in order to remain in pace with the evolving values of their consumers without losing their brands. Such a balance, in which technology enhances human judgment, preconditions the discussion of the role of AI in enhancing intelligence on the market.

Market Intelligence Using AI: Gaining a Competitive Edge

When personalization is based on the individual consumer, market intelligence changes the perspective and puts the large environment where brands function in focus. AI assists marketers to transcend intuition and gives real-time awareness of cultural changes, crises, and opportunities. Real-Time Monitoring: In the case of the 2021 European Super League backlash, AI technology warned brands such as Pepsi against activating irrelevant campaigns, which would present unwanted associations with negative sentiment. Trendspotting: Netflix uses AI to forecast viral trends like the cottagecore aesthetic, and makes timely content (like Bridgerton tie-ins). Crisis Management: When a major fast-food chain faced a food safety scandal in 2022, its AI system detected a 300% surge in negative mentions, enabling rapid PR responses that cut reputational damage by 50%. Financial Intelligence: Bloomberg uses AI to monitor geopolitical developments, including the price of oil, enabling its clients to change investments within a few minutes. Gartner indicates that one out of five enterprises has become users of AI-driven market monitoring to speed up the decision-making process. The cases demonstrate how AI does not only optimize the marketing campaigns, but it offers the brands a type of radar system to identify and predict risks and capture opportunities in the quickest time possible. Gartner indicates that one out of five enterprises has become users of AI-driven market monitoring to speed up the decision-making process. The cases demonstrate how AI does not only optimize the marketing campaigns, but it also offers the brands a type of radar system to identify and predict risks and capture opportunities in the quickest time possible.

Opportunities and Challenges

The possibilities of artificial intelligence present a marketer with a large scope of opportunities, and each positive opportunity is also marked by a set of challenges, which are supposed to be tackled in a prudent manner.

Opportunities and Risks

Opportunity 1: Hyper-personalization

The brands can use AI to analyze their consumer behavior to a significant level and offer them highly personalized suggestions, product recommendations, and marketing messages. This creates greater connectivity and a relationship with customers because of the feeling of knowing. For example, Duolingo leverages AI for hyper-personalization.

Risks: Hyper-personalization, however, may take an excessive toll on the field of intrusiveness. The problem of privacy can be triggered by excessive usage of personal data in implementing some standards, such as General Data Protection Regulation (GDPR) and California Consumer Privacy Act (CCPA). The over-personalization of their targeting can also be seen by the customers as a coercive practice instead of being helpful to them. The Cambridge Analytica case revealed how hyper-personalization in digital targeting can cross digital boundaries when user data is exploited.

Opportunity 2: Real-Time Decision-Making

Through AI-powered analytics, marketers can monitor the campaigns, detect trends when they emerge, and adjust them in real time. It possesses a very high competitive edge in competitive fast-paced markets. Zara integrates AI-powered analytics with real-time sales and social media data to adjust its inventory and design cycles within days.

Risks: It has a weak point in the form of an algorithm dependency that is real time. Poorly trained models will fail to read the data spikes—for example, viral scandals—and will lead to wholly inappropriate/awkward responses, which will hurt brand credibility. PepsiCo's AI-led real-time campaign failed due to negative audience sentiment.

Opportunity 3: The Opportunity to Save Money and Get Efficient

AI automates repetitive work, including media buying, customer inquiries, and A/B testing. This will save on operational costs and allow the marketers to divert more of their resources to their creativity and strategy. Lemonade Insurance, USA, uses AI-powered chatbots to automate customer onboarding and claim processing, and reduces operational costs.

Dilemma: Job loss and complaints about the need to retrain the working population are also linked to the automation process. The lack of proper upskilling of companies will lead to an internal opposition to the undertaking, not to mention the chances of losing the human judgment in matters of operations, where nuance will be an important factor. IBM Watson's automation programs in marketing analytics led to internal resistance and job displacement to adapt to AI-driven workflows.

Opportunity 4: Vision and Visionary Investment in the Market

Prediction, testing of new products, and identification of cultural trends are some of the predictions that the AIs carry out before they become their point of offering. This kind of expectation encourages brands to be innovative without intimidation and to not go out of business. Unilever's "People Data Centre" uses AI to analyze emerging lifestyle trends, food habits, and climate sentiments from millions of online conversations.

Challenge: The predictive models are as biased as the data that they are fed on. It is possible that biased data can be propagated by AI (due to stereotypes or historical inequality), creating campaigns that marginalize/characterizes certain groups of people.

That is why it is obvious that the future of AI in marketing will not be only regarding the ability to use the data to be faster and more accurate, but also the way to make it responsible and ethical. Unless bias and transparency are tackled, the very instruments that are intended to empower the brands will destroy the trust (Figure 2.4).

The Path Forward

AI is not new to marketing practice as brands now make decisions faster, more data-driven, and provide more relevant experiences to consumers. The next step will not be about whether to adopt AI or not, but how to integrate it responsibly. Marketers need to make the data gathering and application processes open, minimize bias in algorithms, and leave the exercise of creativity to people. Those able to reconcile AI's capabilities with the values of their brands will generate sustainable competitive advantages.

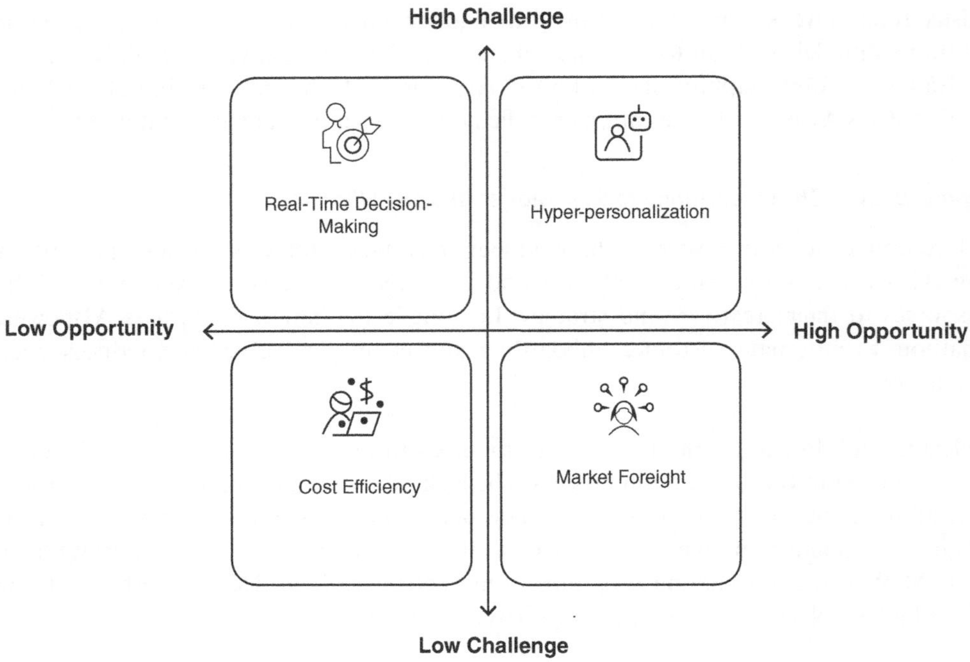

FIGURE 2.4 AI opportunities and challenges in marketing.

CLOSING CASE: HOW COCA-COLA USES AI TO STAY AHEAD IN THE BEVERAGE INDUSTRY

Coca-Cola is one of the most recognizable brands in the world, which is available in more than 200 countries. The company was established in 1892, and it has expanded to become a worldwide giant out of one product. Besides its product, it is known to have innovative marketing campaigns and a good distribution network. It has strongly adopted the concept of artificial intelligence to continue enjoying its competitive advantage in the fast-changing beverage market. The digital transformation of the company is a big transition of the company that uses traditional methods of marketing to data-driven practices that run on sophisticated analytics and AI (Davenport & Ronanki, 2018).

The main component of the AI strategy employed by Coca-Cola is the powerful data infrastructure. The company gathers and uses massive amounts of consumer data across numerous touchpoints, such as social media, mobile applications, vending machines, and retail relationships. Such abundance of information can enable Coca-Cola to better understand the behavior and preferences of consumers, as well as new tendencies (Marr, 2019). As Greg Chambers, the Global Director of Digital Innovation at Coca-Cola, states, AI and digital transformation are not only buzzwords at Coca-Cola but also elements of the business strategy in the 21st century (Coca-Cola, 2022).

One of the most significant illustrations of the best AI practice used at Coca-Cola is the smart vending machines, which have digital screens and use AI. These machines are capable of proposing products to the customer depending on the weather conditions, time of day, and consumer preferences. The technology assists consumers in making their own beverage mixes via the Coca-Cola Freestyle machines that assist in learning consumer preferences and enhancing the consumption experience at the same time (Solis, 2020). Up to this point, the Freestyle platform has studied over billions of drink combinations, providing Coca-Cola with insights into the taste preferences of customers in both demographic and geographical areas (Newman, 2021).

Coca-Cola applies artificial intelligence in the field of marketing and advertising to enhance the efficiency of the campaign and the use of resources. The strategy is part of the larger trends where legacy brands are using AI to coordinate marketing through a variety of channels (Bowers et al., 2024). The predictive analysis enables the marketing departments of the company to know how consumers will respond to different marketing approaches and, therefore, integrate costs and returns on the marketing investment (Chui et al., 2018). As an example, when the COVID-19 pandemic happened in 2020, Coca-Cola used AI-driven analytics to redefine its marketing strategy in a few days since it affected consumer behavior and shifted its marketing strategy from out-of-home to the online realm (Coca-Cola, 2021).

Another aspect of the AI plan of Coca-Cola is social media listening. The NLP and sentiment analysis tools are used to keep track of the brand, consumer sentiment, and trends on various social media platforms in real time (Kietzmann et al., 2022). This aspect allows Coca-Cola to respond to any potential public relation (PR) crisis and leverage the positive references to the brand. According to the Chief Marketing Officer of Coca-Cola, Michelle Peluso, the AI-empowered social listening tools provide an opportunity to interact with consumers differently and enable the company to become a participant in the conversation in real time (Coca-Cola, 2022).

Product development is another field in which Coca-Cola uses AI. Its machine learning is used to ensure that new products are designed to satisfy consumer needs based on their preferences and market trends (Ransbotham et al., 2020). The formation of Cherry Sprite is one of the most common cases that have been created after the examination of Coca-Cola data analytics displayed that people were willing to combine Sprite and cherry flavor in the Freestyle machines (Davenport, 2022).

Coca-Cola AI projects have also come in handy in supply chain management. Predictive analytics is applied by the company to predict demand, manage inventory, and design distribution networks. It is these AI-facilitated solutions that have seen Coca-Cola cut down on its logistics expenditure, and at the same time, expand the availability of its products, particularly in a retail setting where availability is one of the primary drivers of consumer loyalty (Christopher & Holweg, 2021).

Nevertheless, the Coca-Cola AI strategy has certain problems. The company has encountered the issues of data security, the effects of algorithmic bias, and the necessity of the human factor role in the AI decision-making process (Davenport & Bean, 2019). In this respect, Coca-Cola has developed a series of ethical AI principles and governance policies that take into consideration accountability, equity, and consumer data protection (Coca-Cola, 2022).

Coca-Cola is moving into the future and considers to utilize the new technologies like artificial intelligence, Augmented Reality, voice recognition, and blockchain to enhance the business and consumer interaction (Kaplan & Haenlein, 2020). The company is also taking time to do research on new AI technologies, collaborating with universities and other technology firms to stay a pioneer in applying AI in the consumer goods business (Coca-Cola, 2022).

The AI approach of Coca-Cola represents a good illustration of how conventional brands with consumers can accommodate innovative technologies to keep their relevance and development in the online environment. In this way, Coca-Cola has had the opportunity to blend its robust brand and new-age AI technologies to develop an ideal prototype of success in the market today (Kumar et al., 2021).

Discussion Questions

1 What is AI's role in converting customer data into actionable marketing strategies? What implications does this have for consumer trust?
2 In what ways does the distinction between weak AI and strong AI matter for marketers today?
3 Can Gen AI replace human creativity in marketing campaigns, or should it be viewed primarily as an augmenting tool?
4 How can businesses strike a balance between efficiency through AI automation and the need of maintaining human empathy in customer service?
5 What are some of the risks that arise from biased data or over-reliance on AI for market intelligence? How can firms mitigate these risks?
6 In the long term, do you see AI creating sustainable competitive advantages for brands, or does it seem that it would lead to industry-wide standardization of marketing practices?

Assignment Questions

1 Select a global brand of your choice (e.g., Starbucks, Spotify, or Nike). Examine how AI is being used in its marketing strategy and evaluate the effectiveness of those initiatives.
2 Compare weak AI and strong AI in the context of marketing. Which type is more relevant for today's businesses, and why?
3 Design a small-scale AI-driven personalization pilot for an e-commerce company. Outline the data requirements, potential key performance indicators (KPIs), and safeguards to keep in place to ensure ethical use.
4 Analyze the role of Gen AI in advertising and creative content. Provide examples of how it is currently being leveraged by brands today and the way it could be leveraged responsibly to enhance storytelling.
5 Evaluate a recent case where AI-driven marketing practices faced public criticism. Additionally, according to you, what governance measures could have prevented the specific backlash?

MINI CASE: NIKE

Are you interested in purchasing apparel, sneakers, and much more with the digital experience?

Nike is the place that offers the purchase of apparel, sneakers, and a complete digital experience for users. It has transformed into much more than a sports brand; it is now a digitally integrated lifestyle ecosystem. The company has invested heavily in its digital ecosystem, like Nike Digital, the SNKRS app, and even e-commerce. The Nike App uses AI to recommend shoes, apparel, and training plans to its users based on their user activity and purchase history. "Nike Fit" has an AI-enabled scanning tool that measures foot size through the smartphone camera to suggest the correct shoe fit. Additionally, AI models forecast demand for limited-edition sneakers by minimizing excess inventory and maximizing the hype behind these limited-edition sneakers. The SNKRS app is an application used by Nike that utilizes AI to identify bot manipulation and provide loyal customers with exclusive drops. Personalization induced by AI enhances loyalty among the average everyday users and athletes and makes the app more sticky and makes the sales. Although AI does possess all of these benefits in the field of Marketing, it also presents such challenges as problems of transparency. Additionally, the culture of hype and inclusivity is a difficult aspect to balance, and high dependency on data necessitates high governance of privacy. The case study on Nike is a learning lesson to marketers that AI could be applied not only to achieve efficiency in operations but also in brand building. Exclusivity and personalization lead to the improvement of emotional attachment with a brand. Lastly, cultural relevance is also guaranteed by real-time market intelligence, particularly with the younger trend-setting audiences.

HBR Case Links:

- https://hbsp.harvard.edu/product/IES907-PDF-ENG
- https://hbsp.harvard.edu/product/519039-PDF-ENG

Application of Concepts and In-Class Activities

Concept (Kotler Link)	*Application in Practice*	*In-Class Activity/Illustration*
Personalization (Segmentation & Targeting)	AI analyzes customer data to deliver hyper-targeted offers (e.g., Starbucks—weather-based drink offers and Amazon—product recommendations).	Case Exercise: Students are given mock customer datasets and have to design 3 personalized offers for different customer segments. Discuss potential benefits and the relevant privacy concerns.

(Continued)

Concept (Kotler Link)	*Application in Practice*	*In-Class Activity/Illustration*
Generative AI in Marketing Creativity (Integrated Marketing Communications)	Tools like GPT and DALL·E generate ad copy, images, and content prototypes at scale, which enhances creativity.	Workshop: Students use a Gen AI tool to draft two ad variations for the same product. They can then debate the one to choose through A/B campaign.
AI in Advertising (Promotion & Media Planning)	Programmatic advertising platforms optimize bidding and placement, which reduces costs and improves targeting.	Simulation: Groups allocate a $10,000 ad budget across AI-driven channels, then compare the initially predicted ROI.
AI in Customer Service (Customer Relationship Management)	Chatbots handle routine queries, improving efficiency but raising questions about empathy.	Role Play: Half the class acts as chatbot makers, half as frustrated customers. Discuss limits of automation and design escalation rules.
Market Intelligence (Marketing Research & Competitive Analysis)	AI tools monitor cultural shifts, sentiment, and competitor actions to give brands an early signal of opportunities or risks.	Trendspotting Exercise: Students analyze AI-driven social listening dashboards to identify an emerging consumer trend and propose a brand action.

Key Terms

- Weak AI
- Strong AI
- Artificial general intelligence (AGI)
- Big data
- Generative AI
- Personalization
- Programmatic advertising
- Chatbots
- Natural language processing (NLP)
- Predictive analytics
- Customer relationship management (CRM)
- Market intelligence
- Hyper-personalization
- Real-time decision-making
- Ethical AI

References

Bowers, J., Griffin, K., & Silverman, L. (2024, June 4). *The new rules of marketing across channels*. Harvard Business Review. https://hbr.org/2024/06/the-new-rules-of-marketing-across-channels

Christopher, M., & Holweg, M. (2021). Supply chain 4.0: Implementing emerging technologies in supply chain operations. *International Journal of Operations & Production Management*, *41*(10), 1–12.

Chui, M., Manyika, J., & Miremadi, M. (2018). What AI can and can't do (yet) for your business. *McKinsey Quarterly*, *1*, 96–108.
Coca-Cola. (2021). *Annual Report 2020*. The Coca-Cola Company.
Coca-Cola. (2022). *Digital transformation strategy*. The Coca-Cola Company.
Davenport, T. H. (2022). *All-in on AI: How smart companies win big with artificial intelligence*. Harvard Business Review Press.
Davenport, T. H., & Bean, R. (2019). Big companies are embracing analytics, but most still don't have a data-driven culture. *Harvard Business Review Digital Articles*, 2–4.
Davenport, T. H., & Ronanki, R. (2018). Artificial intelligence for the real world. *Harvard Business Review*, *96*(1), 108–116.
Kaplan A., & Haenlein, M. (2020). Rulers of the world, unite! The challenges and opportunities of artificial intelligence. *Business Horizons*, *63*(1), 37–50.
Kietzmann, J., Paschen, J., & Treen, E. (2022). Artificial intelligence in advertising: How marketers can leverage AI to build brands. *Journal of Advertising Research*, *62*(1), 86–103.
Kumar, V., Rajan, B., Venkatesan, R., & Lecinski, J. (2021). Understanding the role of artificial intelligence in personalized engagement marketing. *California Management Review*, *63*(4), 5–31.
Marr, B. (2019). *Artificial intelligence in practice: How 50 successful companies used AI and machine learning to solve problems*. Wiley.
Newman, D. (2021). *Top 10 digital transformation trends for 2022*. Forbes.
Ransbotham, S., Khodabandeh, S., Fehling, R., LaFountain, B., & Kiron, D. (2020). Winning with AI. *MIT Sloan Management Review*, *61*(1), 19–22.
Schrage, M. (2017, August 18). *Great digital companies build great recommendation engines*. Harvard Business Review. https://hbr.org/2017/08/great-digital-companies-build-great-recommendation-engines
Solis, B (2020). *The innovation in customer experience report*. Altimeter Group.

3

AI IN PRODUCT DEVELOPMENT

Learning Objectives

After reading this chapter, you will be able to:

1 Learn about the product development process and the use of AI.
2 Learn about the steps involved in product development.
3 Distinguish between the steps of product development.
4 Learn about the budgeting of product development and the benefits of using AI.
5 Understand the future of AI and its risks.
6 Understand the Anthropomorphism, supply chain, and AI.

OPENING CASE: TESLA-DRIVING INNOVATION WITH AI IN PRODUCT DEVELOPMENT

Tesla is an electric vehicle company that was founded by Martin Eberhard and Marc Tarpenning. It is famous for its innovation in the EV space and uses AI in a lot of its leading innovations. Rather than treating AI as a back-office data tool, Tesla embeds it end-to-end in product development. Tesla's integration of design, software, and systems thinking lays the foundation for this AI-driven, end-to-end product development strategy (Furr & Dyer, 2020). Upstream signal mining converts telemetry, service logs, and customer voice into prioritized requirements; generative-design agents and coupled computational fluid dynamics (CFD)/finite element analysis (FEA) simulations iterate thousands of geometry and materials options before any physical build; digital twins and hardware-in-the-loop benches stress subsystems under rare edge conditions, while shadow-mode evaluations estimate model lift and risk prior to activation; on the line, computer vision detects fit-and-finish defects and a Bayesian optimizer tunes process parameters in real time; postlaunch, over-the-air updates A/B-test

DOI: 10.4324/9781003501862-3

control strategies and user interface (UI) flows, using multi-objective optimization to balance performance, safety, comfort, and energy draw; and life-cycle assessment models surface low-carbon materials and manufacturable alternatives early so sustainability is a design constraint, not an afterthought. Supply-signal forecasts inform design-for-manufacture choices (e.g., pin-compatible components) to keep roadmaps resilient. The outcome is reduced cycles, rate of first-time-right, reduced embodied carbon, and a product that continues to increase in the driveways of customers—giving managers the capacity to make conscious, evidence-based decisions concerning product (Tesla, 2024).

Introduction to AI in Product Development

Artificial intelligence (AI) is transforming a great deal, and product development is no exception: Tesla has re-implemented its entire new-product-development process around AI, mining vehicle telemetry and service logs to translate real-use pain points into ranked requirements; using generative design plus CFD/FEA simulation to explore thousands of part geometries before a single tooling cut; validating control policies in digital twins and shadow-mode testing; detecting fit-and-finish problems on the line with computer vision and tuning process parameters in Bayesian optimizers; and, once a product gets to market. The integration of AI tools into the new product development process can revolutionize how companies ideate, design, and launch their products. Product development using AI includes researching what is popular in the market, creating prototypes, and making sure that production runs as smoothly as possible. The numbers show that AI is becoming important in product development. McKinsey's most recent survey found a big change in how AI is used: Around one-third of the companies polled employ generative AI regularly. Almost around 25% of middle management said they used generative AI tools for personal projects, while 40% of those who answered plan to put more money into AI because of progress in generative AI.

However, despite AI's growing role in product development, organizational complexity and scale often hinder larger corporations from introducing truly innovative products. Unlike agile start-ups which leverage AI-driven insights to rapidly develop and iterate products, many large enterprises struggle with rigid structures, slow decision-making processes, and bureaucratic hurdles. This will allow start-ups to outperform them in innovation and market responsiveness, successfully competing in their territory. Before the rise of private equity in the early 1980s, companies like IBM and HP had special initiatives for new product development within the company. IBM had a program called "wild ducks" wherein they allowed these wild ducks employee got a title of IBM Fellow and could make new things. They were given the privilege of wearing whatever they chose compared to other employees dressed in formal clothes in blue suits, white shirts, and red ties. Their main job was to invent the next new product. While IBM's customer-facing ranks famously wore dark suits and white shirts, the personal computer (PC) team in Boca Raton operated with fewer formalities and more autonomy—a cultural buffer that sped decisions and encouraged rule-bending essential to shipping a radically new product.

AI is revolutionizing product development by enabling businesses to make informed decisions and generate innovative ideas through the analysis of existing data. By leveraging

AI, companies can gain deeper customer insights, optimize resource utilization, and expedite the delivery of products to market. This integration has transformed traditional product development processes by automating repetitive tasks, analyzing vast datasets, and providing actionable information. For example, Netflix employs AI algorithms to analyze viewer preferences and behavior, facilitating the creation of personalized content recommendations and informing decisions on new content production. Similarly, BMW utilizes AI in vehicle design and manufacturing, enhancing efficiency and innovation in its production lines. In the health sector, Navina, an AI-startup, has developed technology that integrates with electronic health records to provide clinical insights, thereby improving patient care and operational efficiency. AI can help businesses work smarter in product development by making better decisions and coming up with new ideas using existing data. AI turns the data you already have—usage logs, tickets, reviews, sensor streams—into clear product requirements (via clustering and large language model (LLM) summarization). Generative design + simulation rapidly explores thousands of options, while causal A/B tests and multi-objective optimization make trade-offs explicit. Example: a dishwasher brand mines warranty + Internet of Things (IoT) data to spot hard-water residue; an LLM frames the requirement, generative design proposes a new spray arm, a digital twin validates it, and a Bayesian field test confirms fewer re-washes with no extra energy.

Result: faster cycles, higher first-time-right, and continuous postlaunch improvement. They can better give customer insights into what they want, use their resources better, and get goods to customers faster this way. AI has become an important part of product development and management. It has changed how companies develop new products by automating boring tasks, analyzing huge amounts of data, and giving useful information.

A huge number of new products hit the market every year. A lot of them say they offer something new and useful. Continuous upgradation of products is helpful to stay in the competition and meet the changing needs of their customers. This is especially important when people start using new technologies. Creating new products can also lead to more ways to market them, which can help grow the market share. Continuous product upgrades are essential for maintaining a competitive edge and adapting to evolving customer needs, especially as new technologies emerge. By consistently enhancing existing products or developing innovative ones, companies cannot only meet changing consumer expectations but also differentiate themselves in the market. Moreover, introducing new products opens up additional marketing opportunities, allowing businesses to expand their reach, attract new customer segments, and ultimately increase market share.

Product development means making changes to existing products or creating new products that look like old ones and selling them in new markets. There are many strategies and methods that can be used to make the product development go smoothly. Also, new ideas are becoming more and more important in the process of making and designing products. Conceptual design is where most product innovation happens. Product development strategy spans smart refreshes of existing offerings and net-new concepts for adjacent markets. To make the journey smooth, teams blend Design Thinking (discovery), Quality Function Deployment (QFD) (voice-of-customer → specs), theory of inventive problem-solving (TRIZ) (inventive principles), Agile/Lean Startup (rapid minimum viable products (MVPs)), design of experiments (DOEs) (parameter tuning), and Stage-Gate (go/kill discipline). Today's conceptual design is powered by AI/machine learning (ML) (clustering pain points, LLM product requirements document (PRD) drafts, generative design), CFD/FEA simulation and digital twins, additive manufacturing for fast prototypes, advanced materials (recycled composites, bio-polymers), IoT/sensors for real-use data, and augmented reality/virtual reality (AR/VR) for immersive testing. A running-shoe brand ingests gait data from its app + in-store pressure mats; AI clusters injury-risk patterns, and Design Thinking interviews refine "jobs to be done."

The Evolution of AI in Product Development

AI has come a long way from simple automation to complex machine learning and deep learning tools. Additionally, early-2000s projects like SRI's CALO and consumer chatbots laid the groundwork for mainstream assistants such as Apple's Siri and Google Assistant—a lineage that continues in today's generative AI agents. At the beginning of the 2000s, AI took its first steps toward becoming a product. Its main goal was to make boring tasks easier to do frequently, so engineers would not have to do tedious calculations and drawings. This was an enormous efficiency improvement with the introduction of computer-aided design (CAD) systems driven by AI. These intelligent systems were characterized by such functions as automatic drawing, real-time design feedback, and more intelligent design tools through collision detection and stress analysis. This is because it enabled engineers to produce stronger and more reliable products within a shorter time. At the beginning of the 2000s, AI started becoming a field of practical application, especially in terms of automated repetitive engineering work. One of the major developments at this time was the adoption of AI in CAD systems, which transformed product development by making it more efficient and precise. New capabilities of these AI-based CAD systems included the automatic creation of drawings, real-time feedback of a design, collision detection tools, and intelligent tools. As a result, engineers would have been able to produce more reliable products of higher strength, consuming less time, minimizing manual work, and errors. For example, Siemens NX software incorporated AI capabilities to predict material behavior based on user interactions and past designs, allowing manufacturers to optimize product designs effectively.

AI is like a smart test track for products: it lets companies "try out" ideas on a computer before they spend money making them. For example, a ceiling-fan brand can feed in common complaints (too noisy, not enough airflow) and let AI quickly trial hundreds of blade shapes virtually, spotting which ones push more air with less noise. Engineers then build only the top two designs, choose the winner, and launch a quieter, more efficient fan faster. Fewer false starts, lower costs, and better results—without the technical jargon.

Where AI Stands Now in Product Engineering

The world of product development is ruled by machine learning and LLMs such as generative AI and ChatGPT. They have become extremely popular within a very short time, as was the case with ChatGPT, which had 100,000 adopters within five days since inception. This demonstrates that they are not merely strong AI tools but also handy in real-life applications. Machine learning can analyze massive volumes of data to identify the most effective methods of creating products, and LLMs provide us with information similar to that of humans on market trends, consumer preferences, and potential features. This AI technology will help companies to remain ahead of the competition and come up with new

TABLE 3.1 Usage of AI across Industries and Companies Globally

Industry	*Company*	*The Use of AI*
Healthcare	Google's DeepMind	It created an AI that can guess the shape or structure of proteins, which is very helpful for learning about diseases, drugs, and making new medicines.
Retail	Amazon	Its recommendation engine uses AI to suggest products based on what customers have looked at and bought in the past.
Logistics	UPS	It uses AI and machine learning to find the best distribution channels, which saves a lot of money and makes things run more smoothly.
Manufacturing	General Electric	AI helps it figure out when its machines need to be serviced, which keeps them from breaking down and costing a lot of money.
FinTech	Mastercard	It uses AI to spot fraudulent transactions, which has cut down on fraud-related losses by a large amount.

products that exceed customer expectations. AI is no longer a luxury in product development, and it is required in much of the industry. The following are some instances of the way big enterprises have utilized AI to enhance their operations (Table 3.1).

Product Development Process (Idea to Execution)

The first step in making a new product is to look for ideas. Some marketing professionals think that finding the best set of unmet customer needs or new technologies is the best way to find new products with the most potential. Another great place to get ideas is from the people in charge. Leaders of some companies, like Andy Grove, who used to be CEO of Intel, are personally responsible for coming up with new technologies for their companies. Many companies are going outside their comfort zones to find new ideas. The outside sources could be consumers, researchers, engineers, universities, labs, and even competitors.

Businesses can get ideas even by looking into the goods and services of rivals and other businesses. Customers may tell them what they admire and do not like about their competitors' goods. Their competitors' goods can be bought, taken apart, and then better ones made.

When the company looks over ideas, it needs to avoid two kinds of mistakes. When a company misses a good idea, this is called a DROP error. Anyone can easily find something wrong with someone else's ideas. Some hesitate when they remember ideas they turned down, while others breathe a sigh of relief when they remember how close they were to dropping an idea that turned out to be a huge success.

Screening is meant to get rid of bad ideas as quickly as possible. The reason for this is that the costs of developing a product go up a lot with each stage. Companies need new product ideas explained and written down on a standard form so that a relevant committee can look them over. There is a description of the product idea, the target market, and the competition. There are also rough estimates of the size of the market, the price of the product, the time and money needed to develop it, the cost of making it, and the rate of return (Figure 3.1).

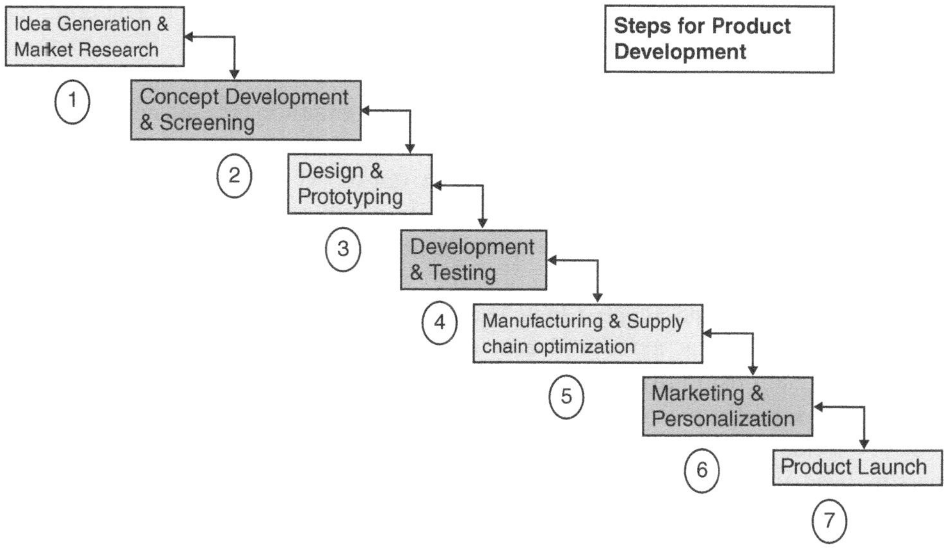

FIGURE 3.1 Steps for product development.

Steps in the Product Development Process

1 **Idea Generation and Market Research**: The first step in making a new product is to look for ideas. Some marketing professionals think that finding the best set of unmet customer needs or new technologies is the best way to find new products with the most potential. Leaders of some companies, like Andy Grove, former CEO of Intel, were personally responsible for coming up with new technologies for their companies. Many companies are stepping outside their comfort zones to find out new ideas. Outside sources could include consumers, researchers, engineers, universities, labs, and even competitors. Businesses can get ideas by analyzing competitor products, customer feedback, and improving upon existing solutions.

2 **Concept Development and Screening**: Companies must avoid two major mistakes when evaluating ideas: **DROP** errors (rejecting a good idea) and **PUSH** errors (advancing a weak idea). Screening helps eliminate weak ideas early since development costs rise significantly at each stage. Companies document product ideas, target market, competition, market size, estimated cost, and return on investment before proceeding.

3 **Design and Prototyping**: The original idea is turned into a tangible concept, and prototypes are created for testing. AI tools assist in rapid prototyping by generating multiple design variations based on set parameters and user feedback. AI can analyze user interaction with prototypes to optimize designs before full-scale production.

4 **Development and Testing**: The product is built and rigorously tested to ensure functionality, safety, and efficiency. AI automates repetitive testing, analyzes sensor data, and predicts product performance in real-world conditions. Example: Tesla AI simulations help automotive companies test vehicle safety without needing multiple physical crash tests.

5 **Launch, Optimization, and Commercialization**: AI tracks product performance post-launch and collects user feedback for continuous improvement. AI personalizes

marketing strategies based on consumer demographics and behavior. The commercial stage incurs the highest cost, but AI can help minimize expenses through targeted advertising and automated market analysis.

6 **B2B Product Development and AI Integration**: AI enhances the business-to-business (B2B) product development process by automating routine procedures and finding new insights in data. Automation tools that are driven by AI facilitate the process of customer engagement, thereby simplifying marketing and operations. Examples: Khoros and 6sense are AI-powered and can provide personalized experiences, which leads to higher conversions and engagement.
7 **AI-Driven Inventory and Supply Chain Management**: AI facilitates predictive analysis of demand forecasting, at a reduced cost of inventory, but with optimal stock levels. Customer Relationship Management (CRM) systems are AI-driven tools that are used to optimize sales through the ranking of leads and the sentiment of customers. Case: The Conversational AI of Drift enhances customer communication by providing personalized and real-time replies.
8 **AI-Enhanced Pricing and Supply Chain Optimization**: AI-based dynamic pricing models change the price dynamically in real-time depending on the volume of orders, market trends, and negotiation. AI applications, such as PROS, can assist companies to arrive at the best prices to apply to various segments. Supply chain platforms that are automated using AI technologies like Coupa streamline logistics, minimize bottlenecks, and forecast maintenance requirements. Case study: AI analytics at Sana Commerce optimizes the marketing process through highly personalized messaging to reach the intended customers.

Idea and Concept Stage

During this phase, developers will come up with new product ideas and work on making them into core concepts. AI can look at a huge amount of information from sources like social media, customer reviews, competitor data, and market research reports to find trends and needs that are not being met in a short time. This helps find chances for innovation and shapes early brainstorming.

Let us say a big software company comes up with the idea of using a new device to cut internet use from several GBs to just MBs. People do not buy product ideas; they buy product concepts. Okay, so this is a product idea. One idea for a product can lead to more than one idea. The first question is: Who is going to buy this? It can be for kids, teens, young or middle-aged adults, or adults over the age of 18. Second, what should this product's main benefit be? Should it be value for money? Third, when is this thing going to be used? Always or for a certain amount of time?

Design and Prototyping Stage

In this case, the original idea is turned into something real, and prototypes are then used to test it. AI tools can help with rapid prototyping by coming up with different designs based on user feedback and parameters that have already been set. AI can also look at how people interact with prototypes to find ways to make them better before they are made on a large scale.

Development and Testing Stage

During this phase, the product is made and tested thoroughly to make sure it works, is safe, and is efficient. AI can automate testing tasks that are done continually, look at sensor data from testing products to find problems, and even guess how a product might work in different real-life situations.

Launch, Optimization, and Commercial Stage

After the product hits the market, its performance is tracked and studied. Based on customer preferences and demographics, AI can be used to make product launches and marketing more relevant to each person. AI can also look at ongoing user feedback and data on how the product is used to find ways to make it better and help shape future versions of the product. The company incurs the highest cost in the commercial stage. But this can be minimized by effective use of AI tools. Too often, businesses are so focused on making a new product that they do not take the time to make a good marketing launch program. Most campaigns for new products also need a set of market communication tools to get people to know about them and then to build preference, choice, and loyalty (Figure 3.2).

B2B Product Development and AI

AI is not just a concept from the future in the B2B world; it is already a useful tool that is making a difference. AI can be used to make B2B businesses more efficient in several ways, such as by automating boring tasks and finding hidden insights in your data. Product managers' new best friend is automation: Not wanting to copy and paste information or send the same email over and over? These boring tasks can be done by AI-powered automation, which will free up the team's valuable time.

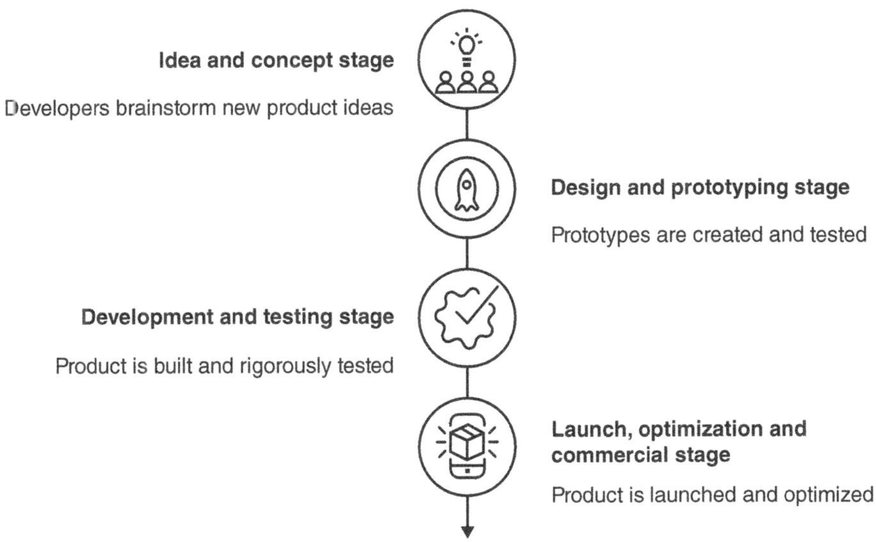

FIGURE 3.2 Product development lifecycle.

Platform for engaging customers The Khoros team combined AI-driven intent data from 6sense with their own behavioral data to give their audience highly personalized, real-time experiences on their website. Each visitor's profile was matched with the right content on customized pages and modules, which led to four times as many demos and twice as many pageviews.

AI can quickly look through huge amounts of data and find trends and patterns that people might miss. This helps people make smarter decisions. This means product managers can use solid evidence instead of gut feeling to make decisions. Personalized customer experiences: marketing blasts that are too general are a thing of the past. AI can personalize interactions with a lot of customers by making product suggestions, emails, and other things more relevant to each person based on their likes and dislikes and how they act. Streamlined supply chains: AI can make a company's supply chain work better by predicting demand, finding bottlenecks, and making sure you have the right amount of inventory at the right time. Customers will be happier, and the business will make more money.

All employees will be more productive: AI can make the whole organization more productive by automating tasks, making decisions better, and streamlining processes.

Want to know what the best AI tools are for making B2B work better? These are some of the best AI tools that you can use in all parts of your business:

For B2B, predictive analytics is like a crystal ball.

Predictive analytics is like a crystal ball that is powered by data. AI can predict sales, demand, and even possible problems before they happen by looking at past data and finding patterns. The way forward is with tools that help businesses make smarter decisions based on data.

Managing Inventory: Find the Right Balance

Having too much inventory can tie up cash, and not having enough inventory can lead to missing out on sales. But how to get to that perfect place? Forecasting tools that use AI can do more than just guessing what people will want. They use real-time market data, news feeds, and even global events to keep your business flexible and make sure your inventory levels are just right.

CRMs with AI: More Than Just Contacts

B2B CRM is what keeps you going. AI can make it stronger, though. AI can make CRM more powerful by looking at how customers act, ranking leads, and even figuring out how people feel. Salesforce Einstein and Pipedrive are two examples. As a result? More targeted advertising, easier work processes, and, in the end, happier customers.

Conversational AI, which is patented by Drift, uses natural language processing to understand and answer prospects' messages. In an open-text format, website visitors say what they want to do, and the experience feels like talking to a real person. Conversational AI is different from other models like it because it was trained on more than 100 million B2B sales and marketing conversations. It is very focused on giving relevant information, qualifying leads, and turning prospects into customers. Conversational AI from Drift makes people 40% more likely to interact with chatbots that only have buttons.

Using Dynamic Pricing to Get It Right

In B2B, prices vary on a legitimate basis, including configuration, quantity, delivery terms, and relationship history, so it is not the changes in price that need to be delivered more frequently, but the quote delivery. In AI-based pricing engines, signals (market benchmarks, win-loss data, inventory and capacity, contract terms, even notes of prior negotiations) are synthesized to come up with a recommended price range for each deal. The sales picks made in that band sound with compelling logic, margin, and fairness are maintained within bounds through the use of guardrails (floors/ceilings, approval rules, and audit trails). One of the suppliers of industrial components leaves three years of their quotes and results; the machine learning model discovers the features that can forecast the probability of winning and margin. On a new RFQ, it will provide a target range (e.g., ₹1.82–₹ 1.95 lakh) and the trade-offs. Response rates are quicker, hit rates increase, and similar customers get similar prices, all without manual recalculation, creating trust.

Supply Chain Optimization: Things Are Going to Go Smoothly

B2B supply chains are like huge webs. AI can help you get out of the mess, though. AI is used by Coupa and other similar solutions to find the best routes, find bottlenecks, and even predict maintenance problems. This keeps your products moving smoothly and makes your customers happy.

Personalized Marketing: Talk to Customers One-on-One

For B2B, account-based marketing is important, but it takes a lot of work. This is where add-ons like the advanced analytics feature in Sana Commerce come in handy. They look at information about customers to help write messages that are very specific to each account and get a response. It is like having a marketing team just for the best profitable customers (Figure 3.3).

Budgeting for New-Product Development

In Table 3.2, you can see how a business might figure out how much it costs to make a new product. Suppose a business is targeting new product launches at a national level. The manager of new products at a big, diversified company that makes packaged goods for consumers looked over 729 ideas made using AI, coupled with other resources costing $500 each. At this point, 81 made it past the filtering stage, and 27 of them made it through the concept-testing stage, which cost $10,000 each. At a cost of $100,000 each, nine passed the product development stage. Three sold well in the test market and each cost $500,000. Each one now cost $7.5 million to make, and when they were released, one did very well. It cost the company $3,110,500 to develop this one successful idea or product, but $15,874,500 was spent on developing 728 ideas that did not work out. The company will have to spend almost $16 million on each new idea it wants to find, if it cannot increase the number of ideas that get through and lower the costs at every stage.

Benefits of Using AI in Product Development

A lot of companies can make product development faster with the help of AI, which is changing the way products are made.

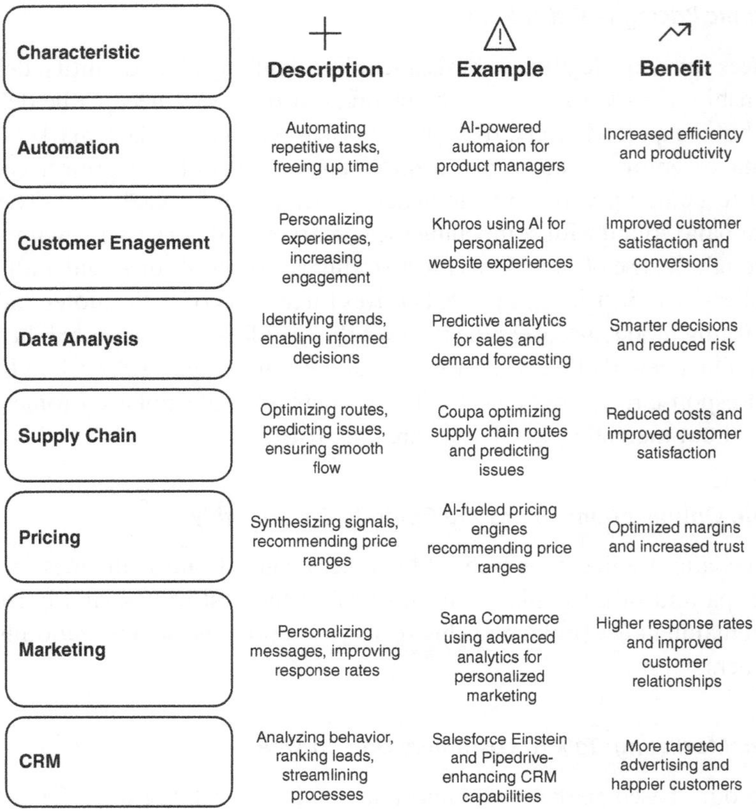

FIGURE 3.3 AI applications in B2B.

TABLE 3.2 Product Funnel Cost model

Stage	*Number of Ideas*	*Pass Ratio*	*Cost per Product Idea*	*Total Cost*
Idea filtering stage	729	1:9	500	364,500
Concept testing	81	1:3	10,000	810,000
Product Development	27	1:3	100,000	2,700,000
Test Marketing	9	1:3	500,000	4,500,000
National Launch	3	1:3	2,500,000	7,500,000
			$3,110,500	$15,874,500

Source: Adapted from Cooper (2019) and McKinsey (2023) product development funnel cost models; Kotler, P., Keller, K. L., Ancarani, F., & Costabile, M. (2021). *Marketing Management* (16th ed.). Pearson Education.

1 **More speed and efficiency**: AI automates tasks that are done frequently during the development process, giving developers and other team members more time to work on other things. This includes procedures like writing code, analyzing data, and simple testing. AI applications suggest possible solutions and spot possible problems as well, which speeds up progress.

AI technologies have processing power that cannot be beat, which lets businesses quickly look at huge amounts of data. Companies can speed up different parts of product development by using AI algorithms, from coming up with ideas and making prototypes to testing and improving the products. By automating tasks that are done repeatedly, businesses can stay flexible and adapt to changing market needs. This cuts down on mistakes made by people and speeds up the time it takes to get products to market. As a result? Companies have an edge over their competitors when their products get to the market faster. Big corporations like Microsoft and Tesla are using AI to speed up development and beat competition.

2 **More innovation, personalization, and creativity**: It does not merely perform work on your behalf, but it also allows you to be creative. Doing complex data analysis and repetitive tasks well, AI allows developers and designers to work on larger projects and generate new ideas. Personalization is a crucial aspect of the modern world, and AI plays a key role in determining the type of products customers desire and creating them according to their requirements. Using customer data, AI can determine the preferences of each particular customer, make recommendation feature to the specific product, and even propose products that can be added to the one he is already purchasing. Such a degree of personalization leaves customers happier, by creating loyalty to the brand, and prompting them to repurchase. The AI models that can generate new designs, variations of products, or even marketing materials are also known as generative AI, which results in the process of the development process being more creative. Firms such as OpenAI are implementing AI in the creation of human-like text formats, translation of a number of languages, as well as the writing of code.

3 **Lower development costs**: AI helps businesses make the most of their budgets for development. By automating tasks, people do not have to do them as much, which saves money on labor costs. AI can also find ways to save money, like giving certain tasks to AI services that are experts in them. AI solutions that are already made, like chatbots, can be less expensive than customer relationship officers. This lets businesses put more money into improving their products' core features and functions.

4 **Better quality and accuracy**: AI is a key part of making sure that products are of high quality. AI-powered tools can also automate quality control steps and find problems early in development. For instance, AI-powered predictive maintenance can tell when equipment will break down, which cuts down on downtime and the costs that come with it. AI technologies help make products better by letting us do more complex simulations, tests, and validations. AI-powered tools can simulate different situations, find possible design flaws, and improve the performance of a product before it is even built as a prototype. This cuts down on the time and money needed for multiple iterations, making sure that the final product meets or beats customer expectations.

5 **Data-Driven Decision-Making**: Data is what makes product development possible, and AI helps businesses find useful information in the huge amounts of data they have access to. AI algorithms can look at past data about products, customer feedback, market trends, and information about competitors to find patterns and guess what trends will happen in the future. Businesses can use these data-driven insights to make smart choices, lower their risks, and improve the way they develop products to better meet customer needs.

Senior Manager of Events and Field Marketing at FullStory, Georgianne Parker, uses AI to make a summary of every event that the marketing team runs. These briefs are sent directly to the sales team, so they are always aware of what their prospects are saying about the brand. In addition, AI helps lower human error and improve code quality by automating tasks like writing and analyzing code.

Risks and Challenges of AI in Product Development

There are a lot of positive sides and opportunities of AI application in the development of the product, though the risks associated with it should be recognized and addressed as well. The following are some of the risks that may arise during the use of AI to create products:

1 **Discrimination and Bias in Data**: It is one of the major issues with the application of AI to create products that it may make unfair decisions. The AI algorithms consume much historical data to make predictions and recommendations. When the information that is used to develop these algorithms is skewed or not just, it may aggravate biases in the product development process. This may result in unfair outcomes, features that exclude some users, and poor implications for some groups of users. In order to prevent bias and ensure unbiased product development, businesses should select and combine their training data carefully.

2 **Lack of openness and ability to explain**: The way AI models are working makes many individuals not understand how they make decisions or suggestions. This secrecy and incapability to clarify is perilous, particularly in those businesses that are controlled or those involving moral concerns. The companies ought to attempt to open AI systems and provide transparent explanations of the outcomes of the results obtained. This not only makes users trust you, but also ensures that you are responsible as well as assists you to make improved decisions during the entire product development cycle.

3 **Moral and privacy issues**: AI technologies will have the ability to collect and process extensive user data, so people are concerned about privacy and moral concerns. Companies should focus on privacy and security of data by seeking consent of users and ensuring they have robust, secure methods to safeguard the sensitive data of the users. The issues of ethics must also be put at the center of AI implementation, which is in accordance with social norms and safeguards the rights of users.

4 **Technical Limitations and Unforeseen Consequences**: Despite the fact that AI has evolved much, it still has certain issues. The AI models may encounter technical issues, such as they are wrong, provide false positives or negatives, or can be attacked by other AI models. Besides this, AI systems may possess unintended outcomes that are difficult to forecast due to their complexity. These technical issues should be identified and addressed, and the risks that could occur should be minimized through testing, validation, and monitoring them at all times (Figure 3.4).

The Future of AI in Making Products

The future of AI in product development is quite bright as it is used to drive innovation, efficiency, and customer-first. With the AI technology continuing to improve, there will be more advanced applications that will alter how products are manufactured. Advances in

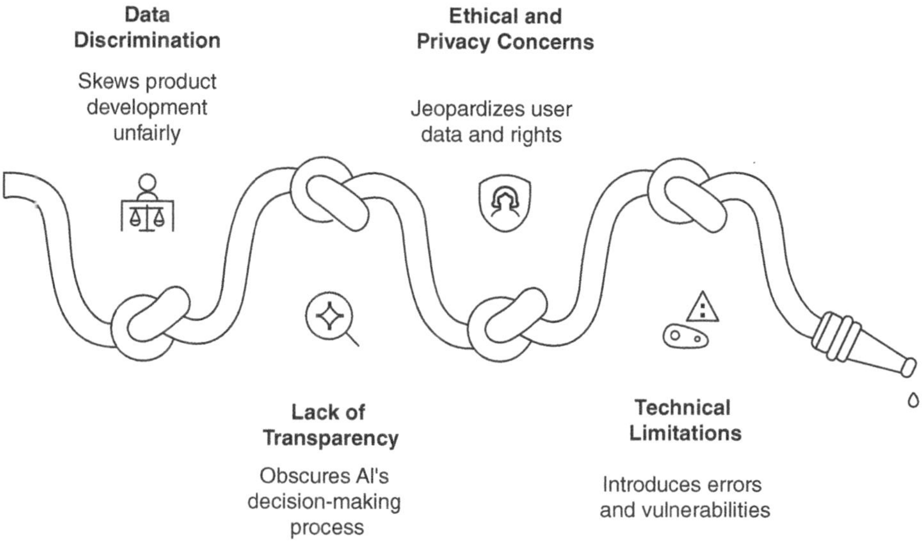

FIGURE 3.4 Navigating AI's pitfalls in product creation.

machine learning, natural language processing, computer vision, and robotics will enable AI to analyze large volumes of data, provide valuable insights, and perform repetitive tasks more precisely and with increased speed. This will provide businesses with the knowledge on how to make intelligent decisions, produce highly personalized products, and deliver customers with genuinely mind-blowing experiences. However, with the advancement of AI, businesses should consider ethics, privacy of data, and recruit AI specialists to assist them in solving the challenges associated with its usage. By embracing the future of AI in product building, businesses can be ahead of the curve and come up with products of tomorrow.

AI and Anthropomorphism

Researchers have found that marketers try to connect emotionally with customers by using stories as branded content or talking through a spokesperson, who could be a real person endorsing the brand or a character made to look like a real person. This method, called anthropomorphism, lets us give other living and nonliving things human traits and behaviors. These characters that look like people can be used to make products, put on packaging, in ads, at retail points of sale, and in other places. With the advancement in AI intelligence level, anthropomorphism can be integrated in the product development. This emotional connection can also be utilized in product development, especially in the designing and packaging stages. Calcium Sandoz's different bottle shapes show how anthropomorphism is used to communicate about the brand through packaging. It comes in the shape of animals like a puppy dog, a giraffe (for kids and young children), and a woman (for women). Each one is meant for a different group of people.

To make their products look like people, product designers use human shapes. Brand consultants use human shapes in logos, icons, or nonhuman endorsers like the 65-year-old Amul Girl, the 122-year-old Michelin Man, or the 50-year-old Pillsbury Doughboy. Some of the emotions that these animated characters use to send messages are happiness, anger, sadness, motivation, and so on. People who buy it are then the ones who give it human traits. Customers who become attached to these animated characters will likely become loyal to certain brands because they have a strong emotional connection to them and therefore form strong brand associations. This connection makes people like the product, buy it again, and again, which leads to brand loyalty.

Anthropomorphism—giving products a humanlike form, face, or voice—used to sit mostly in branding; with AI, it becomes a practical NPD tool. AI mines reviews, social posts, and call-center transcripts to discover the emotions and traits consumers want (friendly, caring, playful), then generative tools turn those traits into candidate forms, labels, and pack shapes while simulators estimate shelf findability, ergonomics, and manufacturability. Affective models predict which faces, colors, and micro-expressions will feel warm (not "uncanny"), and synthetic concept tests quickly compare options by segment (kids, caregivers, women). Voice/clonal-tone models let teams prototype the product's "spokes-character" inside apps or devices, ensuring the same personality flows from packaging to interaction. Postlaunch, telemetry and quick A/Bs refine expressions, shapes, or on-pack stories without a full redesign—closing the loop from emotion → design → market learning.

Example: Building on the Calcium Sandoz idea, a pediatric vitamins team uses AI to analyze parent and child feedback and finds "gentle guardian" cues resonate. A generative 3D tool proposes animal-inspired bottle silhouettes that fit small hands; computer vision forecasts which will pop on cluttered shelves; and lightweight online tests confirm the preferred face and color palette. The result is a child-friendly pack that's easier to spot, easier to hold, and emotionally aligned—improving trial and repeat without sacrificing cost or sustainability (Figure 3.5).

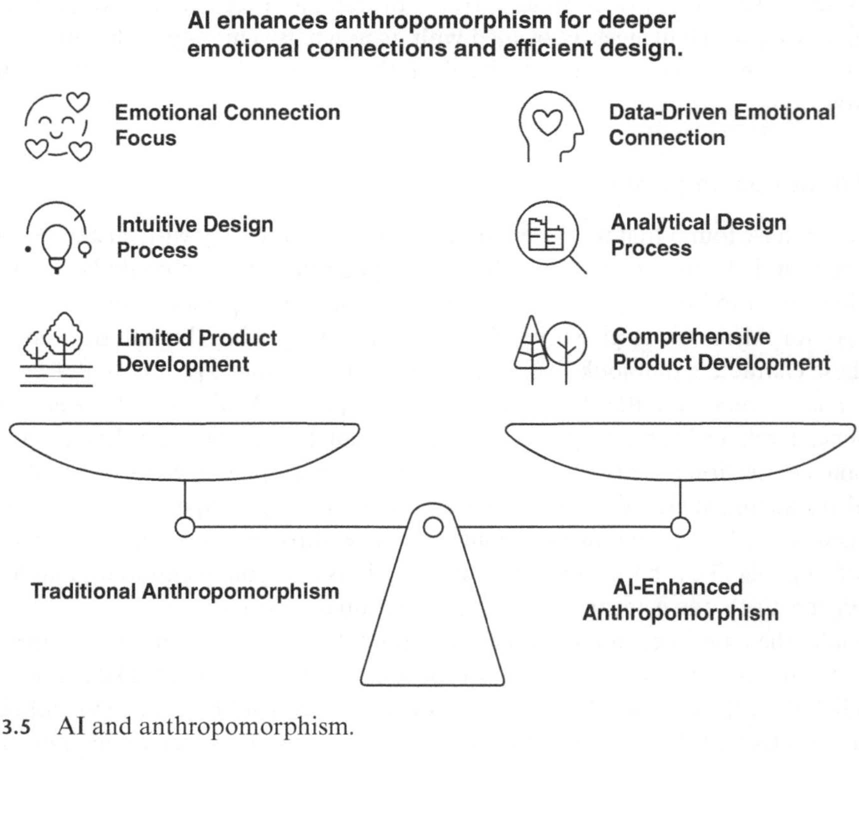

FIGURE 3.5 AI and anthropomorphism.

CLOSING CASE: NIKE AI-POWERED PERSONALIZATION

Nike is the place that offers purchasing apparel, sneakers, and much more with a digital experience, a complete experience for users. It has transformed into so much more than a sports brand; it is now a digitally integrated lifestyle ecosystem. Nike has been strategically integrating AI to enhance customer experience. Starting in 2018, the company began investing heavily in AI and data science, focusing on personalized product recommendations and targeted marketing. Companies are building intelligent experience engines that use data and AI to deliver highly personalized customer journeys—an approach mirrored in Nike's strategy to enhance engagement and customer loyalty (Edelman & Abraham, 2022). This initiative aimed to leverage customer data to provide tailored experiences, increasing customer engagement and loyalty. In 2019, Nike launched Nike Fit and an app feature using AI and augmented reality to help customers find their perfect shoe size. Nike Fit's 3D scans + fit feedback create a live map of foot shapes (width, arch, toe splay) by sport and region. Design teams update lasts and size curves, while generative tools propose midsole/upper patterns tailored to those distributions. Engineering tunes foam densities and knit tensions; PMs pick which variants to prototype and scale. Result: better first-fit prototypes, fewer iterations and returns, and product decisions grounded in real feet.

The company further expanded its AI capabilities with the 2021 acquisition of Datalogue, a data integration platform that uses machine learning to automate the process of turning raw data into actionable insights. This acquisition improved Nike's ability to combine data from various sources, including its app ecosystem, supply chain, and enterprise data, to deliver more personalized and relevant experiences. More recently, in 2024, Nike has been incorporating generative AI into product design, notably with the Athlete Imagined Revolution (AIR) project, which allows designers to create and refine prototypes more rapidly. This has accelerated the product development cycle, enabling Nike to bring innovative products to market faster. (Shopping, 2024). Additionally, Nike is employing AI in advertising campaigns, using generative AI platforms to create more engaging and effective marketing strategies. Currently, Nike continues to expand its AI applications across various areas, including personalized shopping experiences across its digital platforms, optimizing supply chain management through demand forecasting and real-time insights, and enhancing customer service with AI-powered virtual assistants. This ongoing commitment to leveraging AI demonstrates Nike's dedication to staying at the forefront of the industry, driving innovation, and meeting the evolving expectations of its customers (Mathews, 2024).

Discussion Questions

1 Discuss the key concepts of product development and its evolution with AI.
2 Apply the steps for product development to develop a new product of your choice.
3 Apply the budgeting method to a new product development of your choice, describing each cost in detail.
4 Describe the benefits and risks that are associated with using AI.
5 Analyze the application of product design and AI in product development.

Assignment Questions

1 Pick a company of your choice and analyze how it integrates AI into its product development strategy.
2 Apply the budgeting funnel (idea → concept testing → development → test marketing → launch) to a new product of your choice. Calculate the estimated costs and the probabilities of success.
3 Compare two industries (e.g., automotive vs. healthcare) and explain how AI supports their product innovation and how AI use differs industry to industry and per use case.
4 Propose a governance framework to reduce risks of bias, lack of transparency, or privacy violations in AI-driven development.
5 Explain how Anthropomorphism can be used in AI-driven product development. Propose a product design in which human qualities enhance customer engagement.

MINI CASE: DYNAMIC INVENTORY MANAGEMENT SYSTEMS: CASE OF A COFFEE SHOP

Many businesses worry about the costs of having too much or too little stock. Dynamic inventory management systems that AI drives can help with these problems by: Real-Time Inventory Tracking: Keeping an eye on inventory levels and sales trends by using real-time data. Predictive analytics: using advanced analytics to accurately predict demand and make changes to inventory levels based on that. Replenishment orders are automatically sent out based on real-time inventory data and signals that predict future demand. Take the case of a coffee shop chain that is expanding quickly. As their customers' needs changed and grew, they had to keep stockpiling the ingredients they needed to make the food on their menu, which hurt their cafe business. So, the cost of their inventory was going up, and they were worried about throwing away more and more products. By using ThroughPut's AI-powered inventory management, the coffee chain was able to see product demand down to the SKU level and look at inventory turnover rates to figure out how much stock to keep on hand. Because of this, they were able to cut their inventory by 15%, which cut costs and wasted less. As highlighted in "How Machine Learning Will Transform Supply Chain Management," AI and ML are revolutionizing inventory practices by improving demand forecasting and aligning production with real-time sales signals, which is exactly what allowed the coffee chain to cut waste and reduce inventory by 15% (Fountaine & O'Marah, 2024). The coffee chain was able to better balance its inventory levels with AI-driven dynamic inventory management, which saved money and made operations run more smoothly.

HBR Case Links:

- https://hbr.org/2024/03/how-machine-learning-will-transform-supply-chain-management
- https://hbr.org/2023/11/how-global-companies-use-ai-to-prevent-supply-chain-disruptions

Application of Concepts & In-Class Activities

Concept (Kotler Link)	*Application in Practice*	*In-Class Activity/Illustration*
Idea Generation, Concept Screening (New Product Development)	AI goes through customer reviews and market data to surface unmet needs	Students brainstorm product ideas and screen them with AI-like scoring criteria.
Design & Prototyping (Product Design & Innovation)	Generative AI simulates prototypes virtually.	Teams will use a design-thinking toolkit to create prototypes and then consequently simulate customer feedback.
Testing & Commercialization (Product Testing & Launch)	AI-powered quality checks and predictive simulations reduce recalls	Run a role-play launch simulation: teams create a marketing plan with AI-driven personalization
B2B Product Development	AI enhances CRM, supply chain, and dynamic pricing	Topic of Debate: "Is AI adoption in B2B more about efficiency or innovation?"

Key Terms

- Generative design
- Digital twins
- Product development funnel
- DROP error
- Concept testing
- CRM with AI
- Dynamic pricing
- Predictive analytics
- Supply chain optimization
- Personalized marketing
- Anthropomorphism
- Bias in AI
- Transparency in AI models
- Over-the-air updates
- First-time-right

References

Edelman, D. C., & Abraham, M. (2022, March–April). *Customer experience in the age of AI.* Harvard Business Review. https://hbr.org/2022/03/customer-experience-in-the-age-of-ai

Fountaine, T., & O'Marah, K. (2024, March 5). *How machine learning will transform supply chain management.* Harvard Business Review. https://hbr.org/2024/03/how-machine-learning-will-transform-supply-chain-management

Furr, N., & Dyer, J. (2020, February 26). *Lessons from Tesla's approach to innovation.* Harvard Business Review. https://hbr.org/2020/02/lessons-from-teslas-approach-to-innovation

Mathews, A. (2024, July 3). *How Nike is using AI to transform product design, customer experience, and operational efficiency.* AIM Research. https://aimresearch.co/market-industry/how-nike-is-using-ai-to-transform-product-design-customer-experience-and-operational-efficiency

Shopping, A. (2024). How Nike built a personalized AI shopping assistant in 3 weeks | case study. *Rangle.* https://rangle.io/cases/nike-generative-ai-ecommerce

Tesla. (2024). Artificial intelligence & autopilot. *Tesla.* www.tesla.com. https://www.tesla.com/AI

4

AI IN PRICING

Learning Objectives

Having studied this chapter, you are expected to be able to:

1 Provide an explanation of how AI assists and enhances the price-setting process.
2 Explain how information can be used to create smarter, fairer, and more precise pricing mechanisms.
3 Determine the important AI-enabled pricing methods that include dynamic pricing, bundling, and personalization.
4 Implement the playbook of implementation by defining roles, key performance indicators (KPIs), and technology platforms in the organization.
5 Consider the dangers of AI pricing and regulations required to be in place to make it fair, private, and accountable.

OPENING CASE: AIRLINE DYNAMIC PRICING (DELTA)

The prices of airline fares that travel in hours are not collected. They are the reflections of revenue (yield) management: a fixed supply of seats in terms of a fixed demand that increases and decreases over time, day, and event. In the case of Delta, the managerial objective is obvious-sell seats at a profit and not lose customer trust. Price thus serves as a profit lever and as a market signal. When demand is disrupted by storms, concerts, or competitor activity, prices move to balance utilization, margin, and customer experience instead of to pursue short-term spikes.

AI is not a substitute for this logic. Demand forecasting models use route and fare class estimates based on historical bookings, seasonality, remaining capacity, anticipated no-shows, special events, competitor activity, and disruption risk like weather. A layer of

DOI: 10.4324/9781003501862-4

optimization is then used to suggest seat assignments by fare buckets and suggest price increments. Recommendations are executed within specified guardrails: restrictions on daily price change, no spike when there is a claimed emergency and sensitive routes should be reviewed by humans. By deploying data pipelines to the cloud, the time taken between signal and decision is reduced, and AI allows service teams to sift through routine customer requests to ensure that operational noise does not impact pricing decisions.

The sources of accountability with clear escalation paths in the case of indicator drift are the small scorecard-load factor (seats filled), revenue per available seat mile (RASM), spoilage (empty seats at departure), conversion rate, and complaint rate. Such a combination of a disciplined process, real-time learning, and definitive limits in practice allows Delta to react responsively to prices without prejudice to fairness and quality of service. The same discipline is also based on a recoverable sequence: plan pricing goals, demand and price sensitivity, cost estimation and break-even, competition analysis, establish the final price by a decision of a pricing method (value-, cost-, or competition-based) and study the final price with psychological, legal, and fair considerations in mind.

Introduction

The case of the airline implies something simple: under the conditions of changing demand, capacity, and competitive conditions, prices change as well. That is no new reasoning; the power of reading the movements more rapidly, and accurately, is new. Price is a signal to the market and a performance driver across categories. It is as fair, as valuable and as affordable to customers and as margin, share, and cash flow to managers. To get it right, it takes more than a number—it is a process.

In modern practice, the order of the said process can be repeated. The companies make it clear what the prices will be to achieve; the companies research on demand and price elasticity, calculate the cost and a break-even point, and research the proposals of the competitors. This is when they eventually decide to apply a pricing strategy and agree on a final price that would not displease the psychological cues, legal counterpoint, and prerequisites of justice. Economics is safe—willingness to pay, elastic and competitive responsiveness and organizational work is cross-functional, comprising marketing, finance, analytics, and frontline teams. The toolkit has changed. The flow of information on the Internet is becoming effectively continuous; predicting demand and responsiveness modeling; decision-machines can be reprogrammed more quickly; controlled experiments can learn more quickly. They can be implanted and make transparency, prejudice, and acceptable limits a problem. With the equilibrium thus fixed, the next section breaks down the traditional sequence into three building blocks that render the process viable and responsible.

The Price-Setting Process

The price-setting process structures the process of pricing into three interconnected phases, which transform intent into action. Companies start with setting goals and guardrails to base the price determination on strategy and equity. Thereafter, they determine demand sensitivity and cost structures to determine viable ranges and break-even points. Lastly, they benchmark themselves in the eyes of their competitors and use pricing strategies to come up with a defensible figure. Data, models and compliance checks make this workflow stronger, and each decision is profitable and accountable. For example, Apple exemplifies this process through its tiered pricing strategy for iPhones.

Establish Objectives and Guardrails (What Price Must Be—And Must Not Be)

Pricing is based on clarity on what the business is attempting to accomplish. Examples of these goals that a firm can establish include survival in a very competitive market, persistent profitability, an increase in market share, a skimming strategy aimed at recovering the investments in the shortest time possible, or the development of a quality leadership image. All these objectives demand managers to make trade-offs, including compromising volume with margin or compromising increased growth with greater stability. These objectives are converted into guardrails so as to avoid inconsistent or short decisions. Guardrails comprise minimum prices to prevent losses, maximum ceilings to ensure fairness and the proportions of varying prices limit the occurrence of price shock per day. Fairness checks, for example, through discounted vulnerable groups, will maintain the trust and compliance with financial discipline.

Read Demand and Costs (Sensitivity of Customers and Break-Even Point)

Once objectives are set, the next step is to understand how much flexibility exists in pricing. This requires estimating customer willingness to pay, measuring price elasticity, and considering reference prices that shape perceptions of fairness. Observational data, customer surveys, and controlled experiments provide insights into how different price points influence demand. On the cost side, firms distinguish between fixed costs (e.g., rent and salaries) and variable costs (e.g., raw materials per unit) to calculate contribution margins. Using this, managers can identify the break-even point—the volume required to cover total costs at a given price. These calculations help determine the safe pricing corridor and highlight the trade-off between raising margins and sustaining volumes.

Position Against the Market and Set the Price (Relative Stance, Method, and Final Checks)

The fourth and final step is the analysis and translation into a profitable market decision. To position itself at the right relative position, managers examine the degree of rivalry pricing, promotions, and service distinction. To this extent, they adopt pricing strategies, which are cost-based (usually covering the costs with a margin), competition-based (equivalent or below competitors), and value-based (pricing according to the perceived value of the customer). Once a preliminary price has been chosen, psychological design characteristics of rounded numbers, price bundling, or loyalty rewards are considered to improve acceptance and signaling. Price checking would be undertaken prior to finalization to make sure that it is not used in an abusive manner, and it is also not unequal throughout the sales channels. This causes the final figure to be competitive, strategic, and legal (Table 4.1).

TABLE 4.1 Impact and Strategies Used with the Help of AI

Step	*Figures—Example (Local Café)*	*Explanation*	*Strategy Used*	*Impact*
1 Establish Objectives & Guardrails	• Objective: Maintain 20% premium over cost • Price floor: Cost × 1.1 • Max daily change: ₹5 • Student discount: Offered	• Signal quality, protect profitability • Prevent underpricing and price shocks • Ensure fairness for vulnerable groups • Keep pricing stable and goal-aligned	Premium pricing with fairness checks	Builds brand image as premium yet fair, prevents customer backlash and ensures consistent profitability
2 Read Demand & Costs	• Variable cost/cup = ₹40 • Fixed cost/month = ₹60,000 • At ₹80 → Contribution = ₹40; Break-even = 1,500 cups • At ₹85 → Contribution = ₹45; Break-even = 1,333 cups • At ₹75 → Contribution = ₹35; Break-even = 1,714 cups	• Demand and cost define feasible pricing corridors • Higher prices → higher margins, lower sales needed • Lower prices → lower margins, higher sales needed • Shows trade-off between profit and sales effort	Cost-volume-profit analysis	Identifies sustainable price points, quantifies risk of volume loss, and helps balance margin vs. sales volume
3 Position Against Market & Set Price	• Competitor range = ₹75–₹90 • Chosen price = ₹85 • Loyalty program = "Buy 9, get 1 free" • Psychological framing = Avoid .99 • Student discount = Visible at counter	• Premium positioning within competitor corridor • Loyalty programs soften premium • Psychological framing boosts perception • Fairness checks preserve trust.	Competitive positioning with loyalty and fairness elements	Differentiates café as premium but customer-friendly, drives repeat sales, and ensures defensible pricing

Example

In the subsequent chapter, one can see how one can utilize new data, models, decision-making rules, deployment practices, and monitoring to facilitate one among these three building blocks from a workflow without diluting responsibility because one has now defined a workflow with objectives and guardrails; demand as well as costs; position with final price.

Where AI Plugs in Data

The realistic influence of AI on price can only be achieved when presented to the existing pricing procedures. The traditional pricing mechanisms rely on standardized spreadsheets, cost-plus guesses, and competitive specifications. AI may have brought a step forward to process information in huge multidimensional volumes, deliver outcomes in real time, and prescribe (price) actions that maximize profitability, competitiveness, and equitability.

Data Foundations and Privacy

- The data-driven pricing systems are based on data and enable the companies to conduct dynamic, evidence-based decisions as compared to making price-based decisions based on fixed-rule decisions or managerial decisions. A good database requires an amalgamation of several divergent streams—both transactional and customer profile data, market and operational signals—into one pipeline that is capable of being analyzed in real time. This type of integration assists the algorithm in deducing trends of demand, trends of elasticity, and even the determination of the most advantageous prices, which is impossible when using manual processes on a mass scale. However, data prowess is equally a threat in that it can be misused or over-trusted and cause mistrust among the customers, in addition to causing examination by a regulatory body. International laws like the CCPA and GDPR have strict limitations regarding data collection, processing, and usage on the pricing aspects. Corporations must find such a balance through rich datasets in order to enhance pricing accuracy and, at the same time, incorporate guard rails that maintain privacy, fairness, and compliance.
- **Transactional data**: AI-based pricing relies on the basis of transactional records. They take a register of the frequency of purchases, order values, and sales patterns. By doing this, companies would be in a position to identify the high-value customers as well as the demand cycles, besides predicting the price sensitivity. As a case study, an online grocery store, Big Basket, is able to know that there are more items in a basket during the weekend and, therefore, it can charge a small amount of money during that day to deliver the groceries. This will ensure that the decision arrived at regarding pricing is not speculative but based on actual past behavior.
- **Customer data**: Customer-level data exceeds the realms of transactions to demographics, loyalty, and patterns of behavior. AI models use such information so as to target buyers as well as make personalized offers to them. The streaming video online service of such nature could utilize the history of viewing and loyalty to offer student-friendly packages or family packages. Pricing customization will maximize the conversion and retention of the company, but it must be carried out responsibly. For example, AT&T phone company uses price customization.

- **Market data**: External cues such as competitor charges, marketing efforts, and macroeconomic factors can be used to put the offerings into perspective. Companies monitor these variables on a real-time basis to prevent being either over-priced or missing income. To illustrate, a ride-hailing application, Rapido, can dynamically calculate the prices by observing the competitor's surge price in the same location. The integration of market data should make the systems of AI pricing flexible and competitive.
- **Operational data**: Pricing is also influenced by operational constraints, including inventory, cost of production, and even the capacity of the logistics. When there is a shortage, AI may increase prices to control demand and prevent a shortage. When there is surplus inventory, it can be rapidly cleared with discounts. An apparel retailer, Zara, may reduce the prices of the old items that have not been sold by the season before launching the next line. The combination of these inputs is what makes pricing a reality for the customer demand and the reality of business.
- **Consent management**: Intelligent systems should respect direct authorization prior to utilizing individual information in pricing. Customers are expected to know what information is being gathered and its purpose. As a case in point, Emerald Airlines cannot access travel history to offer personalized tickets without seeking permission from passengers. Clear consent creates trust, and it minimizes the risks of regulation.
- **Data minimization**: Gathering of important information minimizes exposure and enhances compliance. The only visit frequency and dollar per visit are sufficient for a coffee chain like Café Coffee Day to design loyalty discounts without knowing all the personal information such as the address history. Minimal data benefits the analytics and ethics.
- **Anonymization**: Anonymization methods eliminate the identifiable information and retain the analytical value. An example of this is an e-commerce site named eBay, which might study the buying patterns of the region by removing names and email addresses and only limiting itself to ZIP codes. This secures the customers and still allows accurate pricing insights.
- **Risks of Non-compliance**: Lack of respect for privacy means fines, damaged reputation, and loss of customer trust in the firm. In GDPR or CCPA, the fines may extend to millions of dollars, and the social targeting could decrease the use of AI-driven systems. The key retailer that makes use of purchase histories without disclosure is likely to lose customer loyalty and is likely to be sanctioned by the regulatory bodies. The trust is thus a strategic and legal requirement. For example, IKEA uses this policy.

Modeling & Decision Engines

- **Demand Forecasting Models**: Demand forecast is used to predict the quantity of sales to be made in the future on the basis of past and external factors. The combination of traditional time-series models (AutoRegressive Integrated Moving Average (ARIMA), exponential smoothing) and the causal machine learning (ML) models, incorporating promotions, holidays, or competitor actions are considered. As an illustration, a supermarket chain may apply ML to forecast the increased demand for soft drinks in the period of heatwaves in summer. Proper predictions will eliminate stockouts, stabilize margins, and prices will show expected changes in demand.

- **Elasticity Estimation Engines**: Elasticity engines are dynamically calculated in estimating the sensitivity of demand to changes in price among segments. These systems keep improving the elasticity curves of various products or customer groups through the constant learning of the transactions. The adaptive learning of this kind makes sure that pricing is at the customer's tolerance and maximum revenue is achieved.
- **Optimization Algorithms**: Linear programming and reinforcement learning are optimization models that balance conflicting objectives, such as revenue, margin, and market share. They take thousands of price cases as an option for selecting a good price scenario. Delta Airlines may use reinforcement learning to make decisions on whether or not to discount the unoccupied seats or wait for the late booking clients. This is what has trade-offs that are systematically carried out as opposed to intuitively.
- **Decision Engines**: The conductor is known as the decision engine and involves the integration of predictions, measures of elasticity, and optimization results at the expense of business rules and guardrails. It prevents the proposals that violate the compliance, fairness, or customer confidence. One such thing is that the engine of a telecom company, like Vodafone, can avoid the sudden price increment on vulnerable consumers, even when it is an optimization in the short term. The ethical and strategy considerations that are made to utilize decision engines render AI-based pricing decisions acceptable.

Deployment, Monitoring, & Governance

- **Deployment**: To succeed, AI-based pricing models should be made operational in enterprise systems. Channel execution is realized through integration with enterprise resource planning (ERP), customer relationship management (CRM), and e-commerce platforms. As an example, the pricing engine of Tata Cliq can be integrated with an online outlet so that it can raise discounts immediately when the inventory accumulates. Smooth deployment means that insights are turned into action without human-induced bottlenecks.
- **Monitoring**: In order to achieve success, AI-based pricing models ought to be operationalized in enterprise systems. Channel performance is actualized by integration with the ERP, CRM, and e-commerce platforms. At Michael Kors, a pricing engine can be connected with an online outlet so that the latter would be able to increase discounts as soon as the inventory gathers. Smooth deployment is an outcome that implies that insights are converted into action without human-caused bottlenecks.
- **Governance**: The AI pricing should be anchored on effective systems of governance that supervise compliance, fairness, and corporate compliance. This can be in the form of cross-functional committees to observe the outcomes and identify the unwanted bias. JP Morgan's audit may include its AI and guarantee that it does not deal with pricing related to the lending processes, and this pricing is discriminatory against some population groups. The sphere of governance is a part of the process of turning AI into a socially responsible decision system, rather than a technically pure tool (Table 4.2, Figure 4.1).

TABLE 4.2 Use of AI across Decision Making

Section	*Key Focus*	*Style Kart Example*	*Impact*
Data Foundations & Privacy	Transactional, customer, market and operational data are integrated into one pipeline. Safeguards: consent, minimization, anonymization.	POS sales + online browsing + competitor crawlers + warehouse stock integrated; GDPR/CCPA consent screens in app.	Real-time demand sensing, accurate inventory match, regulatory compliance, stronger customer trust.
Modeling & Decision Engines	Demand forecasting, elasticity engines, optimization (linear programming (LP), reinforcement learning (RL)), decision engine enforces guardrails & fairness.	ML forecasts seasonal demand; elasticity models for premium vs. discount shoppers; RL balances margin vs. share; guardrail blocks >5% daily hikes.	Pricing precision ↑, revenue/margin balance optimized, fairness preserved.
Deployment, Monitoring & Governance	ERP/CRM/e-commerce integration; KPI monitoring (conversion, margin, churn); drift detection; governance committees for bias & compliance.	AI pricing engine pushes real-time prices to website & app; weekly audits for fairness & policy alignment.	Seamless execution, reduced model drift, bias-free outcomes, alignment with corporate values.
Overall Impact	Data → Models → Deployment → Governance loop	Revenue ↑ 3–5%; Margin ↑ 1–2 pts; Stockouts ↓ 10%; Fairness ensured via caps & student discounts	Competitive edge with transparent, defensible pricing; AI as both profit enabler and governance tool.

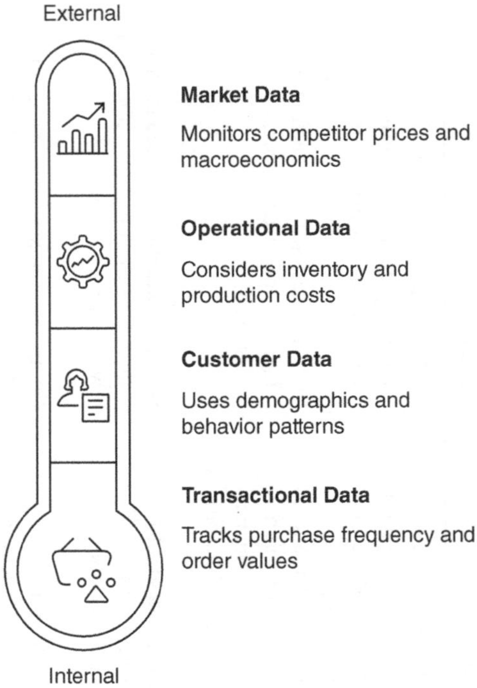

FIGURE 4.1 External and internal data.

AI-Enabled Price Adaptation Strategies

AI-based dynamic pricing enables companies to change prices in real-time according to several factors, such as demand, inventory, and the prices of competitors. As an illustration, one can take a ride-hailing company such as Ola. The demand for rides is brisk during the peak periods, that is, on Friday nights or during major events. This surge in demand is analyzed by the AI-based dynamic pricing algorithm, and raised fares are attributed depending on the available drivers and historical data. This will not only make drivers have a reason to work during the period when the company is busy, but it will also enable the company maximize revenue. The system can be optimized to maximize the price strategies by continuously re-calibration of price sensitivity curve—knowing how much of the customers would be prepared to pay—and also through monitoring the market response. In case users are unresponsive to high prices, the algorithm can decrease the prices to offset the demand in the next peak to ensure customer satisfaction.

Dynamic & Revenue Management

Dynamic pricing helps companies to react on the actions of competitors on a short period of time. As an example, when a competitor ride-hailing service reduces its charges, the AI system can immediately respond to this and respond by altering its pricing to stay competitive without losing revenue. In addition, the system could also introduce discounts or promotions in the off-peak periods to ensure that they attract ridership, hence maximizing fleet utilization. This flexibility not only improves revenue management but also increases customer loyalty since it makes them feel that they are getting reasonable value for their rides. Finally, AI-based dynamic pricing produces a more reactionary and efficient market, which is in the interests of all providers and consumers.

Product-Mix & Bundling Optimization

AI will be essential in streamlining the product mixes and bundling strategies through analyzing the customer tastes and purchasing patterns. As an illustration, a tech firm that markets printers and ink cartridges can be considered. Through AI, the company will be able to determine the cross-product elasticity, as it will enable the company to know how the demand for printers influences the demand for cartridges. This understanding will enable the firm to strategically price these complementary products—giving discounts on cartridges when they sell a printer to customers or packages them at a competitive price.

In addition, AI-powered package experimentation allows companies to experiment with different packages to determine which package will help maximize sales and profit margins, and which packages cause each other to cannibalize. American Airlines, like a streaming service, may test various packages, including specific content not available to other services or family packages, and determine what packages will be most popular with subscribers. The AI system can optimize such bundles with time by examining the customer reviews and feedback and sales statistics to ensure that they satisfy the market requirements and improve overall profitability. The usefulness of this data-driven approach leads to better customer satisfaction, but also loyalty, as it offers customized services that appeal to consumer demands.

Unbundling is a supplement to product mixes and bundling strategies because it offers the customer more flexibility and choice. Whereas, in bundling, complementary products are grouped together to increase the value of the product and maximize sales, unbundling enables people to purchase only those products or features that suit their needs. An example of this would be the case of the technical company selling printers and cartridges, where unbundling would involve selling the cartridges of ink or other printer features individually and attracting customers who may not need a whole package. Using the understanding of AI, businesses can determine which products or features are the most requested when sold separately so that pricing strategies can be in line with customer preferences. This two-pronged strategy of bundling the most common combinations and at the same time offering the unbundled helps companies to serve a greater number of consumers, increasing their satisfaction and possibly increasing total revenue due to targeted sales.

Personalized/Segmented & Test-and-Learn

Price personalization is one of the strongest AI applications in which the pricing strategy is designed to apply to specific customers according to different factors. This will improve customer satisfaction and revenue maximization. This is an in-depth examination of its major aspects:

1 **Segmentation-Based Pricing**:
Segmentation-oriented pricing is one that entails the provision of differentiated prices to different sets of customers. As an illustration, a streaming platform, YouTube Premium, could offer lower subscription rates to students since they have tight budgets. Likewise, the long-term customer might also be rewarded or given special prices due to their long-term interaction with the brand. Etihad Airways can set different prices on the same way

based on the country of origin due to the demand and economic status that differ. The segmentation of the customers enables the businesses to maximize sales, and the pricing would seem fair to the various groups.

2 **True Personalization**:
Personalization is an even more advanced step in which, based on behavioral cues, individualized prices, or discounts are proposed. As an example, ASOS, a global fashion retailer brand, could view the browsing history of a particular customer as well as previous purchases and even the social media interactions to select the best price at which a particular product should be sold. In case a customer has been watching a given item many times but has not bought it, the retailer could provide an individualized discount as a way of persuading the customer into buying the item. Not only does such a degree of personalization boost the conversion rates, but it also boosts customer loyalty since the consumers feel that they are being treated well and that they are understood. To illustrate, the travel booking website can provide personalized offers to the users, depending on their search patterns, providing them with specially designed offers that suit their preferences.

3 **Test-and-Learn Engines**:
Multi-armed bandits and a/b/n testing, which are test-and-learn engines, are important in dynamically testing price points. The systems enable business organizations to distribute traffic to various pricing approaches to determine the most effective ones. As an example, an online marketplace may conduct A/B tests to test customer reactions to the two prices of the same product. Airbnb's strategy continuously real-time further allocates visitors to the most effective pricing strategy, so that the most effective prices are exposed more. This approach is not discriminatory as every customer gets the opportunity to experience different prices. Companies are able to use these engines to optimize their pricing strategies by using real-time information and customers' responses and make their decision-making more informed and better in terms of profitability (Figure 4.2).

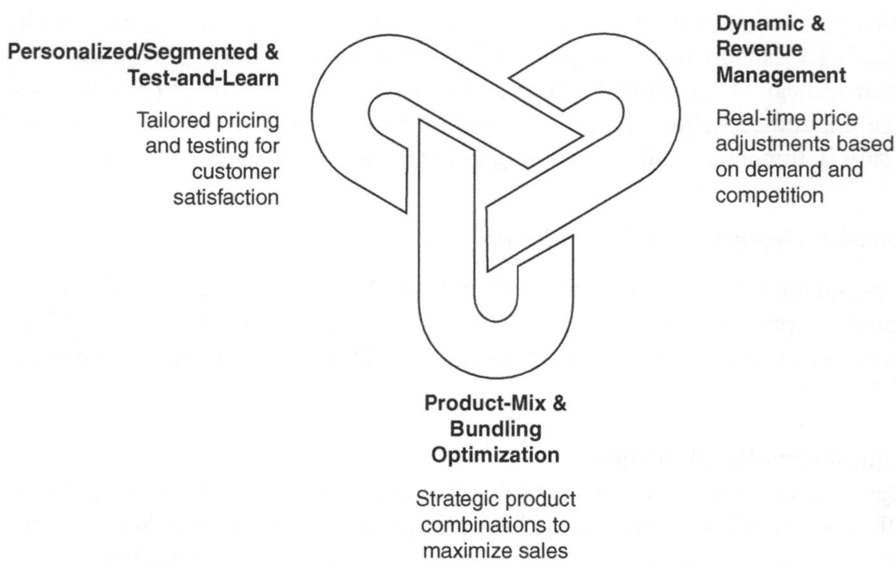

FIGURE 4.2 AI-driven pricing strategy.

Implementation Playbook

The effectiveness of AI in pricing hinges upon the presence of well-established interdisciplinary responsibilities. The task of data scientists is to create and improve machine learning models that could identify tendencies in demand and price elasticity. These models are then checked against strategic objectives of the firm by the pricing analysts, and profitability and positioning will not be compromised. Zalando, a European fashion retailer, uses scientists to build AI models that predict optimal prices across thousands of Stock Keeping Units (SKUs) using demand signals, seasonality, and competitive benchmark.

Organization & Roles

- The effectiveness of AI in pricing hinges upon the presence of well-established interdisciplinary responsibilities. The task of data scientists is to create and improve machine learning models that could identify tendencies in demand and price elasticity. These models are then checked against strategic objectives of the firm by the pricing analysts, and profitability and positioning will not be compromised. Legal and compliance officers protect equality by avoiding biases, such as ensuring that the prices are not discriminatory against vulnerable groups or do not breach consumer protection legislation. Information Technology (IT) professionals and product managers combine AI-based price optimization algorithms with ERP/CRM systems to render them scalable. Otherwise, AI projects can become isolated pilot projects, similar to the case of most retail companies that tried dynamic pricing but never implemented it because of the absence of ownership. For example, Decathlon, a global sports retailer, has integrated its AI-driven real-time updates in-store and online channels.

Experimentation & KPIs

- The initial AI pricing must be limited in scope with pilots on small SKUs, customer groups, or regions to reduce risks while collecting evidence. Singapore Airlines may implement dynamic pricing on a few routes and then extend it to other routes. The key performance indicators (KPIs) are margin uplift, conversion changes, revenue per customer and churn rates, and assist in assessing the impact of AI on improving business outcomes. Learning loops become essential—new knowledge obtained during early tests should be reinserted into the retraining of the models to ensure that mistakes do not increase. An online retailer, such as Amazon, is an example of a company that optimizes its algorithms on a daily basis due to the behavior of the shoppers. This cycle is an iterative cycle that can turn small-scale pilots into scalable systems that optimize continuously.

Platforms, Integration, & Change

- Powerful platforms are required to implement AI pricing. The commonest obstacle is integration with legacy systems (ERP, CRM, Point of Sale (POS)) because many firms have an aging infrastructure. Cloud computing technology like AWS, Azure, or GCP offers scalability to large data volumes and computationally intensive models. Nevertheless, technology in itself is not enough; change management is crucial. Sales

TABLE 4.3 Use of AI for Pricing with Outcomes

Sub-Section	*Focus Area*	*Responsibilities/Key Points*	*Results/Outcomes*	*Examples*
Organization & roles	Roles in AI Pricing	• Data scientists build ML models for demand & elasticity. • Pricing analysts align outputs with strategy. • Legal & compliance ensure fairness and legal adherence. • IT & product managers integrate models into ERP/CRM. • Executive sponsor provides leadership & ownership.	• Robust and fair pricing models. • Scalable implementation with accountability.	1 A ride-hailing firm, Grab, uses data scientists to refine surge pricing while compliance ensures no discrimination in ZIP codes. 2 A luxury brand, Louis Vuitton, prevents over-discounting by aligning AI pricing with premium positioning.
Experimentation & KPIs	Pilots & Metrics	• Start with limited pilots (SKUs, regions, segments). • Measure KPIs like margin uplift, conversion, revenue per customer, churn. • Feed pilot learnings back into model retraining. • Gradual iteration and scaling.	• Reduced risks during early adoption. • Continuous improvement through learning loops.	1 Qatar Airlines AI pricing on select routes before expanding network-wide. 2 Disney + Hotstar tracks churn reduction after introducing AI-driven subscription plans.
Platforms, integration & change	Technology & Adoption	• Use scalable platforms (AWS, Azure, GCP). • Integrate AI engines with ERP, CRM, POS. • Train managers, sales and frontline staff for adoption. • Build transparency to reduce resistance. • Provide continuous IT-business support.	• Elastic infrastructure for scaling models. • Employee and customer trust in AI-driven pricing.	1 Walmart integrates AI pricing across online apps and in-store POS for consistency. 2 Reliance company trains call-center staff to explain AI-customization

staff, managers, and frontline employees need to believe and embrace AI-based suggestions. A telecom operator named Concentrix must be trained to understand how AI-generated pricing suggestions work and how to communicate them confidently to the customers (Table 4.3).

Fairness & Privacy

AI pricing has the unintentional effect of perpetuating social or demographic bias. An example is that because of a perceived elasticity of demand, algorithms can raise the price in low-income ZIP codes in disproportionate ways. This poses reputational and ethical threats. The crucial factor is that transparency may pose a problem to customers who may oppose black-box pricing decisions since they fail to comprehend why they are being charged that way. Companies such as Booking.com were criticized with respect to opaque surge pricing in times of crisis. Also, the issue of privacy is present since AI uses sensitive data of behavior and context, and this should be supported with close consent models under the legislation, such as GDPR. Companies have to balance between individualization and trust in the customer.

- There is a lot of legal questioning on AI pricing. Regulators are keeping an eye on the so-called algorithmic collusion in which independent AI systems may inadvertently coordinate prices among competitors, resulting in fake high prices. Ryan Air, in the airline pricing, the authorities have raised questions about fare similarity due to the algorithmic nature. Another issue is reliability, as the models should be able to withstand even when the stress threshold is exceeded (e.g., when everyone suddenly starts to buy during COVID-19). Otherwise, algorithms are susceptible to mispricing products, cutting their margins, or causing outcry among customers. Strong validation procedures and crisis scenario simulation are thus the key to crisis resilience.
- It should be noted that the company must perform with considerable responsibility to avoid issues such as hacking and other similar electronic crimes. It is noted that the company will be required to conduct its business with a high level of accountability to prevent the occurrence of other electronic crimes like hacking.
- AI pricing systems also need to have clear incident response protocols. Refusals, like mispriced SKUs (e.g., electronics accidentally priced at $1 on e-commerce websites), or surge pricing outrage, may initiate reputational damage. Organizations ought to have rollback procedures in place to revert to past prices in seconds and be able to override algorithms in case they malfunction. There is also a need to communicate with customers in a quick and transparent manner, like the airlines explaining why fares have increased abruptly. Responsibility lines also need to be established in advance: should it be the pricing manager, the data science head, or the executive sponsor? Lastly, there should be post-incident audits to find out root causes and enhance governance. As an example, the surge pricing backlash in DoorDash prompted the firm to institute caps and real-time communication plans (Table 4.4).

TABLE 4.4 AI Usage with Measures and Precautions

Sub-section	*Focus Area*	*Risks/Negative Examples*	*Rectification/ Governance Measures*	*Examples*
Fairness & privacy	Bias, transparency & data use	• AI may discriminate, e.g., by charging higher prices in low-income areas. • Customers may reject "black-box" pricing decisions. • Sensitive behavioral data creates privacy risks.	• Conduct fairness audits to detect bias. • Provide transparent communication on pricing logic. • Use consent-based data collection under GDPR/ CCPA.	1 Bolt faced criticism for surge pricing during crises → added fare caps and clearer messaging. 2 A grocery delivery app, Instacart, was accused of unfair area-based pricing → introduced third-party audits and a fair-pricing policy.

(*Continued*)

TABLE 4.4 (Continued)

Sub-section	*Focus Area*	*Risks/Negative Examples*	*Rectification/ Governance Measures*	*Examples*
Legal & reliability	Regulation, Stress & Security	• Algorithmic collusion risks (e.g., airlines showing similar fares). • Model failure in crises (COVID-19 demand surges). • Vulnerability to cyber threats and hacking.	• Monitor compliance to avoid antitrust issues. • Stress test models with crisis simulations. • Strengthen cybersecurity (firewalls, anomaly detection).	1 Lufthansa Airline regulators probed fare similarity → firms added human oversight to pricing engines. 2 Best Buy, an e-commerce site, was hacked to list $1 electronics → installed anomaly detection and rollback features.
Incident response & accountability	Failures & governance	• Mispriced SKUs or extreme surge pricing cause reputational damage. • Lack of accountability delays corrective actions. • Poor communication worsens customer backlash.	• Predefined rollback and human override procedures. • Clear accountability (pricing manager, data science lead, or executive sponsor). • Transparent communication & post-incident audits.	1 Didi Chuxing, China surge pricing outrage led to caps and real-time customer notifications. 2 Whole Foods online retailer suffered losses from SKU mispricing → created a rapid-response "human override" team.

CLOSING CASE: UBER AI PRICING (LYFT: WOMEN; AI PROMOTIONAL OFFERS)

Uber uses AI algorithms to analyze massive amounts of data in real time to predict when and where demand for rides will rise. These algorithms consider a variety of factors, including historical ride data, traffic patterns, local events, and even weather forecasts.

Assume it is Friday evening, and there is a concert downtown. Uber's AI algorithms would anticipate an increase in ride requests near the concert venue.

As a result, they would proactively raise prices in that area to encourage more drivers to travel there, ensuring that riders could still get a ride despite the high demand. Benefits for Riders and Drivers: While surge pricing may appear to be a disadvantage for riders, it actually benefits them by ensuring that there are enough drivers available to meet demand, resulting in shorter wait times. Drivers are more likely to be on the road during rush hours when prices are higher because they can make more money. Uber's use of AI for surge pricing has been very successful, thanks to data. Uber's own data shows that surge pricing based on AI has cut riders' wait times during peak hours, making customers happier overall. Uber's surge pricing works out well for both riders and drivers.

Where there is a high competition level and price wars may easily erode profits, competitor prices should be watched. With AI systems, businesses can move swiftly by monitoring the pricing strategies of their rivals and what is happening in the market. The approach of Uber demonstrates that real-time data processing can result in dynamic pricing that identifies the optimal balance between profit acquisition and new client acquisition. This competence is useful in markets where the demand is dynamic and the competition is unfavorable.

Uber monitors the competition prices with the help of AI and introduces real-time amendments to the prices of its rides. The AI system examines data on other ride-sharing apps, cabs and public transit to calculate what is a competitive price-wise. In highly demanded areas or periods when there are so many customers, the AI of Uber can adjust the prices to meet the demand and ensure that the rides are not taken up. When the business is not busy, the prices can be reduced to attract more customers. This elastic strategy assists Uber in attracting more customers and ensuring that drivers are paid adequately, hence a balance between the supply and demand.

Discussion Questions

1 What is the role of AI in transforming the conventional price-setting process, and what obstacles do managers encounter when making its adoption?
2 Are companies entitled to employ extremely personalized pricing or does it endanger unfairness toward customers? Discuss.
3 How can transparency enable the development of customer trust in AI-based pricing?
4 What is the solution to organizations achieving profitability and being fair in dynamic pricing by the use of AI?

Assignment Questions

1 Select a company of your own choice (e.g., airline, e-commerce, or ride-hailing). Examine AI's potential to enhance its pricing strategy.
2 Look at a recent example of AI pricing backlash. What was wrong, and how could the mechanisms of governance have averted it?
3 Create a small scale AI pricing pilot with a retail brand. Describe the KPIs, data requirements, and risk controls.
4 Compare AI-driven pricing policies (dynamic pricing, bundling, personalization). Which growth plan will you suggest regarding a subscription-based business, and why?

MINI CASE

During a Friday evening in a large downtown neighborhood, the demand for ride-hailing is high since thousands of individuals are leaving a concert venue. The AI algorithms used in Uber are trained based on millions of historic journeys, and as this breakout occurs, the algorithm predicts it and automatically increases prices in the impacted area. The same can be said about Lyft; the system raises the prices dramatically to bring more drivers on board. Surge pricing is sensible as far as business is concerned. Increased fares will attract more drivers to the busy region and minimize waiting times for riders. The drivers get better wages, and the service will allow them to find a ride even at the time of high demand. Uber's statistics have revealed that surge pricing reduces wait times of riders by a significant margin throughout peak hours, which enhances the overall reliability of the services. But to the customer, it seems like the creation of unfairness in surge pricing. Those who get in the rush zone are charged fares that are two to three times higher than normal without a full understanding of why. Surge pricing has been especially controversial when the surge pricing has happened during an emergency, for example, snowstorm, floods, or even terrorist attacks. Critics maintain that the algorithms seem to take advantage of human vulnerability when there is a crisis.

The lack of transparency in pricing through AI has also been an issue of concern among regulators. The customers are unable to view the reasoning behind the fare rise, which has caused them to accuse the company of making black-box decisions. In other instances, there has been doubt among the authorities that such practices would constitute price gouging, which in some jurisdictions is not legal.

Uber has reacted to this critique by incorporating guardrails in the pricing algorithms. As an example, surge pricing is limited when there are emergencies, and communication with riders has been developed. Uber now does not just display higher fares, but it also explains why fares are higher and how this assists in balancing supply and demand. Lyft has implemented such measures as well (improved transparency and temporary fare limits). The case of surge pricing leads to the identification of the advantages and disadvantages of AI in pricing. On the one hand, AI enables companies to respond immediately to demand, making them efficient and available. Conversely, in the absence of effective governance, transparency, and fairness assurances, the same algorithms may cause damage to trust, be open to scrutiny by the regulatory bodies and undermine the reputation of the brand in the long run.

To marketers and pricing strategists, the case raises a very important question: To what extent do companies consider AI to maximize revenues in the short term, and what boundaries do they consider to keep the fairness and trust intact?

HBR Case Links:

- https://hbsp.harvard.edu/product/H0694Z-PDF-ENG?itemFindingMethod=search
- https://hbsp.harvard.edu/product/525001-PDF-ENG?itemFindingMethod=search
- https://hbsp.harvard.edu/product/R2406M-PDF-ENG?itemFindingMethod=search

Application of Concept and In-Class Activities

Concept (Kotler Link)	*Application in Practice*	*In-Class Activity/Illustration*
Data foundations & privacy (marketing information systems & ethics)	Firms integrate transactional, customer, market, and operational data for pricing; they must safeguard privacy (GDPR, CCPA).	*Case Analysis*: Provide a mock dataset. Students identify useful pricing data vs. privacy risks and draft a "fair use" guideline.
Demand forecasting & elasticity (Understanding consumer demand & price elasticity)	AI forecasts demand (seasonality, events, competitor actions) and estimates elasticity to set safe price corridors.	*Mini Simulation*: Groups forecast next week's café sales using data (seasonality + competitor promo) and recommend price action.
Dynamic Pricing & revenue management (Pricing strategy—dynamic vs. fixed)	AI adjusts prices in real-time (e.g., Uber surge and airline fares), balancing revenue and fairness.	*Role Play Debate*: Customers vs. Uber managers during a concert night. Discuss fairness vs. revenue, then design guardrails.
Product-Mix & Bundling optimization (product mix & pricing)	AI identifies cross-product elasticity to create profitable bundles/unbundles (printers + cartridges, Netflix family plans).	*Group Task*: Teams design 2 bundles from product list (console, games, subscription). Present & vote on most appealing.

Key Terms

- Dynamic Pricing
- Revenue Management
- Price Elasticity of Demand
- Break-Even Point
- Guardrails
- Demand Forecasting Models
- Elasticity Estimation Engines
- Optimization Algorithms
- Decision Engine
- Product Bundling
- Unbundling
- Personalized Pricing
- A/B Testing
- Multi-armed Bandit Testing
- Fairness & Transparency in AI Pricing

Bibliography

Basal, M., Saraç, E., & Özer, K. (2024). Dynamic pricing strategies using artificial intelligence algorithm. *American Journal of Industrial and Business Management*, *14*(2), 15.

Brons, M., Nijkamp, P., Pels, E., & Rietveld, P. (2008). A meta-analysis of the price elasticity of Gasoline demand. *Energy Economics*, *30*(5), 23.

European Commission (2020). White paper on artificial intelligence – A European approach to excellence and trust. https://commission.europa.eu/system/files/2020-02/commission-white-paper-artificial-intelligence-feb2020_en.pdf
Harvard Business Review (2017). *How companies can build fairness into AI.*
Ito, S., & & Fujimaki, R. (2016). Optimization beyond prediction: Prescriptive price optimization.
Kotler, P., & Armstrong, G. (2017). *Principles of marketing* (17th ed.). Pearson Education.
Kotler, P., & Keller, K. L. (2016). *Marketing management* (15th ed.). Pearson Education.
McKinsey & Company (2021). *The future of pricing: How AI is transforming revenue growth.*
Talluri, K., & Van Ryzin, G. (2004). *The theory and practice of revenue management*. Springer.
Uber (Official). (n.d.). *How Uber's dynamic pricing model works.*
Wang, X., Ye, Y., & Zhang, A. (2023). *Scalable nonparametric price elasticity estimation.* UT Dallas Research.

5

AI IN MARKETPLACE AND DISTRIBUTION

Learning Objectives

After reading this chapter, you will be able to:

1 Get more knowledge about the place and AI
2 Insight into Slow-moving stock or Smart logistics
3 Customer buying patterns and inventory management using AI
4 Learn more about Sales channels management with AI
5 Cross-selling and upselling using AI
6 Distribution Operations using AI

OPENING CASE: KROGER

In October 2017, Kroger introduced its "Restock Kroger" initiative, which included a number of performance-enhancing initiatives, such as leveraging data to personalize offers for consumers and improving its technological capabilities, such as its digital value proposition. According to the Food Marketing Institute, 20% of all retail grocery purchases in the United States will be made online by 2022, generating $100 billion in sales. As a result, Kroger is very interested in being at the forefront of technology. In a slide from its presentation at the investor meeting on October 11, 2017, Kroger outlined its plans for collecting and using customer data.

Utilizing all of these inputs—which undoubtedly fall under the category of "big data"—requires sophisticated technological tools, such as artificial intelligence. To combine internal and external data for "convenience, instant gratification, inspiration & solutions," the company has launched a number of technology-driven initiatives.

DOI: 10.4324/9781003501862-5

The "Scan, Bag, Go" app from Kroger will be released soon, enabling customers to scan their own products while they are in the store. The app will alert you when you pass an item you need if you have loaded your shopping list into it. Customers see a real-time total of the items they have bought and the fuel points they have accrued, and downloaded coupons are automatically applied. Checkout is a fast place to verify and pay, and it will get even quicker once Kroger lets users pay with their phones.

Additionally, Kroger announced that it is implementing "Kroger Edge," which are digital panels that replace price stickers on shelves, and that it will start delivering groceries in Arizona using autonomous vehicles from a company called Nuro. Along with warning you about allergies and displaying nutritional data, the panels can also show video advertisements, discounts, and notifications about products on your shopping list. In theory, it also enables the business to dynamically adjust prices across all locations in response to various factors, such as demand trends and weather. Additionally, Kroger uses AI-powered warehousing and personalization. It goes without saying that the biggest supermarket chain in the United States is not going to back down in the face of Amazon and Walmart's competition. The main reason why the distinction between retail and wholesale is becoming more hazy in the United States is because, only three years after its founding, Amazon launched "Amazon Business," which master data management (MDM) estimates is now a $5 billion distributor.

In terms of technology, retail has typically been years ahead of distribution. Over time, a number of innovations in retail, such as price optimization, marketing automation, and inventory management techniques, have "trickled down" to distribution. Distribution leaders must therefore keep an eye on retail since it frequently provides a sneak peek at future developments in our sector. Voice-based purchasing is available with Amazon's Alexa-enabled smart speakers. Both consumers and business clients find the combination of the widest selection of inventory and smart speakers to be highly alluring. By rapidly gaining traction, Amazon can both profit from its AI investments and create obstacles to other business-to-business (B2B) competitors.

Together with humans, modern AI is revolutionizing industries and propelling previously unheard-of levels of creativity, profitability, and expansion.

However, not all AI is made equal. Two essential components of AI are:

1 Automating choices and actions based on the model's output.
2 Acquiring knowledge through a feedback mechanism that makes it increasingly intelligent.

Amazon made a significant investment in AI years ago and is actively developing new skills. They are positioned to gain market share because all of this technology is currently linked to their marketplace. By automating purchasing procedures, customers increase productivity, reduce labor expenses and inventory investments, and increase machine and facility uptime.

Introduction

"Place" (physical distribution) covers the decisions and activities that move products from origin to the right customers—via chosen intermediaries—at the right time and service level. Firms select and support channel partners (discounts, campaigns, service standards), while intermediaries hold inventory, present assortments, negotiate and close sales, and provide after-sales service. Core execution spans inventory control, storage/warehousing, and transportation.

As promotion and search shift to digital touchpoints, customers increasingly choose what to see, where, and when. AI personalizes messages and timing based on profiles and preferences; in operations, AI also automates tasks that are mechanical and repetitive. Example: Alibaba's Xunxi robots automate order picking and packing to materially reduce labor costs. Access and availability remain central to customer satisfaction, and AI now supports place decisions end-to-end: Cobots for packaging, drones for delivery, and Internet of Things (IoT) sensors for tracking and automatic replenishment. Service contexts also use AI: embodied robots can greet and guide customers, though a balanced human environment still matters for satisfaction. Example: Lowe's deploys small shelf-mounted cameras in high-touch aisles; when the system detects a gap (e.g., light bulbs), store devices are alerted to refill immediately.

With the role of "place" framed, we next ground the marketing logic before layering in AI.

Place in Marketing Mix (Foundations)

What Place Delivers

Place in marketing assures efficient availability, convenience, and other service benefits to the products or services for the customers. This involves the richness of the assortment at a place, the length of the queue by customers, accessibility of the product, and the quality of information that is given. The AI enhances these parameters by giving organizations the augmented insights into the trends of demand, accelerating the decision-making process, and standardizing operations in different destinations. Trader Joe's, AI can predict stock outages and propose restocking in time, so that customers can get everything they need when they need it. AI enhances customer satisfaction and operational effectiveness by increasing the level of predictability and responsiveness.

Channel Design & Coverage

The distribution channels are the route that the product takes between the end customer and the manufacturer. The way these channels are run is increasingly changing with the implementation of AI in various stages:

Sales & Marketing: A distributor of building materials uses generative AI as a tool to compose customer-specific emails using the brand voice of the company. Through inputting lead-engine data, that is, active projects and customer profiles, AI generates specific messages that will lead to engagement and sales. This lessens human input when typing emails and enhances relevance and responsiveness. Builders First Source (United States), one of the largest building materials distributers uses AI personalization tools that use customer relationship management (CRM) and project data.

Procurement: An industrial electronics Seimens AI is using AI to conduct an automatic prescreen on supplier bids to significantly reduce the time needed to screen bids. AI-based insights and formatted summaries allow teams to start working on projects 2 months sooner than previously. This not only speeds up operations but also informs and standardizes procurement decisions based on data.

Inventory Classification: A major semiconductor and electronics distributor identifies stock keeping units (SKUs) using a large language model (LLM) to index them to the Harmonized Tariff System (HTS) codes. The pilot project had a near 95% accuracy on millions of items, which significantly reduced the errors made by human hands. This enhances compliance, increases the speed of custom processing, and eases inventory control. Arrow Electronics is a global leader in electronic distribution.

Logistics Documentation: A big distributor in the industry applies generative AI to find any missing shipping or customs paperwork and create full documents automatically. Lead times are reduced, delay levels are minimized, and document preparation time throughout the logistics system is reduced by approximately 60%. For example, Avnet, one of the world's largest electronic distributors, has been piloting generative AI solutions for this.

Customer Service: A global logistics company uses AI to enhance the precision of chatbots and automatically create frequently asked question (FAQ) pages. The customers are able to service themselves in a better manner, which saves on the reliance on human agents and provides a rapid and precise response. AI, therefore, enhances customer satisfaction and the scale of operations. Samsung Virtual Assistant and Self-service support portals help customers with personalized solutions.

Retail Case (Zara): Zara will use AI in production and inventory management. AI-based demand forecasts can optimize the production timetable and volume, and sensors and computer vision can indicate empty shelves so they can be replenished on the spot. This will guarantee that stocks are available in every single store and in the online store, making sure there are no stockouts, missed sales, and the maximization of inventory across all locations.

Performance Basics

AI is reshaping transportation and fleet management through better decisions, automation, and predictive analytics. Teams move from reactive to proactive: machine learning (ML) models find patterns in sensor, camera, GPS, and Point of Sale (POS) data to forecast demand, flag risks, and recommend actions. Autonomous trucks and platooning promise higher safety and efficiency by reducing driver fatigue effects and optimizing fuel. Continuous learning lets systems adapt as conditions change. Dalsey, Hillblom and Lynn (DHL)'s AI platform processes real-time telematics and location data to forecast delivery loads and schedule maintenance before breakdowns.

With foundations set, we now specify where AI plugs into the place system (Figure 5.1).

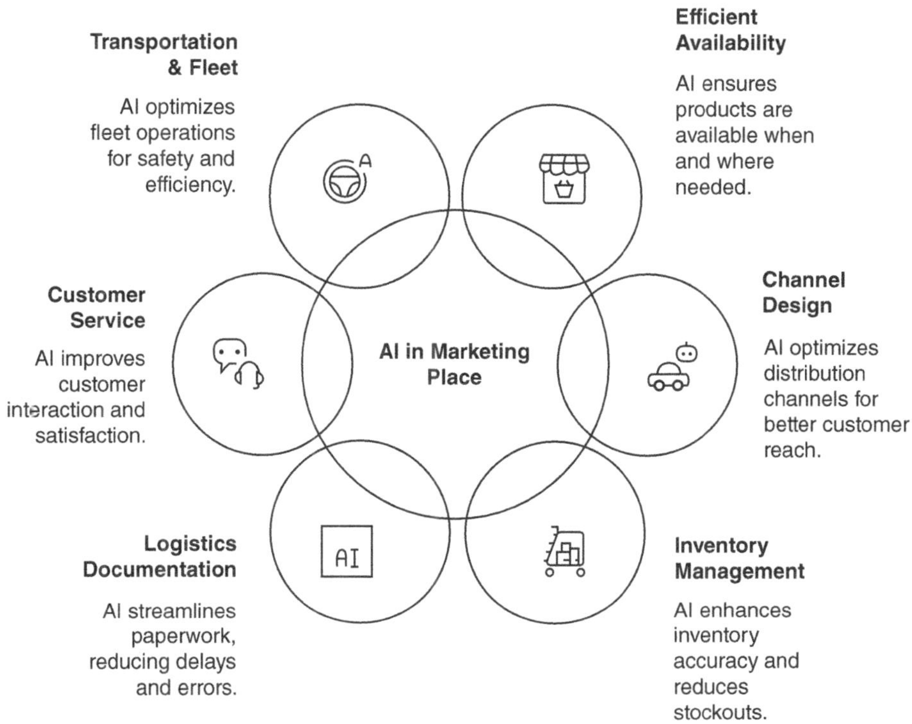

FIGURE 5.1 AI in marketing place.

Where AI Plugs In

AI may change the way in which products are distributed to customers, and make distribution faster, more precise, and demand-responsive. It serves as a smart assistant that constantly tracks sales, stock, and delivery processes and offers improvement at each stage. Analyzing trends across the stores, warehouses, and transportation systems, AI can predict issues before they occur, such as a store being out of stock on a certain item or a shipment being slowed. It also assists in prioritizing the resources so that high-demand products are always ready, and the wastage will be minimized in case of overstocked products. Basically, AI is the foundation of smarter, quicker, and more equitable logistics and inventory choices.

Data Foundations and Privacy

AI can optimally handle clean and accurate data that has been given permission. Examples of the sources are point-of-sale systems, loyalty applications, sensor-based smart shelves, supplier reports, and tracking of the delivery trucks with Global Positioning System (GPS). It is important that the data is complete and reliable, and that it should be checked by timestamps and errors should be corrected, as well as that missing data points should be handled. Meanwhile, businesses should not ignore the principle of privacy, only keeping the information they require and adhering to the regulations of consent. As an example, a supermarket can trace sales using its app to estimate the products required restocking without storing unwanted customer information. Ethical data and clean data will aid the AI in making fair and accurate decisions regarding inventory and distribution. Flipkart integrates AI and relies on rigorous data cleaning, timestamp validation, error correction, and data permission compliance to support accurate demand forecasting, dynamic pricing, and automated replenishment.

Modeling & Decision Engines

The data is used to analyze demand and predict the customer response to changes, and estimate the value of customers in the long term using AI. This will aid in determining how stock is shipped to each store, the priority of items, and how to make substitution arrangements in case one of them runs out. As an illustration, a retailer selling clothing can employ AI to deliver more popular sizes to stores with higher demand, and less of slow-moving products to prevent overstocking. With time, AI works out Strava or trains through outcomes or basic test and trial tactics, such as mini-experiments, to narrow the range of decisions and increase precision in terms of stocking and promotions.

Deployment and Oversight

AI can be used in a batch mode, such as sending weekly inventory orders to stores, or in real time, such as making last-minute adjustments to boatloads or suggesting alternatives when an item is out of stock. Continuous monitoring of AI performance should be done on the basis of simple metrics: whether shelves are stocked, deliveries are on time, or customers are complaining. It is necessary that humans remain within the loop to verify the unusual recommendations, maintain records, and avoid unfair pricing. Carrefour, a grocery chain, can allow the AI to recommend more rapid milk restocking of busy stores, but the managers have to approve the sudden price increases. In this architecture, AI will be able to enhance inventory management, clear slow-moving items, and effectively deliver the products (Table 5.1).

TABLE 5.1 AI Strategies in Distribution

Strategy	*How It's Used*	*Practical Outcome*
Clean & ethical data (4.1)	Collect sales info from POS, loyalty apps, smart shelves, supplier reports, and GPS tracking, while keeping only what's needed and respecting customer privacy.	Fairer and more reliable decisions; e.g., a supermarket restocks fast-selling products without misusing customer data.
Modeling & decision engines (4.2)	AI studies buying patterns, predicts demand, and decides how to send stock where it's needed most. It also tests ideas through small experiments.	Stores get the right products in the right quantities—like popular shoe sizes sent to high-demand locations—reducing waste and stockouts.
Deployment & oversight (4.3)	AI works in both batch (weekly orders) and real time (last-minute delivery updates). Humans stay in the loop to check unusual suggestions or pricing.	Faster restocks, smoother deliveries, and less risk of unfair pricing; for example, busy stores get milk stocked quickly, but managers still approve pricing decisions.

Inventory, Slow Movers, & Smart Logistics

Inventory management is one of the most difficult jobs for retailers and manufacturers. Too much stock wastes money, too little causes loss of sales and disappointed consumers. Unmoved products can quietly absorb profits without being handled in a smart way, and inadequate logistics can make operations expensive and uncertain. Those issues can be handled with the help of AI and its combination of accurate demand forecasting, automatic refill, and smart transportation. The balance between availability of a product, cost-effectiveness, and customer satisfaction is guaranteed by all these levers.

Demand Sensing and Positioning

AI can be used to analyze buying habits of customers, for example, seasonality (Diwali, Christmas), special events (sports tournaments), or weather (wet weather increases umbrella demand). It combines them with external information, such as local trends or advertising campaigns, when forecasting the demand of each SKU in stores or distribution centers. That will help calculate the amount of safety stocks to hold to prevent low stocks. Meanwhile, AI identifies slow-moving products to allow managers to make decisions whether to move them, or combine them with the faster sellers, or provide markdowns. As an illustration, a supermarket can discover that soft drinks are not selling during the winter months; hence, AI can recommend discounting the drinks or bundling them with snacks to make room for the hot drinks.

Replenishment & Allocation

AI replaces the need to use manual checks by applying automated reorder points, activated when stock reaches certain levels that elicit procurement. The rules of allocation then determine the store or warehouse to have priority on the live demand. This minimizes stockout of fast-moving products and prevents overstocking in products that do not sell fast. The outcome is reduced waste levels, reduced markdowns, and less capital invested in surplus inventory. An example is that a fashion store could be automated and order large quantities of Uniqlo types at metro stores and only small quantities in smaller towns where the demand is less. In this manner, stock is matched up, and money is not tied up in inventory.

Transport & Last-Mile

AI is useful in enhancing logistics through the optimization of delivery paths in real time, taking into account traffic, weather, and customer delivery periods. The predictive maintenance tools also alert the managers that there is a likelihood that the delivery trucks will fail, which saves on the unnecessary cost of downtimes. In other instances, autonomous trucks or so-called platooning (convoy of AI-controlled trucks) will lengthen safe working hours and reduce fuel consumption, reducing emissions. Considering the example of an e-commerce company, Alibaba AI will provide an opportunity to reroute a delivery van when one route is slowed down by heavy rain, and also, the customers will not miss packages. This results in quicker, more dependable, as well as eco-friendly last-mile logistics (Figure 5.2).

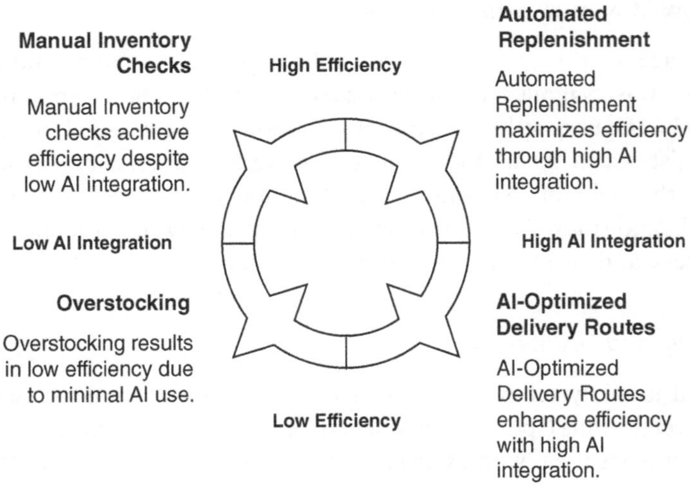

FIGURE 5.2 AI in inventory and logistics management.

Sales Channel Management

The competitive market today is not about just being online and offline but about creating a convergence of customer experience, that is, ensuring that it is seamless and all-inclusive. The customers insist that the brands engage with them during touchpoints, whether when they walk into a shop, order through the assistance of an application, or speak to a sales clerk. The problem companies have to solve is not only to deliver convenience and customization but also to ensure uniformity of pricing, mix, and control across media. AI and advanced analytics play a central part in the organization of these intricate networks, ensuring efficiency and, accordingly, customer delight. For example, Ajio is trying to create AI-powered omnichannel ecosystem across India.

Omnichannel Orchestration

The customers have a growing demand for the flexibility of interaction: some want a personal interaction, others look toward the possibilities of remote interactions, and many enjoy the provision of self-service in reordering their products. AI assists in integrating these modes by processing customer profiles and forecasting the channel that will be effective in a particular situation. As an example, a B2B supplier, BASF, may direct small repeat orders via self-service portals and allocate hybrid sales teams to valued clients. High-tech platforms also provide the opportunity to create hyper-personalized experiences—the sales representatives may have talking points generated by AI, depending on the previous purchases, preferences, and future needs of a buyer. Such an arrangement makes sure that the customers feel heard regardless of the point of contact.

Assortment & Price Coherence

AI helps companies to provide the appropriate combination of merchandise and channel parity. Dynamic suggestions may provide complementary products on what a consumer is viewing or purchasing, and image recognition systems can generate catalogs automatically on e-commerce websites. Pricing is the other frontier: machine learning predictors divide customers into micro-groups based on hundreds of attributes, which enables companies to offer discounts and offers tailored to each customer. As an example, a petrochemicals company claimed to have increased incremental earnings in the range of 100M in the case of the application of AI-based pricing. Nevertheless, transparency should be upheld, that is, having the same prices in different channels that are properly explained in order to prevent any feeling of discrimination or injustice.

Conflict & Governance

The sales channels can overlap, creating conflicting teams or a lack of account ownership. The solution to this is with the help of AI and generative artificial intelligence (Gen-AI), as they can assist in the governance framework and routine work automation. As an example, now, it is possible to automatically draft the request for proposal (RFP)/request for quotation (RFQ) responses, and in the case of the AI assistant of a water-tech company, it created a 1.8M worth of quotes within weeks. Meeting support tools suggest discussions and emphasize follow-ups, leaving sales reps free to develop relationships. Coaching systems act as simulators of customers and can deliver feedback, enabling companies to train many employees in a short period of time, such as an agrochemicals company that used AI-driven coaching to train 650+ professionals. This will guarantee efficiency as well as fairness in the channel operations.

In addition to the simple process of moving SKUs via various outlets, companies have to view the channel network as a strategic product. The architecture of the channel interaction, governance policies that avoid conflicts, and the intelligence layer that ensures that everything remains coherent are all important factors to long-term success. Companies that learn how to manage channels successfully with the assistance of AI not only grow revenue but also gain customer trust, which provides a sustainable competitive advantage (Table 5.2).

TABLE 5.2 AI in Sales Channel Management

Channel Area	*Use of AI*	*Results*	*Brand Example (Success/ Failure)*
Omnichannel orchestration	AI integrates in-person, remote, and self-service sales, predicting which channel works best for which customer.	Customers get seamless, personalized experiences across touchpoints; sales teams focus effort where it matters most.	**Success**: Cosco uses AI to blend online + offline (Go stores, app-based shopping). **Failure**: Sears struggled to unify its online and store experiences, leading to lost customers.
Assortment & price coherence	AI generates dynamic product suggestions, builds automated catalogs, and applies ML for micro-segment pricing.	Higher sales through tailored offers; improved efficiency in catalog management; risk if price fairness isn't maintained.	**Success**: Petrochemical firm gained ~$100M in incremental earnings from AI-driven pricing. **Failure**: Swiggy faced backlash in some markets for "surge pricing" seen as unfair during emergencies.

(*Continued*)

TABLE 5.2 (Continued)

Channel Area	*Use of AI*	*Results*	*Brand Example (Success/ Failure)*
Conflict & governance	Gen-AI automates drafting proposals, meeting prep, and sales coaching simulations, reducing friction among teams.	Faster responses to customers, improved training, and better governance of overlapping channels.	**Success**: Agrochemical company trained 650+ staff using AI coaching. **Failure**: Early Salesforce AI pilots showed bias in lead prioritization, frustrating sales teams before fixes were made.

Network and Distribution Product Management

Distribution product management entails considering the whole flow of products, which consists of suppliers, manufacturers, distributors, retailers, and ultimately customers as a product. It implies that all the chain processes, including vendor management, packaging, warehousing, and logistics, have to be thoroughly planned and constantly optimized. Other companies go further to use blockchain to enhance the process of traceability, so that customers and regulators can directly observe the origin of a product in a given supply chain, and how it transited the supply chain.

The logistics activities in such an arrangement extend far beyond getting boxes into and out of the places. They are supply planning (determining the quantity of stock on hand), temperature control (essential to medicines or frozen food), security (to discourage theft or tampering), fleet routing (selecting the shortest delivery route), tracking (understanding the location of each order), and warehousing (maximizing the use of storage space). The end objective is quick and waste-free satisfaction that has a direct positive impact on profitability. To illustrate this, a dairy company that is monitoring temperature conditions during transportation with the help of AI can save millions of dollars by preventing spoilage.

The commercial aspect of distribution is also modified by AI, which will make the interaction with the customers smarter. Offers made based on a shopper real-time location, like proposing the purchase of products, can reduce cart abandonment. Suppose that a customer is buying running shoes online, an AI bot can point out a time-sensitive purchase in local pickup in a local store, which will make the purchase more attractive. Bots also generate social proof by persuading choices with messages such as Great choice! 200 other customers purchased this last week, which is an effective method of conversions.

The sale is followed by 24-hour AI-assisted service agents such as Amelia or Interactions. They can screen the problems like the delivery status, warranty complaints, or payment questions, and direct human agents based on the tone detection (suspecting that a customer feels frustrated) and propose the most appropriate answers. This enhances efficiency as well as customer satisfaction.

To scale all these capabilities, organizations should consider developing a concise governance structure:

- Role definition (who manages the vendors, who observes Key Performance Indicators (KPIs), who is the customer service).

- Offered KPIs (accuracy of delivery, order cycle time, return rate, customer satisfaction).
- Establish a change management plan that will help the employees easily adapt to the AI-powered work modes.

Examples: consider an example of a pharmaceutical company, Pfizer. It has been in a position to apply AI in supply planning and temperature regulation to ensure the timely and safe delivery of medicines. At the same time, its chatbot can provide answers to patient inquiries regarding dosage reminders or refills so they can handle more complex cases. Clear KPIs like 95% on-time delivery and less than 1% spoilage can help measure success. It is this combination of operational and customer-facing AI that has made the entire distribution chain a competitive product.

Implementation Playbook

The playbook that accompanies the shift between strategy and action should be clear. The most efficient AI and distribution ideologies would not accomplish rollout without planning. Companies must coordinate people, processes, and technology as they build protective walls to address risks. This section of the document explains the crucial steps. IBM uses a formal Deployment playbook that aligns data scientists, supply chain managers, compliance teams, and AI specialists before any AI rollout.

Organization & Roles

The approach of accountability is a well-constructed one. A number of companies have a distribution council that includes supply chain leaders, marketing, analytics, and store operations leaders. This council defines RACI (Responsible, Accountable, Consulted, Informed) in a manner that will ensure that each is aware of what he or she has to do when there are disruptions or new initiatives. One of these is that during any unforeseen arrival of online grocery orders, store activities can use substitutions, analytics signals, demand spikes, and marketing notifications to inform consumers about modifications. Escalation and override authority should also be preassigned, for example, the setting of the surgical pricing limit or replacement regulations Target, so that a decision can be made immediately.

KPIs & Experiments

Definitive measurements aid in success measurement. Examples of KPIs are on-shelf availability (OSA), fill rate, on-time in-full (OTIF) deliveries, inventory turns/ Gross Margin Return on Inventory Investment (GMROII) (efficiency measure), pick accuracy/time, last-mile cost, customer complaints, or substitution rates. In a bid to do better, companies usually carry out controlled experiments. As an illustration, a retailer could experiment with lower delivery charges based on flexible time slots to boost the efficiency of fulfillment, or could experiment with AI-generated planogram prompts to enhance shelf availability. The results are facilitated by the standard reporting formats that enable the results to be compared and scaled across the regions.

Platforms & Change

Implementation is in technology. Companies must consider revisiting their Warehouse Management System (WfMC), Transport Management System (TfMC), and Order Management System (OfMC) to identify whether they are appropriate and efficient today and going forward. The build vs. buy issue is also critical, as there are companies that invest in their own custom artificial intelligence and those that use third-party tools. Beyond technology, there is a win-or-lose scenario in the teaching of employees to operate equipment and processes without becoming uncomfortable. The customers also require transparency: the company cannot conceal the price of delivery, replacement, or warranty services, or the customers will be unsatisfied. In one case, FedEx tells a customer beforehand that they promise to deliver within a certain time.

Risk rules also need to be clear in order to produce a robust execution. They include anti-unfair price mechanisms when the demand is high, the availability of substitutions that meet the needs of satisfied customers, and backup measures anytime the system has failed. By combining people, KPIs, and platforms with clear rules and regulations, firms can expand the scale of AI-driven distribution responsibly and confidently (Figure 5.3).

Risks & Governance

As AI and automation open significant sources of efficiency, new threats arise. In the absence of proper governance, the companies may suffer the wrath of the customer, regulatory fines, or even failure of their systems. Having guardrails that are constructed around fairness, privacy, legal compliance, and reliability will guarantee that innovation will be sustainable. Microsoft has developed an internal responsible AI to govern how AI is built and deployed.

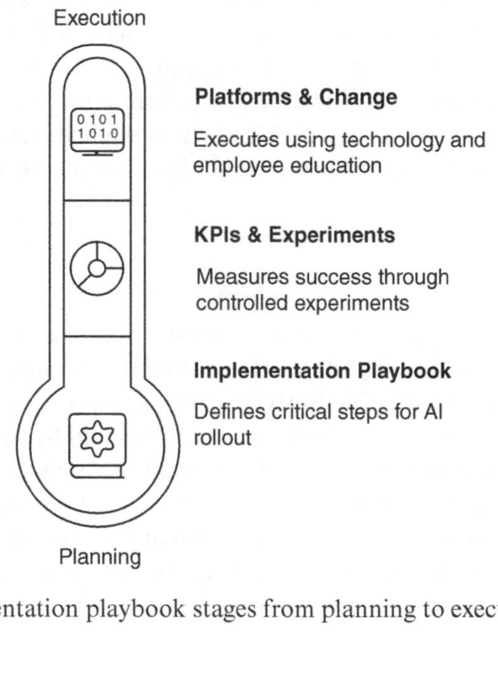

FIGURE 5.3 AI implementation playbook stages from planning to execution.

Fairness & Privacy

The AI systems should be made to treat the customers equally. As an example, an online grocery site must not be geo-biased, in which case customers in a specific region are always offered more favorable delivery times than those in other regions. Firms should also observe data privacy by only collecting data that is necessary (data minimization), utterly utilizing it to the intended purpose, and obtaining proper consent from customers. Transparency is essential—in case AI recommends product replacement, the customers must clearly see why and can make a choice. Dark patterns: Dark patterns should be avoided, for example, the attempt to position high-margin products in the guise of recommendations. An easy fairness protection measure is to post the eligibility regulations, that is, who is eligible to get the same-day delivery as Prime members of Amazon.

Legal & Reliability

During periods of high demand, distribution AI must not violate consumer-protection rules, pricing, and anti-gouging legislation. As an example, algorithms should not be expected to artificially raise the prices of bottled water in times of natural disasters. Competition risks also exist: with the pricing algorithms learning off each other, there is a risk of them colluding by mistake, leading to regulatory action. The ability to withstand a shock, like cyberattacks or data being scraped by rivals, also requires reliability, meaning systems must be robust to withstand such a shock. To overcome these risks, the companies must possess incident playbooks, enabling quick responses, rollback/kill switches to shut down defective models, and auditable logs to hold them responsible. Reporting to the customers, regulators, and other partners often helps to avoid losing trust in case of disruptions. Azure by Microsoft has a well-established AI incident response framework.

Ethical & Social Impact

Businesses are not only expected to conform, but also consider the broader implications of AI-centered distribution to the community. As an example, warehouse and logistics automation may cause the loss of manual jobs, and the retraining and the fairness of the transition might be subject to discussion. Sustainability is another concern since AI can reduce waste levels by optimizing routing and packaging, but it should not make people buy more due to hyper-targeted marketing. Social segregations can also exist in relation to the bias of AI decision-making, for example, South Africa is not prioritized as much as an urban customer. Ethical governance mechanisms will encourage businesses to audit models to identify undesired bias, publish sustainability reports, and engage with society that has undergone technological change. One scenario is the case of Unilever who has pledged to be responsible in its supply chain as it continues with its sustainability agenda by using AI.

CLOSING CASE: EBAY

All facets of the eBay marketplace are integrated with AI, which anticipates the needs and desires of both buyers and sellers, motivates consumers searching for something unique, supports business owners hoping to expand, and makes the platform more user-friendly.

With multiple levels of complexity, it is one of the most reliable international marketplaces. eBay lacks its own warehouses, delivery routes, retail locations, and inventory. With 1.2 billion listings and millions of buyers and sellers in 190 markets, it uses AI to bring structure to an otherwise unstructured world. Its advantage is in that challenge. We use more than 20 years of data and customer insights to train our algorithms and improve the intelligence of our AI. The AI learns and gives feedback each time a user engages with the marketplace, enabling us to improve the user experience. Deep learning advancements have sped up the progress by enabling us and others to make longer strides in data processing.

Overall, eBay employs a four-pronged strategy: enhance the user experience, develop and implement the infrastructure that best suits eBay's particular requirements, integrate core and domain AI science into everything it does, and make sure that everything is done with the user experience in mind.

Through computer vision, recommendation systems, machine translation, natural language processing, search, personalization, insights, and discovery, eBay creates and implements AI at scale to improve the user experience on our platform. It makes use of AI to enhance our comprehension of user intent in natural language processing and unit measurement. This knowledge is applied to the condition of the goods, pricing ranges, and shipping circumstances in addition to our varied groups of buyers and sellers. eBay uses AI to comprehend context and display a wide range of pertinent products for improved search diversity. For instance, searching for "smart home" yields a number of pertinent results, including brand, condition, price, and smart home protocol (e.g., Wi-Fi and Bluetooth), as well as smart home compatibility (Alexa, Google Assistant, Apple HomeKit, Nest, Philips Hue), so the buyer can choose what best suits their needs.

By investing in technology and using AI, eBay is strengthening its relationship with its sellers and relieving them of this burden. For sellers who might not have access to advanced AI-powered tools, it creates an even playing field. Sellers can then concentrate on sourcing, closing deals, and expanding their companies. Data, metrics, and analytics are managed by its platform, which we then present to our sellers in order to support their success. The core of eBay's mission is to support sellers by investing in tools, technology, and our platform.

By using natural language processing to refine the search for the best-matched item, it can shorten the time it takes to list products. Sellers benefit from improved product descriptions and details while also saving time. By offering sophisticated promoted listings on eBay and more precisely customizing its ads off of eBay through ad science, it pushes the limits of its first-party ad experiences and enhances user engagement. By doing so, it keeps enhancing the shopping experience and encourages customers to explore more of our worldwide inventory.

With 190 markets, eBay facilitates international trade by facilitating e-commerce transactions. eBay is advancing machine translation technology. The goal is to develop a single AI system that can process various languages and expedite the process for customers who shop abroad. According to a study on the eBay platform's machine translation from English to Spanish, the system's impact on global trade based on US exports increased exports by 17.5%. It aims to provide sellers with improved insights regarding pricing, sourcing, and shipping. It is dedicated to utilizing machine learning to assist sellers in determining the optimal prices to help an item sell, determining when to look at or list a particular product to obtain the highest market value, and improving their own marketing to draw in customers. Every development team at eBay collaborates with several remote teams. We developed a tool called ShipShip to help keep information flowing so that everyone is aware of the various projects they are working on.

Another AI-powered tool has been released by eBay to help sellers save time and effort when creating product listings. In just a few seconds, eBay will create draft listings with suggested categories, titles, and item details for sellers who upload batches of product images using the new magical bulk listing tool. Sellers can post their listings to the marketplace once the details have been checked for accuracy.

The enchanted bulk listing tool can produce multiple drafts at once and process hundreds of photos in a batch. In the upcoming months, eBay intends to extend the tool's availability to additional categories and nations. Currently, US Seller Hub users can use it to list in the Sports Trading Card category. According to preliminary data, the tool considerably shortened the time needed for users to list items when they were creating trading card listings.

Discussion Questions

1. Discuss the key concepts of place, and distribution and the use of AI.
2. Apply the discussed concepts of AI and distribution in a product industry of your choice in a detailed manner.
3. Describe the benefits and risks of using AI in place and distribution.
4. Analyze the application of AI in sales channel management, cross-selling, upselling, and customer buying patterns.

Assignment Questions

1. How can Zara use AI to balance online and offline inventory distribution?
2. In what ways can Amazon Fresh apply AI to improve last-mile delivery?
3. How should a competitor respond to a petrochemicals firm earning $100M from AI-based pricing?
4. Would you approve of AI's recommendation to cut rural supply due to low demand? Why or why not?
5. Design a three-phase AI adoption plan (short, medium, long-term) for a mid-size distributor.

MINI CASE: BIGBASKET'S AI JOURNEY IN DISTRIBUTION

BigBasket, one of India's leading online grocery platforms, faced growing challenges as demand surged during the pandemic. Customers wanted faster delivery, fresh products, and fair prices, while the company had to manage thin margins, unpredictable demand, and logistics complexity across multiple cities. Traditional forecasting methods were not sufficient to handle the real-time fluctuations in demand for groceries like milk, bread, and vegetables, which could vary by neighborhood, weather conditions, or even local events.

To tackle this, BigBasket invested in AI-driven distribution. First, it used demand sensing models that analyzed sales data, app usage patterns, and even weather forecasts to predict what products each warehouse should stock. For instance, during a week of heavy rains in Bengaluru, AI predicted a spike in instant noodles and ready-to-eat items, prompting timely restocking. This reduced both stockouts and wastage.

Second, AI optimized last-mile delivery routes. Delivery executives were assigned routes based not only on location but also on predicted traffic, customer time preferences, and package sizes. This cut delivery times by nearly 20% in pilot areas. At the same time, predictive maintenance tools helped reduce breakdowns of delivery vans, ensuring reliability.

Third, BigBasket experimented with AI-based pricing and assortment management. The system suggested micro-offers to specific customer groups, such as discounts on fruits for health-conscious buyers or bulk offers on staples for large families. While this personalization drove higher sales, the company also had to maintain transparency to avoid perceptions of unfair pricing. However, challenges remain. Some customers complained about substitutions—such as receiving a different brand of rice when their preferred one was out of stock. Internally, store managers worried about over-reliance on algorithms, fearing that local knowledge was being ignored. Regulators are also keeping a close watch on pricing fairness in essential goods.

BigBasket's case shows both the opportunities and risks of AI in distribution. It highlights how AI can improve demand prediction, inventory flow, and last-mile delivery, but also raises important governance and customer trust issues. If you were on BigBasket's distribution council, how would you balance AI-driven substitutions with customer trust and satisfaction?

HBR Case Links:

- https://hbsp.harvard.edu/product/UCT035-PDF-ENG?itemFindingMethod=search
- https://hbsp.harvard.edu/product/R2406M-PDF-ENG?itemFindingMethod=search
- https://hbsp.harvard.edu/product/S25011-PDF-ENG?itemFindingMethod=search

Application of Concepts & In-Class Activities

Concept	*Application in Practice*	*In-Class Activity*
AI in demand sensing	Forecasting demand using sales data, weather, and local events (e.g., BigBasket stocking instant noodles during rains).	**Activity**: Give students sales + weather data and ask them to forecast which items should be stocked more/less.
Slow-mover management	Identifying and handling low-selling SKUs via bundling, markdowns, or delisting.	**Activity**: Students analyze a list of slow-moving products and design an AI-backed strategy to clear them.

(*Continued*)

Concept	*Application in Practice*	*In-Class Activity*
AI in last-mile logistics	Optimizing delivery routes and predictive maintenance of fleets (e.g., Amazon Fresh and BigBasket).	**Activity**: Role-play exercise where teams redesign delivery routes under constraints like traffic or peak demand.
Omnichannel orchestration	Integrating online, offline, and self-service sales to give a seamless customer experience.	**Activity**: Break students into groups—each group designs an omnichannel AI solution for a retail brand (e.g., Zara and Reliance Smart).
Fairness & governance	Ensuring transparent pricing, ethical data use, and avoiding bias in distribution.	**Activity**: Debate: *"AI-driven personalized pricing is unfair—agree or disagree?"*

Key Terms

- Demand sensing
- Inventory turns
- Slow-mover management
- On-shelf availability (OSA)
- On-time in-full (OTIF)
- Last-mile delivery
- Predictive maintenance
- Omnichannel orchestration
- Dynamic pricing
- Micro-segmentation
- Assortment coherence
- Substitution rules
- Distribution council
- Algorithmic collusion
- Governance framework

Bibliography

Agatz, N., Campbell, A. M., Fleischmann, M., & Savels, M. (n.d.). Challenges and Opportunities in Attended Home Delivery. *Operations Research/Computer Science Interfaces*, 379–396. https://doi.org/10.1007/978-0-387-77778-8_17

Barreto, L., Amaral, A., & Pereira, T. (2017). Industry 4.0 implications in logistics: an overview. *Procedia Manufacturing*, *13*(1), 1245–1252. https://doi.org/10.1016/j.promfg.2017.09.045

Carbonneau, R., Laframboise, K., & Vahidov, R. (2008). Application of machine learning techniques for supply chain demand forecasting. *European Journal of Operational Research*, *184*(3), 1140–1154. https://doi.org/10.1016/j.ejor.2006.12.004

Martin, K. (2019). Ethical implications and accountability of algorithms. *Journal of Business Ethics*, *160*(835-850). https://doi.org/10.1007/s10551-018-3921-3

Mattila, M., Yrjölä, M., & Hautamäki, P. (2021). Digital transformation of business-to-business sales: what needs to be unlearned? *Journal of Personal Selling & Sales Management*, *41*(2), 1–17. https://doi.org/10.1080/08853134.2021.1916396

Mittelstadt, B. D., Allo, P., Taddeo, M., Wachter, S., & Floridi, L. (2016). The ethics of algorithms: Mapping the debate. *Big Data & Society*, *3*(2), 1–21. https://doi.org/10.1177/2053951716679679

Sperandio Milan, G., Dorion, E., & da Rosa Matos, J. A. (2012). Distribution channel conflict management: A Brazilian experience. *Benchmarking: An International Journal*, *19*(1), 32–51. https://doi.org/10.1108/14635771211218335
Verhoef, P. C., Kannan, P. K., & Inman, J. J. (2015). From multi-channel retailing to omni-channel retailing. *Journal of Retailing*, *91*(2), 174–181. https://doi.org/10.1016/j.jretai.2015.02.005
Waller, M. A., & Fawcett, S. E. (2013). Data science, predictive analytics, and big data: A revolution that will transform supply chain design and management. *Journal of Business Logistics*, *34*(2), 77–84.

6

AI IN IMC

Learning Objectives

1. Understand how silos (separate teams by country, product, or function) can confuse customers and weaken a brand.
2. Learn what a Chief Marketing Officer (CMO) can do—act as a helper, advisor, or service provider—to get teams working together.
3. Know how to set up cross-team groups, shared networks, and a common planning system so people cooperate without losing local flexibility.
4. Practice keeping one clear brand message while still letting local teams adapt it for their market—using clear rules and shared goals.
5. Build a media-neutral marketing plan that brings ads, public relation (PR), social, events, sales, and data together and uses the feedback to improve fast.

OPENING CASE: BURBERRY

Burberry is a British-based luxury fashion brand that has long been recognized for its classic offerings and timeless designs, but it has developed in recent years into a digitally oriented company. Historical and legacy elements are integrated into Burberry's image; however, things are skewing toward the utilization of smart technologies in various aspects of the business. In 2023, Burberry's investment in information and communications technology (ICT) was approximately $76.9 million, a considerable amount of which will be invested in AI, big data, Internet of Things (IoT), and cloud systems. This displays Burberry's transition toward contemporary, data-centered feedback in regard to marketing and further operational management.

AI is a central aspect of Burberry's journey. AI adds value and assists in actionable decision-making related to customer data from numerous places, including their

DOI: 10.4324/9781003501862-6

brick-and-mortar stores, the Burberry mobile app, the Burberry website, and the Burberry social media platforms. AI-powered systems identify specific customer behaviors, learn from them, and adapt in real time. Thus, customer experiences have changed from passive responses to active engagements and interactions. Instead of relying on traditional customer segments, Burberry uses real-time personalization, allowing communication to be more targeted, relevant, and adaptable.

The core principles of IMC, cohesive and proper messaging, are a focus of Burberry's AI. It allows for proper coherence and message alignment when communicating over various channels. For example, when a customer receives a personalized email, a display ad, and participates in a chatbot, Burberry has aligned its messaging using AI, so the customer hears the same message in various media. AI helps create relevant content without being repetitive, personal content without being intrusive, and all campaigns leverage the same tone, offer, and message, regardless of channel.

Burberry's personalization initiatives have been effective. Burberry's in-store tablets and AI-powered loyalty programs afford them a 50% lift in repeat customers who engage with the Burberry personalization systems, as they suggest items that suit the customer's profile, provide styling recommendations for items, and offer exclusive content for loyal customers. While Burberry is creating personal connections with everyone by leveraging customer preference data to anticipate what they may want, the AI-assisted systems keep customers engaged. Creating this deeper engagement and sense of loyalty to the Burberry brand will never be a bad thing.

The standard content strategy has been modified as well. Today, Burberry leverage their AI tools to summarize what campaigns are performing, rigorously evaluate who engaged with the campaigns, and adapt content across different platforms. For instance, visuals, wording, and formats are all subject to continual updates based on live customer feedback and choices made about behaviors. Campaigns no longer have fixed attributes or channels; they are always altering, and through this more agile approach to SIMC, Burberry can dynamically improve its messaging to specific audiences without the risk of diluting the Burberry image.

Finally, AI assists Burberry in fighting counterfeits. As part of this commitment, Burberry has adopted Entrupy's image-based recognition technology, which uniquely uses AI to analyze products at the microscopic and aesthetic detail level. With a 98% accuracy rate for identifying counterfeit goods, this tech offers Burberry another level of protective measures while maintaining consumer confidence. In this way, the brand makes sure that only authentic products get through to market while focusing on both brand respect and consumer confidence.

Customer care has changed since AI chat systems are now handling everyday inquiries, suggesting products, and directing customers to stores. Chatbots have developed and are now more accurate, consistent, wait less, and are assertive, meaning a brand can utilize human effort effectively enough, yet be just as effective in supporting their customers. Most importantly, they will always capture the tone or style with which a particular luxury fashion brand is associated.

While Burberry's use of AI in IMC may seem like efficiency, these are functional ways of improving customer experience in a more systemic way, while being able to maintain the brand identity, and while using real data that allows for more accurate crafting of messages. Burberry's embracing of digital tools illustrates the way that luxury brands can remain valid, yet still function with the differentiating and surrounding factors that the brand values they were built on, i.e. loyalty, security, creativity, or social management and communication. It has generated better campaigns, better connections, and improved outputs.

Introduction to AI in IMC

Marketing communication is no longer just print ads or scheduled TV commercials. Today, brands exist in a connected space where customers are interacting across multiple channels, and often at the same time. Integrated Marketing Communication (IMC) gives order to these dispersed messages. It ties all communication tools together, from digital media to in-store displays, into a single and consistent mode of communication with the customer or business, in a format that will make sense to that customer.

Artificial intelligence (AI) is engaged in the IMC process, not simply as a tool to support communication, but as a major part of the IMC process, allowing for the opportunity for other non-AI tasks. It enables the real-time analysis of massive amounts of data to refine targeting, timing, and message consistency for each channel. Algorithms look for patterns, recognize customer affinity, and even react to predict responses. Communication becomes faster, more relevant, and more personal (while still being managed as consistent and brand-appropriate).

With AI, every customer interaction becomes more intelligent. From website chatbots to email product suggestions, each exchange responds to what the customer wants. Marketers no longer must guess. AI finds what works, tests different versions, and improves results automatically. This helps close the gap between what brands say and what customers are looking for. It also improves how messages are delivered, especially in digital spaces where speed and accuracy are key.

AI does not replace human planning. Instead, it helps make that planning more effective. Marketers use AI to adjust content, plan budgets, and manage repetitive tasks. Jobs that used to take days can now be done in seconds, with support from real data instead of guesses. Personalization can be done on a larger scale. Insights are available all the time. Most importantly, communication stays well-managed and consistent, even in large and detailed campaigns. That is the real benefit AI brings to modern IMC: smarter processes, better coordination, and results that can be clearly measured. Coca-Cola uses AI personalization for marketing campaigns across digital, social media, vending machines, and retail channels.

Overview

AI is changing how marketing communication works. From planning to execution, AI tools now play a significant role in how brands connect with their audiences. The focus has moved away from disconnected messages to real-time, coordinated communication. IMC provides the right setup for using AI. These systems bring speed, accuracy, and alignment, which match the goals of clear messaging, focused targeting, and coordination across platforms.

Today, brands like Unilever manage substantial amounts of data coming from many channels. AI helps make this easier by connecting and analyzing the information. Instead of working in separate teams, marketing groups now share a common view of customer data. Content, timing, and channels are planned based on what the data reveals. Improvado, a US-based platform, uses AI to bring together marketing data from various sources. This gives brands one reliable place to guide their IMC decisions.

One of the biggest advantages of AI is speed. It can process data in seconds, allowing marketing teams to act quickly. Campaigns can adjust automatically when customer behavior shifts. Brands no longer must wait for reports; they make changes while the campaign is still running. A recent study found that 90% of marketers now use AI to support faster decision-making. Having quick access to reliable insights helps brands stay relevant and competitive in fast-changing markets. Pepsi used AI to collect data from live taste events, process responses instantly, and adjust digital ads and influencer posts in real time based on audience reactions in different cities.

AI also helps teams stay on the same page. Sales, advertising, PR, and digital teams often face challenges in keeping their messages consistent. AI tools give them a shared system, using dashboards, alerts, and performance data to keep everyone aligned. This structure helps IMC work more smoothly. Conflicting messages are reduced. Time spent fixing mistakes goes down. Every platform can deliver the same message with the right timing and context.

AI improves audience segmentation, too. Algorithms look at demographics, behavior, and intent to build detailed customer profiles. Campaigns can then target the right groups with more relevant content. AI continues to update these segments by learning from new data and feedback. This takes brands beyond basic targeting and moves them toward precise audience matching. IMC improves as communication becomes more personal, without losing control or consistency.

In the end, AI supports what IMC is built for, clear, coordinated, and consistent messaging. It helps brands scale personalization, avoid waste, and stay aligned across channels. Decision-making becomes sharper, content moves faster, and customer interactions feel more connected.

Role of AI in IMC Effectiveness

IMC success is when the right message is delivered across the right channel, to the right audience, at the right time. Consistency is the goal, and there are so many combinations of channels, formats, and audience preferences that it can be a challenge. AI simultaneously creates order through the chaos. AI looks at what works and monitors what does not, and can recommend campaigns to drive better results, while not robbing any creative concept or strategic thought.

AI supports the effectiveness of IMC by helping to coordinate efforts at all levels of a campaign, whether it is campaign planning, campaign implementation, or post-campaign reporting. AI tools provide teams with data and insights to improve accuracy and remove inaccuracy. Whether it is deciding on audience targeting, types of content to create, timing of a live event, or selecting which channels to deploy, there is always data to support and inform the decision. This reduces the chances of a mismatch between what the brand wants to say and what reaches the audience. Teams work with more clarity and use data to guide important decisions from the start.

However, full use of AI across the entire IMC process is still limited. Only 30% of agencies, brands, and publishers have adopted AI throughout all stages of their media campaigns Most only use it for specific tasks, such as automation or simple targeting. This limited use holds back the full benefits of AI. Without connected systems, feedback loops remain incomplete, and campaigns miss chances to improve through continuous learning.

AI helps IMC work better by adding clarity, speed, and control to complex campaign environments. Creative work, media planning, and message consistency all improve with the help of AI tools and real-time feedback. While many teams are still not using AI to its full potential, the results so far point in a clear direction. As more marketers go beyond basic uses, AI will continue to shape how integrated communication delivers stronger and more consistent outcomes. Mercedes-Benz applies AI not only in its cars but also deeply into its marketing communications ecosystem to ensure the right message reaches the right audience at the right time across all channels.

AI in Advertising

Advertising will continue to be one of the fastest-moving and most dynamic elements of the marketing mix. With the rise of digital platforms and shifts in audience behaviors, campaigns need to be developed faster, smarter, and with more creativity than ever. AI is changing how brands approach advertising, through ideation and strategy, optimization, and tracking. AI tools can now run large-scale ad testing, optimize targeting, and shorten the launch of campaigns. The advertising process has gotten faster, but key focus areas based on the audience will be more important than ever.

The optimization process does not cease going live. AI tracks individual ad performance across all platforms, analyzes audience engagement trends, and can simultaneously adapt settings. Adaptations mean that high-performing ads can double down on outreach, while ads that have a lower performance can be paused or changed in real time. The feedback loop fosters better outcomes and reduced waste. Campaigns become more agile and economical, even as targeting continues to improve as the AI learns about specific groups most likely to respond to content. Loreal tracks engagement on beauty ads across Instagram, TikTok, and YouTube, and AI boosts winning creatives and pauses low-performing ones instantly.

The prediction of AI in advertising only represents the shift that is happening. By 2025, the AI advertising market is expected to be $40 billion at a continued rate of growth annually of about 20 percent. This pace suggests more brands are opting to automate decision-making vs. continue with manual processes. AI will not only drive efficiencies, but it will also allow even more creative testing. Brands will be able to experiment with more ideas without overwhelming teams or pushing deadlines.

With AI, IMCs can be implemented faster, more accurately, and consistently. It enables creative work to be scaled, but in a more measured way. The messages are always active, responding to the actions and reactions of the audience without fragmentation. It also facilitates tracking and improvement of the results. As more brands begin to integrate AI advertising technology, the anticipated IMC return will become stronger, and perceived risks will decrease, thus reinforcing the notion that AI value is no longer a theoretical concept, but a measured and constant factor with each released DISCONNECTED ad.

AI in Enhancing Public Relations & Customer Service

Public relations and customer service are both critical components in determining how consumers perceive a brand. Each relies on regular or ongoing engagement, immediate replies, and up-to-date information. AI offers a heightened level of speed and process control for both functions. Brands can respond to an audience's inquiry on multiple platforms and in real time, address data request questions when they occur, and measure public sentiment as it is happening. As communication continues to grow and upon which relationships are built, AI is imperative for building trust and sustaining relationships.

AI will be further developed to learn as it adds value from completing individualization (or personalization). AI identifies replies to be sent again based on tracking the history previously undertaken by customer history, behaviors, or past interactions. Instead of sending the same reply, the AI chatbot maintains trust at the individual level while delivering the response needed or action required. Individualization reduces frustration and improves the experience overall. AI allows customers to have a sense of acknowledgement from the brand, even when a staff member is not present and identifiable. This combination of automation and reacquainting in both PR and operational style roles can enhance customer relationships derived from the brand.

Samsung Galaxy Note 7s Crisis management was based on sentiment measurement tools and the analysis of key public reactions. AI can direct brands to rising or increasing issues. AI improves PR and customer service by speeding up responses, increasing accuracy, and making messages more personal. Conversations flow better across all platforms. Information stays consistent with the brand voice. Customers get a smoother experience without adding pressure on human teams. As more organizations start using AI in these areas, their communication becomes more responsive, better coordinated, and ready for the challenges of today's fast-moving environment (Figure 6.1).

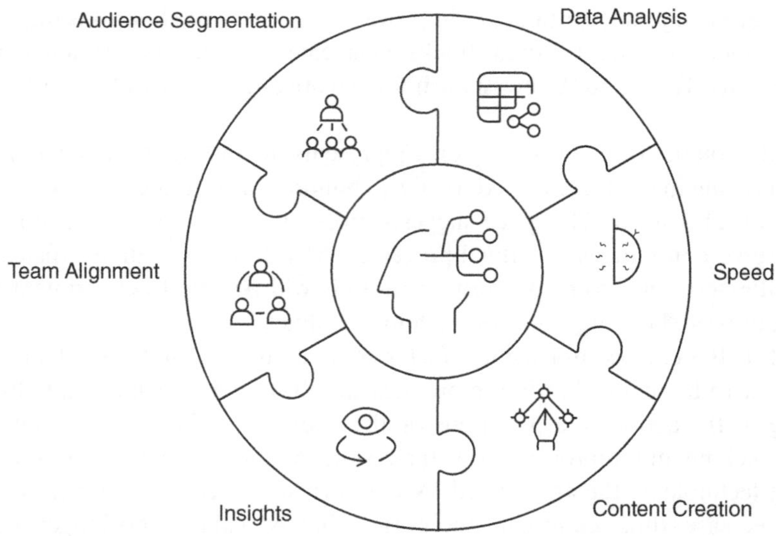

FIGURE 6.1 AI's role in marketing communication.

Role of AI in IMC

AI is now a significant part of how brands structure IMC. As customers are beginning to engage in more platforms, the demands for coordination, speed, and personalization are ever-increasing. AI helps take some of those demands off by sifting through vast amounts of data, recognizing audience behaviors, and automating communications in a variety of formats. This allows brands to maintain one voice while addressing the differing needs of audiences in-real-time. AirAsia uses an AI-powered chatbot across its website, mobile app, WhatsApp, and Facebook Messenger.

Personalization, Predictive Analysis

Personalization is now a basic expectation in marketing. People no longer respond to generic messages. They pay attention to content that matches their interests, habits, and timing. IMC must treat personalization as essential, not optional. AI supports this shift by spotting patterns, adjusting content, and helping brands deliver relevant messages while keeping communication consistent. Predictive analysis strengthens the process by forecasting customer behavior before it happens.

AI connects different data points to build detailed audience profiles. Information like age, location, purchase history, browsing behavior, and past interactions all contribute to this understanding. These profiles allow brands to speak more directly to customer needs. Predictive analysis takes it further by anticipating future actions based on current behavior. This shifts marketing from being reactive to being proactive. Campaigns can adjust before the customer takes the next step, leading to better timing and higher engagement.

Rep, a US-based company, uses AI to personalize website content in real time. Their platform combines predictive analysis with visitors with intent to adjust product displays, site navigation, and messaging. Each visitor sees content shaped by their behavior. The website responds automatically, without human involvement. This kind of personalization feels natural and improves session length, click-through rates, and conversions.

With predictive analysis and personalization, we are providing richer and more fitting communication. User behavior determines the messages we send, and it is expected and sent at what is predicted to be the best time, which is personal to the user.

Automation: Real-Time Engagement

Real-time engagement plays a key role in today's communication strategies. Customers now expect fast responses, timely interactions, and consistent messaging across platforms. Delays reduce interest. Gaps in communication can damage trust. IMC works better when brands respond quickly and in a meaningful way. AI supports this by making automation possible. Brands can connect instantly with their audience without adding to the team's workload or losing control over message accuracy. Automation makes communication easier across different platforms. AI watches customer behavior, sends instant replies, and adjusts message flow based on what users do in real time. Every touchpoint becomes a chance for feedback.

Speed alone is not enough. Relevance and timing matter just as much. AI looks at patterns and adjusts messages based on context. Real-time feedback adds even more control.

AI tools measure how people respond and adjust messages as needed. If engagement is low, the system might evaluate a new format. If interaction is high, the message can be shared more widely. Surveys, responses, and usage data help build a live performance map. Brands can change content, tone, or timing while the campaign is running. This keeps communication useful and engaging as things progress. Adidas uses AI-powered real-time engagement during campaigns and product drops. When launching limited edition sneakers or collaborations, AI tracks social media trends, website traffic, and app activity in real time.

Content Creation

Content plays a significant role in every marketing communication strategy. Whether it is emails, social media posts, landing pages, or digital ads, brands rely on content to build their identity and influence their audience. IMC requires all this content to stay aligned, consistent, and focused on the target audience. AI helps support these goals by automating content creation. This saves time, reduces manual work, and speeds up campaigns.

AI tools allow marketers to produce content quickly without lowering the quality. Text generation models can create emails, blog posts, product descriptions, and ad headlines from simple prompts. These language models learn from existing data, follow tone and style guidelines, and adjust based on the platform or audience. This makes content scalable, but not repetitive. Approximately 35% of marketers currently use AI to create content because it allows them to meet tight deadlines without overstretching their creative team.

Writesonic is a UK content creation platform that uses AI authors to generate blogs, ads, emails, and product content across many formats. Brands use it to create a large amount of content without the need to create large teams or extend timelines. It also supports many different tones, formats, and languages, which makes it useful for any global IMC strategy that needs scale but does not want to lose the alignment it typically sees with multi-channel approaches.

Relevance tools adjust tone, language, and structure to match audience behavior and platform style. A LinkedIn post may need a formal tone, while Instagram captions rely more on visuals and storytelling. Emails follow personalization patterns. AI improves content creation by speeding up the process, adding variation, and reducing the workload. Campaigns stay consistent. Messages adjust to suit the audience's needs. Communication stays clear across platforms. As these tools get better, more brands will begin using them for everyday content work, making IMC easier to manage, quicker to deliver, and better suited to changing audience expectations.

Content Channels

IMC requires brands to communicate across many platforms, each with its own format, audience, and tone. Managing these differences manually can take time and often results in inconsistencies. AI simplifies this process by customizing content for each platform. Messages stay true to the brand's voice while adapting to the needs of different channels. This improves audience reach, keeps communication clear, and helps with more organized campaign planning.

A Russian platform, PublBox, implements this approach. PublBox utilizes AI to execute social media marketing by personalizing, scheduling, and optimizing content with the content adapted to each platform. The automated function repurposes the content in order to fit a variety of formats, which ultimately assists with visibility and reach. Campaign messages become more organized, and the messaging remains consistent. The team's time is saved while building presence on social media, without having to come up with different strategies for each platform. Tracking performance also adds even more value. AI tracks how content performs with recommendations on where improvements need to be made; if the content is not gaining traction on a platform, it is reworked.

AI-powered content channel management improves IMC by keeping messages aligned, timely, and suited to each platform. Brands can reach broader audiences, speak in a consistent tone, and adjust content with precision. Teams save time, engagement improves, and strategies stay connected across all platforms. As more tools focus on managing content per channel, integrated communication will become easier, more effective, and better suited to the needs of today's multi-platform audiences.

Content Optimization

Content optimization plays a key role in improving the performance of IMC. Strong content by itself does not guarantee visibility or audience engagement. Brands need to make sure their messages are clear, easy to find, and well-organized. AI helps with this by reviewing existing content, spotting performance gaps, and suggesting improvements. This leads to sharper communication, better reach, and stronger alignment across platforms and channels.

MarketMuse, a platform based in the United States, shows how AI supports content research and optimization. It reviews current content, recommends updates, and helps improve structure and depth. It also assists with content planning by identifying topic gaps and comparing performance with competitors. Marketers use it to make sure content matches both audience needs and campaign goals. This reduces guesswork and leads to better results. Teams create content with purpose, backed by data.

AI improves content optimization by making content more effective, not just faster. Brands shift their focus from content production to content performance. Messages connect more clearly, content ranks better on platforms, and audiences stay engaged for longer. Integrated marketing strategies benefit because every content element is aimed at achieving clear, measurable goals. As more organizations use AI for content refinement, campaign results will improve through better structure, higher visibility, and greater accuracy (Figure 6.2).

AI Technology in IMC

AI technology is radically transforming the world of IMCs, an industry with a background in linear campaign flows and manual coordination development. The way that brands are using AI is enabling full-on usage and efficiencies in marketing communications output, as they are making content decisions, considering live performance, and publishing synchronized messages across advertising platforms. Campaigns are accelerating, messages are more consumer specific, and without further integration, more linkages to technology give you greater clarity and control over a highly complex communication system that has grown more integrated with IMC.

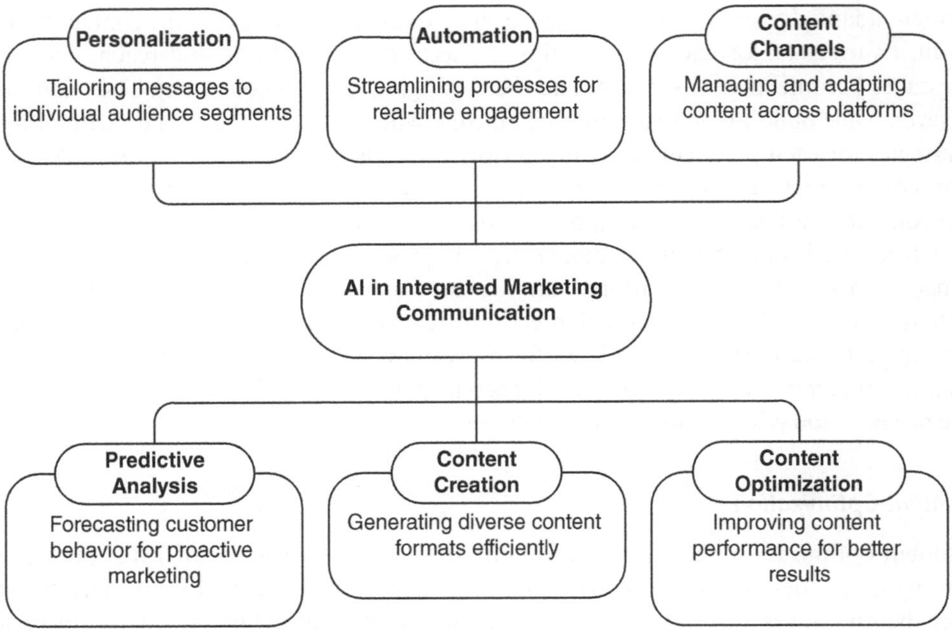

FIGURE 6.2 Enhancing IMC with AI.

Yarnit, an India-based platform, helps simplify this process. It uses AI to manage content creation, campaign execution, and analytics in one place. Marketers receive real-time suggestions, performance feedback, and content options without needing to jump between tools. This reduces workflow complexity, shortens timelines, and gives more structure to integrated campaigns.

Brands learn what resonates and what causes drop-off. This feedback comes during the campaign, not afterward. Teams can fine-tune tone, visuals, or timing while the audience is still engaged. Gumloop, a US-based platform, specializes in this area. It gathers social media data, runs sentiment analysis at scale, and delivers clear insights. This helps brands track public opinion and recognize changes over time. As a result, communication becomes more in tune with the audience's emotional state. IMC gains a level of real-time awareness that keeps messaging timely and relevant.

Scalability also improves with AI. Brands can run multiple campaigns across languages, regions, and audience types without growing their teams. AI handles variations, generates reports, and keeps all content within brand guidelines. Large campaigns are easier to manage. Brands stay agile. IMC expands without losing control or structure. Natural language processing (NLP) improves how AI interprets and responds to input. Chatbots understand what customers are trying to say. Tools recognize tone, urgency, and emotion.

Thus, AI simplifies the complexity of IMC. Campaigns move faster, reach more people, and adapt in real time. Tools help brands scale, measure, and fine-tune every message. As adoption grows, AI will continue to shape communication by creating smarter campaigns, clearer insights, and better results across all formats and platforms.

Benefits of AI in IMC

AI adds measurable value to IMC by improving how brands connect, engage, and respond across channels. Marketing strategies become more structured. Execution gets faster. Insights arrive without delay. Teams gain visibility into what is working and what is not. AI transforms communication into a continuous, data-driven process that leads to smarter decisions, higher returns, and consistent brand messaging across every touchpoint.

Automation also improves internal coordination. Marketing teams manage multiple platforms, formats, and channels. AI streamlines these workflows, removes task duplication, and automates approvals. Claudefront, a UK-based platform, uses AI to automate multi-platform reports and workflow insights. Teams no longer spend time manually tracking performance. Reports are generated automatically, and dashboards point out key gaps. Communication becomes more focused, and execution improves without added complexity. AI also boosts accuracy. Campaigns become more consistent when intelligent systems manage content. Errors are reduced, and messages stay aligned with brand tone and platform requirements.

Scalability becomes easier to manage. AI supports communication across languages, time zones, and audience segments. Real-time analytics provide constant feedback. AI tools collect and process data continuously.

AI also improves reporting. Manual formatting errors are reduced, and reports become more precise. Claudefront's automation engine delivers clear performance summaries across platforms, tracking conversions, spending, and engagement. Marketers base their decisions on verified insights. Campaign comparisons, audience responses, and platform performance become easier to understand. Strategy becomes data-driven and more agile.

AI improves IMC by increasing speed, accuracy, and relevance. It automates workflows, personalizes content, and tracks performance across every platform. AI turns data into decisions, and decisions into results. As more teams adopt these tools, communication will become more focused, more effective, and more aligned with what audiences want. IMC will continue to grow, powered by intelligence, guided by data, and ready for scale.

Challenges of AI in IMC

AI offers clear advantages in IMC. However, the path to full-scale adoption comes with several challenges. AI systems require strong data foundations, cross-functional collaboration, and regular updates. Many organizations find it difficult to align these needs with their existing processes. This gap between AI's potential and its daily use in IMC continues to limit results. To fully benefit from AI-powered strategies, brands need to address these underlying issues.

Technical challenges remain common. Around 70% of marketers report difficulties in implementing AI due to complex systems, integration problems, or a lack of infrastructure. AI tools must connect with customer relationship management (CRM) platforms, content management systems, and campaign dashboards. When systems remain disconnected, workflows break down. Campaign consistency weakens when AI cannot access complete data sets. Without proper integration, communication becomes fragmented, undermining the structure of IMC efforts.

Skill gaps present another barrier. Marketing teams need to understand how AI tools work, how to interpret results, and how to apply automation to strategy. Ascend2, a US-based research company, highlights skill shortages and integration difficulties as two of the main barriers to AI adoption. Their studies show how internal resistance and the lack of clear implementation plans slow progress. Communication teams need more than access to AI; they also need training, real-world examples, and support from leadership. Without this foundation, AI projects fall short of expectations.

Privacy issues are also becoming increasingly problematic. Many AI processes involve personal-sensitive data, like browsing history or shopping practices. Privacy laws can be rigid, and marketers must ensure compliance. Marketers must think of data protection, consent tracking, and anonymity, if necessary. It only takes one action, incident, or experience to lose the trust in years of brand building. Viable, a US-based voice-of-the-customer platform, demonstrates that with an AI platform, privacy and insight can coexist. The platform pulls important feedback from consumers on any number of things while keeping within the confines of consumer data protection and process. Companies like Viable show that it is possible to prioritize both performance and privacy simultaneously. IMC can also benefit from using these types of AI tools because they can maintain both ethical standards and a meaningful understanding of their audience.

Lack of alignment or integration across the organization is another hurdle. AI tools usually require some level of integration between marketing, information technology (IT), compliance, support teams, and whatever else might be required to get going. If teams are unable to establish and implement a plan based on the clarity of communication about every collective step, their strategy will likely stall. The result causes a campaign to stall out. IMC strategies are often enhanced when tools are selected based on real-world needs, going forward, usability, and long-term goals—as opposed to hype, or who the vendor is making promises to them.

Another challenge is incomplete feedback loops. AI tools can deliver a lot of information. Cultural resistance of organizations is another challenge for AI adoption. Teams operating in previous styles of work-group teams rely on trust and may resist facilitating trust with data and automation. Organizational leaders may have a previous control of the environment and do not want to give it up. Creative talent may see automation as replacing jobs.

Global campaigns do offer other challenges. Laws about data, content style, and language are considerably different compared to other jurisdictions. AI applications will strive to adjust to the locally relevant laws without delivering an inconsistent narrative or message globally. No one platform will be translatable in every market. It is common to need content customization locally. IMC needs to merge content consistency globally while strengthening its impact locally. AI needs to facilitate both.

Despite these challenges, the AI opportunity in IMC is very real. Any technical difficulty, data privacy concern, talent shortage, or bordering organizational consideration can be accomplished by design and implementation. Resources like Viable and research insights from Ascend2 are available that offer models that mitigate those considerations. This is the case no matter the design solution: compliance framework, staffed roll-out plan, or simply being smart with data (Table 6.1).

TABLE 6.1 AI-Enabled IMC and Outcomes

IMC Area	*What AI Enables*	*Brand Example*	*Tool/Approach*	*Outcome*
Workflow speed & reporting	Auto-reports, faster approvals	Claudefront	AI reporting + workflow insights	Quicker cycles, less manual work
advocacy & referrals	Find happy users, collect/share reviews	Deeto	AI advocate discovery + automated referrals	More trusted content across channels
Voice-of-customer insights	Privacy-safe feedback analysis	Viable	NLP on customer feedback with privacy controls	Faster insights without risking compliance
Personalization at scale	Tailored content and offers	Netflix	Recommender systems for titles/creatives	Higher engagement and relevance
Dynamic pricing guardrails	Real-time pricing with fairness checks	Uber	Surge algorithms + policy thresholds	Better revenue while protecting trust

Emerging Trends in IMC

AI offers clear advantages in IMC. However, the path to full-scale adoption presents multiple challenges. AI systems demand strong data foundations, cross-functional collaboration, and continuous updates. Many organizations struggle to align these requirements with existing processes. The gap between AI's potential and its day-to-day application in IMC continues to limit performance. Brands must address these gaps to realize the full benefits of AI-powered communication strategies.

Technical challenges remain widespread. Around 70% of marketers report difficulties in implementing AI due to system complexity, integration issues, or lack of infrastructure. Platforms must connect with CRM tools, content management systems, and campaign dashboards. Disconnected systems interrupt workflow continuity. Campaign consistency is affected when AI tools cannot access complete datasets. Without proper integration, communication becomes fragmented, which weakens the structure of IMC strategies.

Skill gaps present another challenge. Marketing teams need to understand how AI tools work, how to interpret the data they produce, and how to connect automation to strategy. Many professionals still lack this knowledge. AI adoption becomes uneven. Some departments move ahead while others fall behind. IMC struggles when AI is not applied consistently. Campaigns lose their balance, and communication weakens due to differences in skill levels across teams.

Ascend2, a US-based research provider, identifies both skill shortages and tool integration as two major obstacles to AI adoption. Their studies highlight how many organizations face internal pushback and lack detailed implementation plans. Communication teams need more than access to tools. They need proper training, clear examples of use, and strong leadership support. Without this kind of structure, AI efforts slow down or fall short of expectations.

The cost of AI adoption is also a barrier. Many tools come with subscription fees, setup charges, and a need for technical support. Smaller businesses or teams may not have the required budget. This delays or limits AI use. When only a few parts of the process are automated, the overall value drops. IMC works best when AI is used across the full system, not just in parts.

Unrealistic expectations can slow down adoption as well. Some teams expect immediate success, forgetting that AI needs time to learn and improve. Without patience or proper setup, early results can be disappointing. Tools get abandoned. Resources are wasted. IMC efforts suffer when planning is rushed or based on assumptions rather than strategy.

Misalignment between departments can also slow things down. AI tools often require coordination between marketing, IT, legal, and customer service. If these teams are not working together, delays and confusion follow. Strategy becomes fragmented. Campaign timelines stretch out. IMC needs cooperation across all departments. Without it, AI tools may serve narrow interests instead of shared goals. Clear planning around ownership, data flow, and access is essential.

Confusion around tool selection is another problem. The market offers hundreds of AI tools, each with its own strengths. Without a clear plan, teams may use too many tools at once. Overlapping features cause confusion. Integrations fail. Results become inconsistent. IMC functions better when tools are chosen based on long-term strategy, not just short-term appeal or trends.

IMC succeeds when communication is clear, consistent, and built on trust. AI should support these goals. Without the right foundations, the tools meant to improve communication can end up making it harder. But with careful planning and responsible use, AI can become a reliable part of every communication strategy. It can help brands stay coordinated across platforms, engage audiences with confidence, and deliver stronger results with less effort (Figure 6.3).

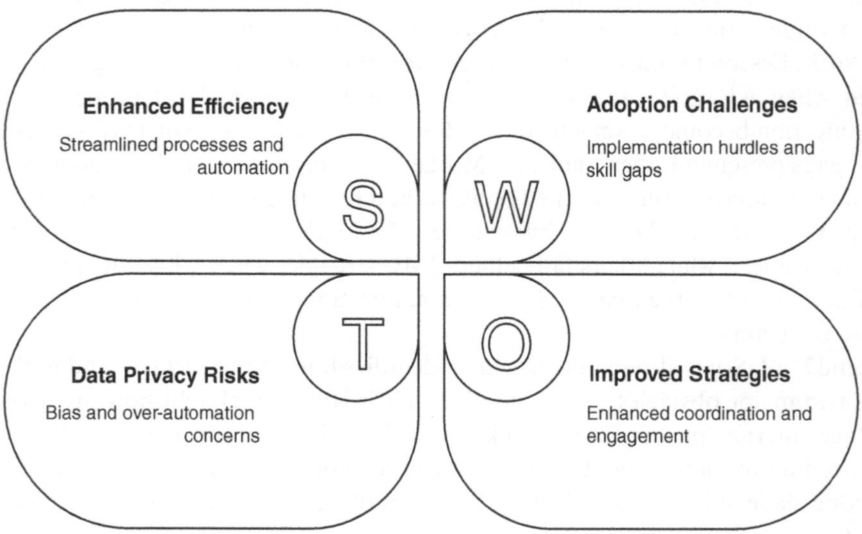

FIGURE 6.3 AI in IMC.

CLOSING CASE: SAMSUNG

Samsung has a strong presence in the consumer electronics industry, and it is the world's leading company because of its innovation in smartphones, televisions, appliances, and connected devices. With such a vast range of products and an active global audience, Samsung has to be consistent but flexible with its communications. Marketing for Samsung is not just about promoting the products it creates. Marketing supports Samsung's identity as a company and its brand identity, which are both centered around technology. With the increasing role of AI, Samsung is better able to stay clear, concise, consistent, and relevant in its communication.

Samsung's additional adoption of AI has benefited the company in dealing with the complexities of multi-country campaigns in a more precise fashion. Since more than 80 countries sell Samsung products, Samsung is relying on AI-enabled tools to tailor content that is sensitive to the region, language, and platform. Campaigns can be created that align with regional trends while still maintaining an overall brand message that ties the campaign together. Other things considered in developing AI-enabled messages are engagement and relevance. Creating relevant communication preferred by Samsung's clients allows the company to move faster. The brand is able to connect with customers while staying on brand and ultimately maintaining control over the quality and structure of its messages.

Personalization provides another way to become more effective in marketing. Beyond the messaging or the means of communication, Samsung is using AI algorithms to enhance content personalization on its digital properties. For example, a visitor reviews product recommendations, offers, and banners based on their browsing records, device utilization, and preferences. While the message being presented in every case is different depending on the user, the brand identity is the same. The communications and structure with regard to the brand are constant, but the content is dependent on the user's browsing action. The use of AI-based personalization results in increased engagement, builds trust, and assists in developing long-term customer relationships.

Samsung is continuing to improve and develop more robust campaigns, communication, and creative collateral through the use of AI-enabled analytics. The AI analyzes the actual content in real time and is able to analyze individual campaign components as well as how the overall campaign performs on multiple platforms and in different regions. Samsung can turn AI to improve the overall content itself and the design of campaigns in real time by editing headlines, visuals, and calls-to-action based on what has already proven to perform better. The system actively identifies strategies that are succeeding or improving, and what aspects need to be modified or edited. Teams respond more quickly. Campaigns stay flexible. IMC benefits from this data-focused approach, where each change helps keep the message consistent across all platforms.

Customer support also includes AI-powered chat tools that give instant replies across Samsung's platforms. These systems help answer questions, guide purchases, and connect people with service centers. The tone matches Samsung's brand style. The replies are accurate and informed. Support becomes a part of the IMC approach, dependable, easy to access, and in line with the larger communication strategy.

AI-based social listening tools help Samsung track public opinion about product launches, service problems, and overall brand image. These tools collect feedback on a large scale and turn it into useful insights. Communication plans can be adjusted quickly. PR teams respond more accurately. Campaign messages change based on how people react. IMC becomes a more flexible system, backed by real-time data and messaging that stays in line with the brand.

AI also helps Samsung organize internal processes across marketing teams, partner agencies, and global offices. Shared dashboards, automatic reports, and AI-managed content systems help keep campaigns on track. Teams use the same data, follow shared rules, and work at the same pace. This results in communication that feels coordinated, even when managed across different regions and product lines.

Samsung's use of AI in IMC is part of a bigger approach, using smart systems to manage complexity more easily. Campaigns stay true to the brand, messages update in real time, and communication stays consistent at every step. The brand remains clear, up to date, and connected. AI does not just support Samsung's marketing; it also shapes how the brand speaks, responds, and interacts in today's fast-changing digital environment.

Discussion Questions

1. Where have you seen "silos" in real life (school clubs, group projects, or part-time jobs)? How did they cause confusion?
2. Why is one clear brand message important? What goes wrong when each team makes its own version?
3. The chapter suggests cross-silo teams and networks. What would make students actually join and share?
4. Should a CMO control everything or mostly coach and support? Why?
5. What does "media-neutral planning" mean to you? How could it stop fights between ads, PR, and social media teams?

Assignment Questions

1. Pick a brand you know: Identify two silos it likely has (e.g., Product lines or countries). Explain one brand problem those silos could create and how to fix it.
2. Play a CMO: In 8–10 bullet points, design a "non-threatening plan" to get silos teams to share data and follow one planning template.
3. Local adapt, global consistent: Write 1 page guideline showing what parts of a brand message must stay the same worldwide and what parts the local team can change. Include 3 examples of each.#

MINICASE: GLOWCUP

GlowCup is a mid-size Indian beverage brand selling ready-to-drink iced tea and fruit coolers. It grew fast by letting teams work on their own—split by product, channel, and region. Soon, the brand felt messy: different taglines, "Chill the Day," "Sip the Sun," "Feel Fresh, Feel Free," clashing colors and photos, random event sponsorship, and three separate retailer proposals for one national promo. Shoppers were confused, a key retailer cut shelf space, and budgets were spread thin with little impact. There was a new CMO who did not take over with everyone. Rather, she was a facilitator. She unveiled a single-page brand plan (target, one promise, three proof points, shared assets). She established one main message, the GlowCup: Refresh Your Moments, and a simple visual design. Regions might be adapted, but not the core. She created a weekly cross-silo group (Glow Grid) to discuss wins and reuse designs. Campaigns were rendered media-neutral: one and the same story was released in short videos, influencer tastings, in-store displays, and improved Amazon pages. An asset library facilitated the ability to remain on brand. Two measures followed the progress: recall of the core line and weekly incremental sales, with the support of the chief executive officer (CEO).

Six months later, the brand recall increased to 47%, retailer satisfaction increased, GlowCup was awarded a national summer endcap, the reuse of assets reduced the cost of production by 18%, and social interaction doubled. The lesson: it is not necessary to kill silos--link them. Defined brand center, common tools, and media-independent implementation combine piecemeal efforts into a more effective, less costly, and quicker brand machine.

HBR Case Links:

- https://hbsp.harvard.edu/product/IN1530-PDF-ENG?itemFindingMethod=search
- https://hbsp.harvard.edu/product/IM1189-PDF-ENG?itemFindingMethod=search
- https://hbsp.harvard.edu/product/UV9088-PDF-ENG?itemFindingMethod=search

Application of Concepts

Concept (Kotler Link)	*Application in Practice*	*In-Class Activity*
Segmentation & targeting (STP)	AI groups customers by behavior/value so messages go to the right micro-segments.	**Card Sort**: Teams cluster 12 "customer cards" and write a one-line message for each cluster.
Personalization (1:1 Marketing)	"Next-best-message" engines pick the best offer/time for each user to lift clicks and sales.	**Journey Board**: Place 6 customers on a funnel and choose a tailored nudge for each.
Testing & Optimization (A/B, Metrics)	AI runs A/B tests (subject lines, thumbnails) and auto-shifts budget to winners.	**Mini A/B**: Create 2 captions; class predicts the winner and states the one-line hypothesis.
Brand safety & ethics (Privacy/Bias)	Guardrails for GDPR/CCPA, bias checks, and approvals keep AI content safe and fair.	**Policy Sprint**: Write a 5-line "AI use policy" for the campus club's social media.

Keywords

- AI in marketing
- IMC
- Segmentation
- Targeting
- Personalization
- A/B testing
- Optimization
- Omnichannel
- Privacy
- Bias/ethics

Bibliography

California Office of the Attorney General. *California Consumer Privacy Act (CCPA/CPRA)*. https://oag.ca.gov/privacy/ccpa

Davenport, T., Guha, A., Grewal, D., & Bressgott, T. (2020). How AI will change the future of marketing. *Journal of the Academy of Marketing Science*. https://doi.org/10.1007/s11747-019-00696-0 *(overview + related works)*

Davenport, T. H., & Ronanki, R. (2018). Artificial intelligence for the real world. *Harvard Business Review*. https://hbr.org/2018/01/artificial-intelligence-for-the-real-world

European Commission. *General Data Protection Regulation (GDPR) — official portal*. https://gdpr.eu/

Kotler, P., & Keller, K. L. (2022). *Marketing Management (16e)*. Pearson. https://www.pearson.com/store/p/marketing-management/P100003045842

McKinsey & Company (2024). The State of AI in 2024—and a half-decade in review. https://www.mckinsey.com/capabilities/quantumblack/our-insights/the-state-of-ai-2024

NIST (2023). AI risk management framework (AI RMF 1.0). https://www.nist.gov/itl/ai-risk-management-framework

Shankar, V. (2021). How artificial intelligence (AI) is reshaping marketing. *Journal of the Academy of Marketing Science*. https://doi.org/10.1007/s11747-019-00696-0

7

ROLE OF AI IN BRAND MANAGEMENT

Learning Objectives

1 Explain what AI does in branding and why it matters today.
2 Describe how AI supports core brand tasks: positioning, communications, and brand experience.
3 Identify real examples of AI in action and link them to brand outcomes like trust and loyalty.
4 Analyze the benefits AI brings and the risks.

OPENING CASE: BANK OF AMERICA

Bank of America is one of the leading US banks when it comes to using AI in real, practical ways. Its focus is clear on the numbers: $13 billion is spent each year on technology, and $4 billion of that goes into new areas like AI. Branding today is about more than campaigns or visuals. It is shaped by how people experience and view the brand. By making AI part of its main structure, the bank makes sure its image reflects speed, accuracy, and a strong focus on customer convenience.

Erica, the bank's AI assistant, plays a key role in this change. Since its launch in 2018, Erica has managed over 2.5 billion interactions. As of 2025, it has 20 million active users. Every time someone uses Erica, it strengthens the idea that the brand is dependable and always available. Whether it is checking a balance or sending reminders, Erica's steady performance helps create a familiar tone. Over time, that tone becomes part of the brand itself. AI is no longer just a support tool. It helps shape how the brand communicates across millions of digital interactions.

DOI: 10.4324/9781003501862-7

The effect goes beyond what customers see. Inside the bank, AI supports more than 90% of employees each day through different platforms. This includes AI tools that help with coding, which have improved developer productivity by more than 20%. It also includes training tools and simulations, with over a million sessions completed last year. These tools help build a more efficient and future-ready work environment. That internal progress shapes how people view the bank from the outside, as a company that is modern, capable, and dependable.

Customer support plays a significant role in building brand trust. Bank of America has cut information technology (IT) help desk calls by 50% through AI. This shows how better efficiency adds to customer confidence. At the same time, tools used by Merrill and the Private Bank managed over 23 million interactions in 2024. These are not just faster services. They reflect smarter ways of staying connected, which support the brand's promise of clarity, access, and innovation for all types of clients.

Personalization is also a key part of branding, and AI helps make it possible on a large scale. By studying past behavior, choices, and real-time activity, AI adjusts messages for each person. Whether it is a product alert or a financial tip, the message feels specific and timely. This kind of attention helps build emotional connections, which are important in turning users into loyal customers. Personalized service leaves an impression.

Today, most customer interactions happen on digital platforms. AI helps Bank of America keep the same voice across all channels, including mobile apps, websites, and chat services. From the tone of replies to the timing of messages, AI keeps everything consistent. These smooth experiences shape how people view the brand. Over time, customers come to expect a certain level of quality. Meeting that standard repeatedly builds long-term trust and recognition.

AI also helps guide brand decisions. The bank collects feedback, fixes problems, and makes updates based on real customer usage. This ongoing process leads to changes in products, communication style, and service quality. As a result, the brand feels active and responsive. When customers see improvements based on their own concerns, their trust increases. They feel heard, which builds a stronger connection with the brand.

All of this is supported by strong technical expertise. Bank of America holds more than 7,400 patents, with around 1,200 related to AI. More than half of those have already been granted. These innovations give the bank full control over how AI works within its own systems. Technology is not just added in. It is designed to reflect the bank's values from within. This thoughtful approach helps keep the brand steady as it grows and becomes more digital.

Introduction to AI in Brand Management

AI has now transitioned from merely a supporting role to one of active engagement in crafting brand experiences. This includes automating responses, a key component of how brands interact with people; personalizing content; and facilitating a new means of connection with organizations. The objective hasn't changed: build trust, enhance recall, and inspire loyalty. The methods in which they operate have changed, with brands relying on data, predictive approaches, and automation to be accountable for their brand identity in real time.

Brand management requires planning and action. AI fits both. Planning tasks related to strategy—audience analysis, trend monitoring, and content development can benefit from the AI capabilities of speed and breadth. Execution tasks, including maintaining consistency in specific messages, identifying a relevant tone, and engaging in real time for relevance, can also be more efficient. More power equals more control to present the brand in a consistent manner: fewer errors, less waiting, and experiences feel more connected. This is where AI adds efficiency through clarity, speed, and consistency. Burberry uses AI personalized email campaigns, WeChat chats in China, and real-time AI insights for store associates to provide personalized styling.

Consumer expectations continue to evolve. They want speed, relevance, and meaning in their lives, and AI supports those expectations for organizations in the more personalized manner they expect, by learning based on patterns and uniquely applying them across processes to achieve improved outcomes. By tracking behaviors, preferences, and feedback, organizations can respond in substantially improved ways over time. Instead of responding to everyone's requirements consistently the same way, brands can use AI adaptive meaningfully. That meaningful level of presence directly connects to interpretation and generates longer-term loyalty.

Brand visibility is solely determined by its consistency of presence. AI supporting the same voice, tone, and message across organizational media channels, whether through emails, Apps, advertising, etc., has consistent and aligned communications. The individual experiences build on brand recognition over time. They create memory links to values associated with the brands that are positive or not—for example, trust, innovation, and simplicity. Multiple experiences give people the same signal across different currencies and contexts, which embeds a brand in their thinking.

AI also has long-term responsibility for the brand health and monitoring it consistently for value-driven responses to people. This includes monitoring user habits, sentiment tracking, and engagement. Brands can modify their delivery based on these patterns. The organization needs to shift direction meaningfully to show it actually cared at to value individuals, especially in the competitive space. Brands that adapted rapidly with their relative durability were best positioned to create meaningful impressions. AI becomes the tool to keep brands present while continuously connecting.

Define & Relevance of AI in Branding

AI in branding refers to the use of smart systems that assist in creating, managing, and improving brand-related tasks. These systems use data, algorithms, and automated tools to perform functions that once required human effort. The focus stays on improving consistency, reach, and relevance. AI does not replace the brand idea. It supports how that idea appears, responds, and grows in a fast-moving digital space.

Branding today goes beyond messaging. It includes visual design, customer tone, feedback response, and even real-time engagement. AI tools manage all these areas quickly and accurately. Brands now train AI systems to follow their values, language, and design rules. The results stay consistent across touchpoints. Whether in websites, emails, or ads, the brand personality remains clear. That level of consistency helps increase brand recognition and recall.

Relevance matters in a crowded market. AI helps brands stay timely and tuned in. It picks up signals from user data like behavior, location, and habits, and adjusts brand responses. The experience feels personal, not random. Targeted content appears when needed. Offers match past choices. Tone fits the mood. That level of relevance improves how people connect with the brand. More engagement often leads to stronger loyalty.

The rise in AI investment shows its growing impact. AI in marketing is expected to be worth $47.32 billion in 2025, growing at a rate of 36.6% compound annual growth rate (CAGR) until 2030. Around 92% of businesses plan to invest in generative AI in the next three years. These numbers show a shift. Brands are no longer just trying out AI. They are building their future around it. AI now plays a key role in modern branding strategies.

AI also supports creativity at scale, such as Nutella's campaign in Italy, where AI generated 7 million unique jar labels. Each label followed brand guidelines but had a distinctive design. These labels led to strong local engagement. People shared them, collected them, and posted them online. The brand stayed visible without heavy spending. AI helped Nutella create personalized value while keeping its global image.

AI allows brands to talk to people, not just groups. Responses change based on who is listening. Content adjusts to what people care about. The brand becomes more human, even though a machine manages interaction. That mix of scale and care creates long-term value. AI adds the structure. Brands add the meaning.

Evolution of Branding Strategies

Branding strategies have changed a lot over the past two decades. Earlier, the focus was on visibility through mass media, static campaigns, and broad messages. Today, branding goes deeper. It focuses on individual experience, real-time engagement, and measurable outcomes. AI plays a significant role in this change. Brands no longer rely on assumptions. They study data, predict behavior, and adjust messages in real time to stay relevant.

Digital platforms created the need for new branding methods. With customers having more control and shorter attention spans, brands had to become faster and smarter. AI helped meet these needs. Smart systems manage everything from audience targeting to performance tracking. They give insights into what works, what does not, and what needs to be improved. Brands can now adjust their approach during a campaign without starting over. That kind of flexibility changed how branding decisions are made.

Personalization moved branding into its next stage. Generic messages became less effective. AI now helps deliver highly personalized content that speaks to specific user needs. AI-driven marketing personalization increases conversion rates by 25% and reduces customer acquisition costs by 37%. The results are clear. Brands that use personalization not only save resources but also build stronger relationships. People are more likely to respond when content reflects their needs or interests.

Smaller brands use AI to grow faster without spending more. Tomorrow Sleep company in the USA used an AI-powered content platform called MarketMuse to improve its search engine optimization (SEO) strategy. As a result, it increased organic traffic without depending on large ad budgets. The brand reached more people, ranked higher, and appeared more trustworthy without changing its core identity or tone.

The role of branding will keep changing. AI brings both new chances and new questions. Success depends on how well brands manage the balance between using smart tools and keeping their identity. The strategy should guide the tools, not the other way around. AI does not define the brand. It supports how the brand grows, connects with people, and stays meaningful in a changing world.

Why AI Matters in Brand Management Today

Brand management has moved from controlled messaging to real-time interaction. Audiences now connect across multiple channels, expect relevance, and want quick responses. AI supports this change by bringing automation, smart tools, and personalized features into brand-building tasks. These tools help brands stay visible, consistent, and quick to respond. No industry is left out. AI now plays a key part in managing how brands communicate, grow, and connect in a fast digital world.

The wide use of AI shows growing trust. Around 88% of marketers now use AI in their daily work. Another 69% feel positive about its effect. These numbers show a clear change in attitude. AI is no longer seen as optional or experimental. It now helps with decision-making, customer interaction, and tracking brand performance. Brands that adjust early gain better control, accuracy, and stronger audience connections.

Brand identity now grows through a better understanding backed by data. AI observes user behavior, preferences, and how people respond. Based on that, it helps shape messages, adjust tone, and aim content at the right people. Campaigns no longer rely on broad guesses. Every step is guided by information. This kind of accuracy helps brands create moments that feel relevant at a large scale. People begin to know the brand not just by name, but by how it acts in the moment.

Efficiency improves across every step. AI tools write content, test designs, and suggest keywords. They manage reports and track user actions. This automation frees up time, so teams can focus on creative ideas while the system takes care of repeated tasks. Branding can grow without extra pressure. With 56% of companies already using AI, the level of competition is rising. Brands without AI often fall behind, not by choice, but because they cannot move as fast. Consistency also gets better with AI-supported processes. Automated checks help make sure tone, language, and visuals stay within the brand's style. Every message, no matter the platform, shows the brand's true personality. Mistakes drop. Gaps close. Users feel a clear sense of who the brand is, whether they are visiting a website, reading an email, or chatting with support. A strong brand image builds better recall and long-term trust. Canva uses AI tools like Magic Write and AI design assistants to generate brand-aligned templates, layouts, and content. It ensures brand colors, fonts, and tone stay consistent across presentations, social posts, and ads while saving time for teams.

AI is important because building a brand today depends on it more than telling stories. What really is effective is being relevant, quick, and well organized. The right message must reach the right person at the right time. AI helps make that happen. It adds speed to decisions, clarity to plans, and structure to how brands communicate. In today's world, creative ideas alone are not enough. Brands need smart tools to guide those ideas in the right way.

Role of AI across Branding Spectrum

AI continues to reshape branding at every level. From planning to execution, AI plays an active part across the entire branding process. Brands no longer rely only on creativity or instinct. They now combine those elements with data-based systems. That shift has changed how brands look, speak, and respond. Every interaction reflects a higher level of accuracy, control, and quick response powered by smart tools.

Predictive analytics is central to this change. Volkswagen used AI to forecast results in ad buying, which led to better placement and a 20% increase in sales. The system tracked reactions, evaluated different formats, and updated campaigns during the run. This ability to adjust spending helped Volkswagen get better results without increasing effort or cost. AI made the brand more effective with the same resources.

Data collection was once limited to simple surveys or delayed feedback. Now, AI manages substantial amounts of data from many channels in real time. Every click, search, scroll, and pause becomes part of the feedback loop. Brands get a better view of user interests, goals, and feelings. That information shapes the brand's message. Changes happen quickly. The brand speaks in a way that feels current and aware. Content creation has changed too. AI tools can now create text, images, and video by following brand guidelines. They keep the tone, colors, and message while adjusting the layout for different platforms. Campaigns are delivered faster. Creative teams save time. More content gets tested. The best versions get scaled. The ones that do not work are dropped quickly. The brand stays visible without losing its consistency or control.

Inventory planning is now linked to branding in new ways. PatPat, a children's clothing brand, uses AI to predict demand, manage stock, and match campaigns with inventory levels. This leads to better coordination between supply and marketing. Ads reflect what is in stock. Messages stay honest and current. No customer feels misled. This match between what is promised and what's available builds trust. The brand feels organized and dependable.

Ad spending becomes more effective with AI. These tools evaluate different versions of the same message across formats, platforms, and time slots. Performance data comes in right away. Brands keep what works and drop what does not. Money is spent wisely. Messages improve. There are fewer mistakes. Volkswagen's results prove the value; AI cuts waste and increases returns. This same idea is now used in many industries.

AI also shapes branding by taking over routine tasks. Setting up campaigns, tagging assets, and checking results no longer need manual effort. Teams can focus on planning and content. AI manages the rest. Output increases. Branding grows in both reach and depth without overloading the team. Work becomes smarter and more focused. Brand testing also improves with AI. Tools simulate how users might react to packaging, taglines, or design updates. Real people give feedback faster and in larger numbers. Brands test before launching. That lowers the chance of failure. Changes are quicker to make. AI supports careful testing that protects brand image while trying out innovative ideas. Results arrive faster. Decisions improve.

AI does not replace creative thinking. It helps bring those ideas to life. Plans move faster. Execution becomes stronger. Branding becomes an ongoing cycle of feedback, changes, and delivery. The process does not stop. Each update reflects smarter planning. Each post supports the bigger picture. AI keeps the brand active, aligned, and moving forward (Figure 7.1).

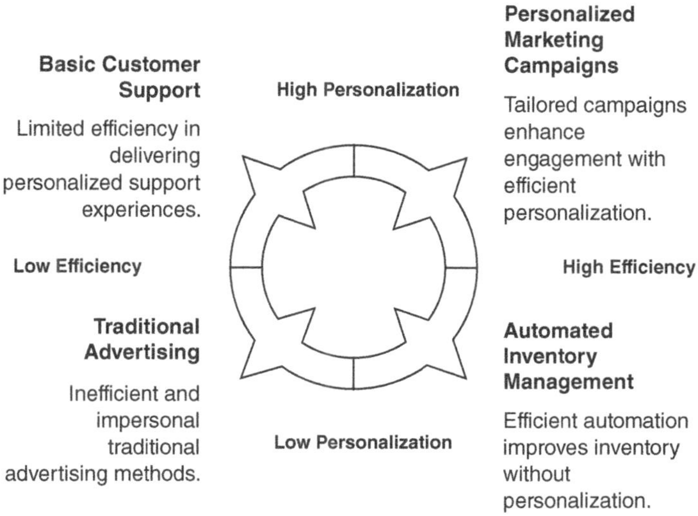

FIGURE 7.1 AI's impact on branding processes.

Application of AI in Brand Management

AI supports brand management by managing key functions across planning, communication, engagement, and analysis. The goal stays the same: keep the brand relevant, consistent, and easy to recognize. AI adds more accuracy and speed to tasks that were once manual and slow. With the rise of real-time data and growing customer expectations, brand managers now use AI systems to simplify choices and conduct actions more quickly across different platforms. McDonald's uses AI through its Dynamic Yield Platform, which adjusts digital menu boards in real time based on weather, time of the day, popular items, and regional preferences—without using McDonald's visual or verbal brand identity, it helps in maintaining a consistent global brand while responding faster and more intelligently to customer behavior, culture, and trends.

AI in Brand Positioning

Brand positioning defines how a brand is seen in the minds of its audience. It reflects the value, promise, and identity that make the brand different. AI strengthens this process by providing real-time insights, quicker feedback, and accurate audience grouping. Brands no longer rely only on traditional surveys or fixed studies. They use AI tools to understand where they stand, how they are viewed, and what changes could help them stay relevant.

Positioning works best when it matches what customers expect. AI helps understand those expectations by studying wide patterns in behavior. Brands gain clearer knowledge about what people care about, how they engage, and what grabs their attention. That knowledge leads to better positioning. Messages become more focused. Identity becomes clearer. The brand's value is easier to explain. It starts speaking directly to the people it wants to reach.

Visual storytelling plays an important part in positioning. BMW used generative AI to create art-based, personalized ad campaigns shown directly on cars. This method highlighted exclusivity, creativity, and innovation. These are traits that matter in luxury space. The campaign helped people see BMW not just as a car company, but as a modern luxury brand shaped by design and technology. Strong positioning also improves through testing and slight changes. AI-supported platforms let brands test how audiences might react before anything is launched. Feedback comes in faster. Brands try different tones, messages, or designs in safe settings. The best ideas move forward. Weak ones are removed early. This process lowers the chance of mistakes and brings more confidence to brand choices. Positioning becomes steadier, quicker, and more in line with audience thinking.

Real-time adjustments powered by AI help brands stay in tune with shifts in emotion, culture, and competition. Brands no longer guess what people feel. They see it in the data. The outcome is clearer positioning. The brand speaks directly, adapts quickly, and stays grounded in what matters to the audience. That steady connection adds long-term value across various categories and markets.

AI in Brand Communications

Brand communication influences how audiences receive, understand, and respond to messaging. AI gives brands organization, speed, and scale to brand communication. Brands are using AI in the spheres of writing, tuning, and revisions of language for video and audio texts across any media. Then the data-driven framework can follow suit in language, tone, and the timing of the messaging. The consistent process is to get the messaging out to fit the brand, and that elicits action with clarity and consistency.

Predictive tools provide valuable feedback on how decisions are made in communication design. Predictive AI can prioritize and identify specific styles of designs or formats more quickly for the highest response. There is no guesswork around planning or brainstorming of copy, design, layout, or call-to-action buttons. Each aspect of the message is viewed holistically as part of the tracker for the individual in real time. It has been shown that AI-provided predictive analytics based on the activity of user data can optimize click-through rates by up to 30%. Reducing decision paths for a user helps teams invest less energy shaping the cognitive steps and deliver more targeted messaging stories where there is even greater accountability on performance outcomes.

The importance of consistent communication across all touch points is critical when talking about building a brand. AI can help with common points of parity in language, tone, and critical points regarding the type of communication, for example, email, social media post, app message, or digital ad language. Automation tools may simply do a final review of the written content and note anything that does not sound, look, or feel consistent with the brand voice. Teams can fix problems before going live. This level of control supports a steady brand image across all platforms. A steady voice builds trust and keeps people coming back.

Copywriting now combines creativity with machine learning. JP Morgan Chase used an AI tool called Persado to create ad copy that lifted click-through rates while staying true to the bank's tone. The AI studied language patterns to find what connected best with readers. The result was not just more clicks, but messaging that clearly matched the bank's image, professional, trustworthy, and straightforward.

Feedback plays a significant role in planning communication. AI tools scan comments, reviews, and replies to understand public feeling. These patterns reveal what people enjoy or reject. Messages improve based on how the audience truly feels, not just assumptions. Scalability is another area where AI stands out. Brands that work across different regions or languages need a large amount of content that still feels personal. AI takes care of translations, adjusts tone, and tweaks phrases to match local culture. This helps brands stay united globally while sounding natural in each market. The result is communication that feels personal, even when delivered at scale.

AI in Brand Experience

Brand experience includes every interaction a person has with a brand, from the first impression to after-sales support. AI improves this journey by offering quicker responses, more personal options, and interactive help. The experience does not feel one-sided anymore. AI makes it active and engaging. Customers enjoy more control, smoother guidance, and faster service. All of this adds to satisfaction and shapes how people view the brand in daily use.

Interactive features support real-time connection. Tools like AI chatbots, voice assistants, and visual interfaces now play a strong part in the brand journey. Nykaa, the global beauty brand, introduced an AI chatbot and a virtual artist feature that helps users pick products and try on makeup virtually. These tools answer questions, suggest shades, and show how looks might appear on the user. That kind of help turns online shopping into a useful and pleasant experience.

Both speed and accuracy matter in each step. AI allows brands to respond quickly, which cuts down on frustration. Automated systems manage frequent questions right away while keeping the tone and message in line with brand values. Customers receive replies that match the brand's voice. Fast, helpful answers leave a good impression. When service runs smoothly, the full experience feels dependable and well-designed.

Visual experiences also improve with AI tools. Features like virtual try-ons, product previews, and guided views help people explore from anywhere. This makes the process easier and removes guesswork. Customers feel more confident about what they choose. The journey feels smoother, and doubt goes down. This often leads to higher satisfaction and more repeat visits. AI helps close the gap between physical and online interaction.

AI recommendation systems play a strong part in shaping brand journeys. Based on what people do online, the system suggests content, offers, or products at the right time. The right moment adds value. AI also makes experiences more flexible. When behavior changes, the system reacts. The layout shifts. Messages change. Options get updated based on the situation. A returning visitor will see something different than someone visiting for the first time. This makes the brand seem more in tune with each user. People stay more engaged when tools respond to them. Personal AI chat tools and smart suggestion engines have already increased customer loyalty in many industries.

The full brand experience does not stop at service; it builds memory. AI helps make sure every step of the journey keeps the same level of quality. From browsing to buying to asking for support, each part feels connected. That kind of smooth experience becomes something people remember and talk about. AI helps create that impression, one clear and helpful moment at a time.

Benefits of AI in Branding

AI brings measurable value to branding by making communication smarter, making decisions faster, and engagement more personalized. The technology adds precision across the entire brand-building process. Companies can reach the right audience, at the right time, with the right message. That accuracy reduces guesswork and improves return on effort. As a result, branding shifts from reactive messaging to proactive experience-building across all customer-facing touchpoints.

One of the biggest gains comes from enhanced targeting. AI studies behavior, preferences, and context to identify high-intent users. Messages are sent when users are most likely to engage. Timing improves. Relevance increases. Conversion rates follow. Reports show that AI users achieve 25% higher conversion rates while reducing customer acquisition costs by 37%. Better targeting means better efficiency in both budget and customer attention.

Consistency improves brand strength. AI ensures every communication, across all platforms, follows set guidelines. Language remains consistent. Visual elements stay aligned. The system flags off-brand material before it reaches the public. That control protects brand identity. Over time, consistent messaging builds a stable impression. People remember brands that sound and look the same across emails, apps, ads, and support.

Speed is another key benefit. AI automates time-consuming tasks like content creation, testing, and distribution. Campaigns launch faster. Adjustments happen in real time. Delays reduce. Performance increases. Faster execution also enables brands to ride trends without missing the moment. The brand feels responsive and informed. That adds credibility and keeps the brand visible when it matters most.

Brand communication becomes more impactful with AI support. Tools suggest which words, images, or tones drive better engagement. Teams make data-backed choices rather than relying on assumptions. Master Card improved ad engagement by using AI-generated copy. The brand message stayed on point, while response rates increased. Such optimization adds value without requiring major structural changes.

Customer experience also improves with AI integration. Smart systems power virtual assistants, chatbots, and service tools. Users get quick answers, personalized support, and helpful suggestions. The interaction becomes smooth and satisfying. Starbucks built "Deep Brew," an AI engine that personalized product recommendations and improved store operations. The brand experience feels effortless, both in-store and online, strengthening emotional connection.

Inventory and product alignment also benefit from AI-driven prediction. Stitch Fix uses machine learning to recommend clothing based on customer data. Suggestions fit better. Returns reduce. Satisfaction increases. That precision builds trust. Customers rely on the brand to make decisions for them. Over time, that confidence improves retention and turns occasional buyers into long-term users.

AI strengthens decision-making through real-time feedback. Brands do not have to wait weeks for results. Dashboards display live performance data, sentiment shifts, and user behavior. Teams adjust mid-campaign based on clear signals. Less waste. More accuracy. Better timing. Decisions get backed by fresh data, not just forecasts. The brand feels current, informed, and always one step ahead.

Automation allows teams to scale faster. Brands manage more content, more campaigns, and more segments without extra pressure on staff. Risk management improves with

AI. Monitoring tools detect negative sentiment early, flag policy violations, and alert teams about unusual activity.

Cost efficiency rises across branding efforts. Smarter targeting means fewer wasted impressions. Faster execution means fewer delays. Predictive tools prevent overproduction and underperformance. Personalization reduces returns and boosts repeat sales. Combined, these benefits lower overall branding costs. Global AI marketing spend is expected to reach $40 billion in 2025. The shift continues because results justify the investment. Market expansion is becoming easier. AI adapts content for regional audiences while maintaining brand identity. Localized versions stay relevant without losing core values. Language, imagery, and tone shift according to data. Global campaigns run with local accuracy. The brand feels present everywhere, yet familiar in each place. That reach, backed by AI, builds authority without diluting identity.

Long-term brand value grows with a stronger emotional connection. AI enables brands to focus on relationship-building, not just transactions. Every step, starting from discovery to support, feels intentional and designed for the user. That level of care drives brand affinity. Brands do not just sell more; they build reputations that last. AI becomes a quiet driver of perception, consistency, and emotional engagement. Nestlé is another example.

Challenges of AI in Branding

AI offers many advantages for marketing, and at the same time faces multiple obstacles. Brands that are using AI are being faced with problems that range from public trust to the boundaries of the systems themselves. The more an organization permits AI to impact its communications decisions, the more accountability it takes. Failings in judgment and mistakes are more visible. Gaps are more difficult to ignore or overlook. The more brands rely on automated decisions in marketing, the more they must be cognizant of reputational risk management in order to protect organizational identity, brand, equity, reliability, and consumer trust. Unilever is one of the world's largest fast moving consumer good (FMCG) companies, which uses AI to make branding faster, more efficient, and globally consistent while staying locally relevant.

Brand trust exists in content quality, and AI does not deliver 100% accuracy with every generated request. Messenger errors, inaccurate visual outputs, or erroneous recommendations can happen. Apprehension arises from errors. The residual effects are long-lasting. AI systems require proprietary data source(s), regular updates, and ongoing monitoring. If these mark points are absent or neglected, even the best AI system will produce output that reflects brand messaging that diverges from previous brand positions. The totality of the branding output suggests branding has an urgent quality, or semblance of a disconnected brand, all of which diminishes brand association, rather than enhances it.

Finally, bias is an ongoing consideration for brands producing outputs and establishing their brand identity with AI-generated text. One of the superpowers of an AI system is that it learns from past data—and if that past data is biased, it will model and amplify that biased pattern in its outputs. Ergo, AI can generate content with assumptions as simple as stereotypes to a given output, or missing one of the most significant population segments, or missing a social equity question altogether. About 43% of organizations (or have even heard of an organization that has dealt with bias of some sort in AI systems) have had various forms of content or communication bias in AI systems. This represents reputational risk—biased communication that consumers become aware of will change perceptions about branding non-bias and segregate consumers who have the desire to support fairness, equity, or inclusion.

Ethical concerns also affect how people respond to AI-led branding. Consumers value transparency. When messages appear automated without disclosure, trust can fall. Overuse of AI-generated content raises questions: Who made the message? Why does it sound generic? Around 49.5% of businesses fear data privacy or ethics risks when using AI. Responsible brands need to address these questions openly before relying heavily on automated communication.

Creative depth poses another challenge. AI can generate content quickly, but often lacks emotional tone or cultural understanding. Branding thrives on nuance. Minor changes in language or design create big differences in impact. AI may miss those details. Without human review, campaigns risk sounding flat or robotic. Emotional connection weakens. People notice when messages feel mechanical or out of touch.

Context handling presents a key limitation. AI struggles to read emotional or situational context. Messages that work in one setting may fall flat elsewhere. Tone may shift unintentionally. In branding, even small tone mismatches affect perception. A cheerful message during a sensitive event can appear careless. Human input remains critical in shaping how messages appear across moments and moods.

Overreliance on automation leads to brand dilution. When AI manages too many functions, brand voice may start drifting. Messaging loses its unique flavor. Competitors using similar tools might end up sounding alike. Differentiation fades. The brand tone becomes generic. Strong branding demands balance. AI should assist, not dominate, the creative and communication process.

Data quality directly affects AI output. Poor data inputs result in poor recommendations. If the system trains on outdated or irrelevant data, the content misses current needs. Branding then feels disconnected from market shifts. Audiences lose interest. The system does not fail because of flaws in AI, but due to a lack of fresh, clean, and relevant information. Compliance and regulation also slow down adoption. Data privacy laws continue to evolve. AI systems that collect or use customer data must follow strict rules. Any misstep can lead to legal trouble or public scrutiny. Brands using AI must build safe, secure, and transparent systems. The pressure grows as more customers ask where their data goes and how brands use it.

Training AI systems takes time and cost. Brands need to invest in custom solutions, review models, and update algorithms. Pre-built tools often lack the depth to serve specific brand needs. Small or mid-sized brands may struggle to match the speed and quality of larger competitors. That gap creates inequality in AI-driven branding performance across different business sizes.

Employee roles also change under AI influence. Automation reduces the need for some tasks but increases demand for new skills. Teams need to learn how to manage, evaluate, and adapt AI tools. That shift requires training and a mindset change. Without support, confusion grows. The brand process suffers. Teams need both creative insight and technical knowledge to succeed in an AI-supported branding structure.

Measurement becomes difficult when AI touches multiple touchpoints. Attribution grows complex. Brands struggle to isolate what worked: was it the content, the delivery, or the timing? AI adjusts constantly, often without a detailed explanation. Without clarity, teams cannot fine-tune performance. Branding becomes harder to optimize. Results appear strong, but causes remain vague.

Short-term gains can distract from long-term brand building. AI systems chase engagement, not always alignment. Clicks rise, but meaning drops. Campaigns win attention but miss emotional depth. Brand voice weakens when driven only by what performs fast. AI helps reach more people, but it does not guarantee stronger bonds. Long-term loyalty comes from trust, consistency, and relevance. Those elements need human insight.

Final control remains important. Brands need systems that allow oversight. Full automation risks detachment. Brand managers must shape output, adjust tone, and approve direction. Feedback loops between human teams and AI tools create the best results. Without those checks, branding suffers. Technology performs best when guided, reviewed, and refined, not left to act alone (Table 7.1).

TABLE 7.1 AI Applications in Branding

Branding Area	*What AI Does*	*Success Example & Result*	*Failure Example & Lesson*
Targeting & personalization	Finds the right audience and moment	Hotstar (India) uses recommendation AI to match shows to users → higher watch time and retention.	Target (predictive coupons) once revealed a teen's pregnancy via analytics → shows why sensitive signals need strict privacy rules and opt-outs.
Creative optimization	Tests copy/images to lift response	Heineken used AI to write and test ad copy → better click-through and lower cost per lead.	Toys "R" Us released an AI-generated brand film that felt impersonal → creative AI needs human tone checks and brand storytelling.
Service & customer experience (CX) (Chat/Assist)	Answers fast, personalizes support	Pret A Manger (UK) powers offers and store ops → smoother experiences and higher ticket size.	Microsoft Tay chatbot went off-brand on Twitter → always add strong guardrails, filters, and human oversight.
Product Fit & Merch	Recommends items, tags content	Warby Parker uses ML to pick clothing per user → fewer returns, higher satisfaction.	H&M faced backlash for AI auto-tagging/ mislabeled items → keep humans in the loop and validate training data.
Dynamic pricing	Adjusts prices in real time	Decathlon uses repricing algorithms to stay competitive → higher conversion and inventory turn.	Uber surge pricing during big events drew fairness complaints → add caps, clear messaging, and "fair use" rules.
Content consistency	Enforces tone, format, visuals	LEGO uses AI checks before publishing → fewer off-brand posts, faster approvals.	Generic "automation-only" rollouts that push unreviewed assets → brand voice drifts; keep human brand editors.

CLOSING CASE: GUCCI

Gucci stands as one of the most recognized luxury fashion brands globally. Known for bold design, exclusivity, and strong cultural influence, Gucci continues to lead by blending heritage with innovation. The brand holds a strong connection with younger, digitally active consumers. To stay aligned with this shift, Gucci has introduced AI tools to strengthen its digital presence and reinforce brand relevance without losing its luxury identity.

The fashion industry feels pressure to remain fast, fresh, and relatable. Gucci uses AI to accommodate the industry expectations while remaining true to its own identity. AI serves a supportive function, enabling Gucci to survive every touchpoint of its branding, from campaign planning to direct consumer response. The brand applies smart tools not only to produce better internal processes but to improve consumer-facing experiences too. The brand maintains a connected and cohesive experience by taking advantage of those multiple streams.

AI helps Gucci with audience understanding. The brand employs AI-based systems to inform its understanding of customer behaviors, preferences, and purchasing patterns. These pieces of information are used to inform the brand's campaigns, product placements, and strategies for individual platforms. Things like messages are congruent with intent. Offers are congruent with context. That level of individualization allows Gucci to retain exclusivity while remaining human enough across consumer segments. Luxury branding gets smarter, not simply louder.

Gucci utilizes AI too for creative testing and the ideas behind a campaign. The brand tests its visuals or narratives before putting them in front of audiences with AI-based simulations. The creative phenomena are guided by audience feedback, cultural tone, and aesthetic preferences. Therefore, while the creative remains taut, the feedback loops build confidence. The process makes the brand riskier, and experiences remain resonant without recycling familiar ideas.

Digital try-ons and AI chat features are part of the brand experience every Gucci customer is exposed to. The online shopper connects with Gucci products in an interactive manner. The brand employs AI think tools to help shoppers select the correct sizes, match accessories, and complete purchases based on behavior. The digital process as a whole is intentional and seamless. Customers equate Gucci with luxury, but equally with convenience and care. Each of those parts of the experience builds emotional bonds and consequently improves brand interaction online.

Gucci uses AI to continuously track its impact using social listening to monitor its brand. Brand managers track mentions of their brand online, reactions to their campaigns, and shifting sentiments. Brand managers take note of what has positive sentiment and what may require corrective actions using sentiment analysis. Consequently, fast responses to issues reduce reputational risk to the brand, and positive sentiment gets its time in the sun. The brand maintains its tuned frequency to the global audience without losing its consistency in tone.

Gucci also uses AI to produce exclusive digital content experiences for valued users. Personal offers, first access to, and targeted campaigns represent deeper insights into who the high-value customers are in comparison with others. Inside Luxury branding, consumers expect some relevance and recognition. In contrast to other emotions, AI proved useful for meeting that expectation. So that the content feels rare and not random. The experience feels curated and not generalized. The brand preserves its identity while extending its repeated one-to-one connections.

Gucci demonstrates that AI genuinely can enable and contribute to luxury branding without deteriorating its standards. The brand bridged tradition and technology expertise. In every instance of AI applied to the brand, Gucci aligned the values of creativity, quality, and exclusivity. The AI is not the brand's service or value. It is sharpening the brand's voice, extending its outreach, and perfecting the experience. Gucci exemplifies that AI can be effective when guided, meaning it can substantiate the essence of its brand even in the most sensitive image spaces.

Discussion Questions

1 Where can AI add the most value to a brand: positioning, content creation, or customer experience? Why?
2 How do we keep a consistent brand voice when using generative AI across many channels?
3 What ethical risks worry you most, and how should a brand manage them?
4 Should brands disclose when content or chat replies are AI-generated? How might that affect trust?
5 When should humans overrule an AI brand decision? Share a real or hypothetical example.

Assignment Questions

1 Pick a brand: Identify 3 current or potential AI uses. For each state, the brand goal, data needed, success metric, and one risk + migration.
2 Write a reusable AI + prompt+ style guide that would make a content model produce on brands' posts.
3 Draft a simple policy covering data sources, bias testing, disclosure rules, and escalation when AI outputs may harm brand trust.
4 Outline the key tiles you would track weekly for AI-driven brand activity and why matters.

MINI CASE

Swift Cart is a regional online grocery app. When it expanded to three new cities, its messages felt messy: push alerts shouted discounts, emails talked about recipes, and social posts were just jokes. To fix this, the team made a simple "Brand Voice" guide for their AI tools: be friendly and helpful, save people time, no hard sell, celebrate small wins for busy households, and don't shame anyone about food waste. They trained the AI on approved wording, product names, and allergen lists. They also set guardrails to stop risky health claims, force allergen warnings, and avoid stereotypes. From one creative brief, AI wrote versions for every channel: a main headline, a 15-second reel, and an app banner. Humans still checked anything with nutrition claims, and legal reviewed required notes. The AI also learned local context and highlighted the right local vendors. Results after eight weeks, brand consistency score went up from 58 to 86, fewer people turned off push alerts (down by 22%), and conversions on AI-made bundles rose by 9%. There were mistakes. One reel told people to freeze leafy greens for months, and partner farmers complained. Swift Cart removed it, added rules about produce tips, and launched a "Farmer first" content series co-created with suppliers. Another issue: AI kept saying budget to seniors, and they didn't like the tone. The team updated prompts to focus on dignity and independence and added a respect check before posting. By the end of the quarter, AI wrote about 60% of first drafts, humans edited them all, satisfaction with messages rose from 4.1% to 4.5%, trust mentions increased 14%, and repeat purchases grew by 7%. If you were SwiftCart's marketing lead, what is the next guardrail or checklist item you would add before the next city launch—why?

HBR Case Links:

- https://hbsp.harvard.edu/product/511137-PDF-ENG?itemFindingMethod=search
- https://hbsp.harvard.edu/product/W20939-PDF-ENG?itemFindingMethod=search
- https://hbsp.harvard.edu/product/525052-PDF-ENG?itemFindingMethod=search

Application of Concepts

Concept (Kotler Link)	*Application in Practice*	*In-Class Activity/Illustration*
Brand voice governance (Integrated marketing communications)	Build a unified style guide (tone, claims, inclusivity) and plug it into AI tools so all emails, ads, and chat replies stay on-brand.	Give students a short style guide and 5 mixed AI copy drafts; teams "greenlight or redline" each draft and rewrite one to fit the guide.
Human-in-the-loop content (Content strategy & organization)	Set a workflow where AI drafts, humans fact-check/sanitize, legal approves sensitive claims, and publishing is version-controlled.	Map a swimlane diagram for roles (AI → editor → legal → publish). Students spot bottlenecks and propose service level agreements (SLAs).
Personalization & modular assets (Segmentation/Targeting/Positioning)	Create modular copy/creatives (headline, call to action (CTA), image) and let AI assemble variants per segment while respecting brand rules.	Provide 3 segments and a content "lego kit." Teams assemble one compliant ad/email per segment and justify choices.
Brand Safety in programmatic (Media & IMC Planning)	Use allow/deny lists, contextual filters, and risk scores so AI media buying avoids off-brand placements.	"War room" drill: a brand ad appeared next to harmful content. Students set new guardrails and a recovery plan (message + channels).

Keywords

- Brand governance
- IMC (integrated marketing comms)
- Style guide
- Human-in-the-loop
- Personalization
- Modular assets
- Brand safety
- Programmatic buying
- Contextual targeting
- Measurement & uplift testing
- Data privacy (GDPR/CCPA)
- Crisis playbook & guardrails

Bibliography

Bleier, A., & Eisenbeiss, M. (2015). The importance of trust for personalized online advertising. *Marketing Science*, *34*(1), 136–163. https://doi.org/10.1287/mksc.2015.0930

Davenport, T. H., Guha, A., Grewal, D., & Bressgott, T. (2020). How artificial intelligence will change marketing. *Journal of the Academy of Marketing Science*, *48*(1), 24–42. https://doi.org/10.1007/s11747-019-00696-0

Goldfarb, A., & Tucker, C. (2011). Privacy regulation and online advertising. *Management Science*, *57*(1), 57–71. https://doi.org/10.1287/mnsc.1100.1246

Lambrecht, A., & Tucker, C. (2013). When does retargeting work? Information specificity in online advertising. *Journal of Marketing Research*, *50*(5), 561–576. https://doi.org/10.1509/jmr.11.0503

Malthouse, E. C., Maslowska, E., & Franks, J. (2019). The role of artificial intelligence in personalized engagement marketing. *Journal of Advertising*, *48*(4), 334–342. https://doi.org/10.1080/00913367.2019.1585306

National Institute of Standards and Technology (2023). *Artificial intelligence risk management framework (AI RMF 1.0) (NIST AI 100–1)*. https://doi.org/10.6028/NIST.AI.100-1

Renda, A. (2023). From the GDPR to the AI Act: A blueprint for AI governance in Europe? *Computer Law & Security Review*, *50*, 105904. https://doi.org/10.1016/j.clsr.2023.105904

8

AI IN MARKETING STRATEGY

Learning Objectives

1 Understand the evolving role of AI in modern marketing strategy
2 Apply AI concepts to strategic marketing models
3 Evaluate the impact of AI on content personalization and delivery
4 Assess the integration of AI in digital advertising and market research
5 Analyze real-world business applications of AI in marketing

OPENING CASE: AMAZON

Amazon stands as a global leader in how AI reshapes marketing strategy. As one of the most customer-focused companies, Amazon relies on AI to manage massive volumes of consumer data. Every action on its platform, clicks, purchases, and searches, feeds its AI systems. These systems then drive personalized suggestions, real-time pricing, targeted advertisements, and timely communication. The result is a dynamic, user-specific experience that enhances engagement and conversions.

The company uses AI beyond basic recommendation engines. Algorithms track consumer behavior, analyze product preferences, and identify shifting interests. AI enables Amazon to understand needs and offer relevant options even before a customer actively searches. The speed, accuracy, and precision of AI-based decisions support Amazon in retaining customers and increasing purchase frequency. AI builds the bridge between user intent and seamless product discovery.

In its marketing strategy, Amazon considers AI as a decision-making assistant. It supports demand forecasting, email targeting, product ranking, and ad placements. Machine learning systems decide which product to show, when to show it, and who should see it. AI also

DOI: 10.4324/9781003501862-8

helps Amazon segment audiences, allowing micro-level targeting based on patterns, behavior, and purchase intent. This creates sharper campaigns with higher conversion probabilities.

Personalization is where Amazon finds high returns on AI integration. Shoppers receive suggestions based on real-time browsing, past transactions, or similar consumer profiles. Emails and push notifications carry product links chosen through predictive analytics. Product pages are customized to each user's activity, increasing the likelihood of interest and interaction. AI curates what each user sees, shaping their journey from browsing to buying.

AI also plays a key role in pricing strategies. Amazon adjusts prices multiple times a day using dynamic pricing algorithms. These systems compare competitors' rates, track demand shifts, and evaluate stock availability. Price changes are not random; they are responses driven by data. Each shift aims to stay competitive while maximizing margins. AI delivers faster and smarter pricing decisions than human teams could manage.

Beyond website and app experiences, AI powers Amazon's advertising model. Brands advertise through Amazon Ads, which uses AI to show sponsored products to the right users. Ad placements rely on what users are searching, buying, and browsing. AI ensures the visibility of products now of the highest relevance. That adds value for both sellers and shoppers.

AI reduces manual work and speeds up content decisions. Automation takes over repetitive marketing tasks, allowing teams to focus on creative planning and strategy alignment. AI filters data, highlights trends, and presents insights. The system learns over time and improves results across marketing channels. Decision loops become tighter. Actions become more precise. Results become more consistent.

Amazon's use of AI shows how technology transforms traditional marketing into data-driven operations. Marketing becomes a combination of insights, prediction, and automation. AI no longer acts as just a support tool. It drives key outcomes. With AI at its core, Amazon sets a high standard in how businesses can turn data into measurable performance across the customer journey.

Introduction to AI in Marketing Strategy

Artificial intelligence (AI) is changing the way businesses think about marketing. From automated decision-making to real-time customer engagement, AI adds speed, precision, and relevance. The shift is clear; AI has moved beyond optional support and now plays a central role. As competition rises and consumer expectations grow, marketing teams turn to AI to stay relevant and deliver a timely impact.

The global AI market crossed $184 billion in 2024, reflecting its fast-growing importance. With a projected growth rate of 37% annually through 2030, the momentum continues. AI's influence is not limited to technology sectors alone. Reports show that up to 14% increase in global Gross Domestic Product (GDP) by 2030 could come from AI-led productivity gains. Marketing stands out as one of the early and active users of this shift.

Marketers have started depending on AI to manage daily tasks and make better choices. Over 88% now use AI in some form each day. Campaign planning, audience targeting, and performance tracking, AI plays a role in all of them. The shift is also organizational.

Around 78% of companies already use AI in at least one area. AI is no longer a future plan. It has become part of everyday decisions.

The value is visible in numbers. About 80% of marketers report higher efficiency due to AI. Over 70% believe AI can outperform humans in key tasks like content selection, timing, and targeting. Around 63% of companies using generative AI see clear productivity benefits. These numbers underline a growing trust in AI-led decisions. BMW uses AI to personalize marketing campaigns, analyze customer behavior, and deliver targeted ads in real time. AI-generated visuals and chatbots ensure consistent brand communication.

Marketing and sales functions use AI more than any other business area, except Information Technology (IT). Around 56% of companies apply AI to streamline operations. About 51% use it to handle fraud and cybersecurity. The adoption goes beyond cost saving. Companies now see AI to improve speed, accuracy, and relevance in decision-making.

Define & Importance of Marketing Strategy

Marketing strategy works as a structured plan that directs how a business reaches its audience, promotes products, and achieves specific goals. It includes defining objectives, selecting channels, positioning offers, and evaluating results. Without a defined strategy, marketing becomes scattered and reactive. A clear approach ensures that every action aligns with brand goals and delivers measurable impact.

A strong marketing strategy starts with understanding the audience. Businesses study consumer preferences, buying behavior, and engagement patterns. Based on these insights, they choose suitable platforms, build targeted messages, and set realistic performance benchmarks. A focused plan allows consistent communication, improves resource allocation, and helps brands stay competitive in shifting markets. KFC uses customer data from app orders, social media, and regional taste preferences to understand its audience and shape its marketing strategy. It helps in maintaining consistency and staying competitive in fast-changing food markets.

Marketing efforts without a plan often lead to wasted budgets and low engagement. Strategy adds direction and structure. It answers key questions: what to sell, who to target, how to promote, and when to act. Marketers can set timelines, assign responsibilities, and predict campaign outcomes with better clarity. Structure reduces trial-and-error decisions.

Technology has expanded how strategies are built and executed. AI-powered tools now support audience segmentation, message customization, and campaign optimization. Marketers use AI to scale content, schedule updates, and analyze feedback. Platforms like Bloomreach offer AI-based personalization on a scale, allowing e-commerce brands to deliver customized content in real time. This improves relevance and boosts response rates.

AI improves each part of that structure. From planning to execution, AI makes strategies more relevant and more effective. Businesses that combine strategic clarity with AI-driven insights build better connections and stronger results.

The Role of AI in Reshaping Traditional Strategic Framework

Traditional marketing strategies followed a linear path. Teams set fixed goals, followed standard timelines, and used broad segmentation. Decisions relied heavily on past

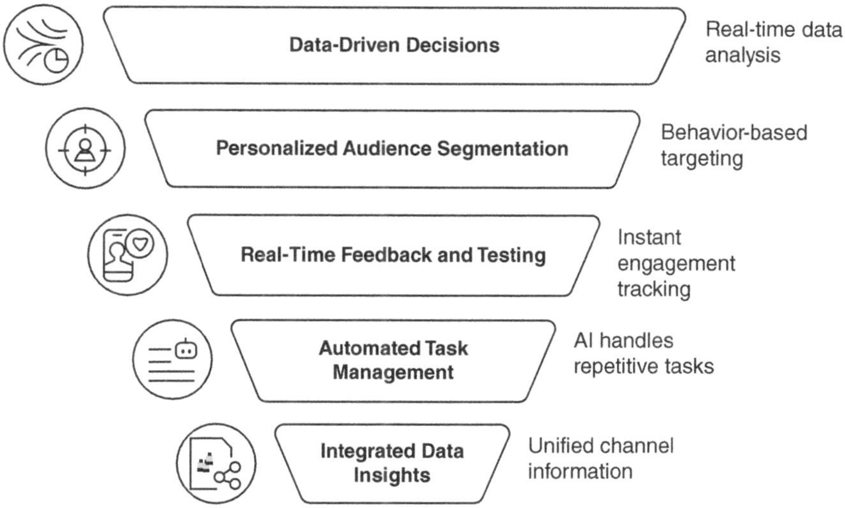

FIGURE 8.1 AI-driven marketing transformation.

performance and intuition. Once campaigns were launched, adjustments were rare and slow. That method worked in stable environments but often failed to keep pace with shifting consumer behavior and rising expectations.

AI has challenged and updated this outdated approach. Data now drives decisions. AI tools study consumer patterns, market shifts, and campaign feedback in real time. Instead of fixed plans, strategies now evolve based on continuous learning. Marketers test faster, adapt quicker, and respond with greater precision. Traditional methods now seem too rigid and slow.

AI improves how businesses segment audiences. Retail brands like Levi's old model used to segment customers mainly based on gender and income levels—for example, advertising premium denim to high-income urban men aged 25–40, everyone in that group received the same message, regardless of their preferences. AI also brings speed to testing and feedback. Marketers once waited weeks to measure impact. AI tools now track engagement instantly. Teams can adjust wording, timing, or platform in real time. Performance improves without halting the campaign. Strategies remain active and flexible. That responsiveness adds value to every marketing decision.

Instreamatic, an audio advertising technology company, uses AI to reshape audio campaigns. Their system personalizes messages for each listener. Instead of one-size-fits-all radio ads, AI creates dynamic audio content based on user behavior. Brands get more engagement. Listeners hear more relevant content. Traditional ad formats lose ground to smarter, data-led systems. Modern strategy means moving from fixed plans to flexible systems (Figure 8.1).

Integration of AI in Long-Term & Short-Term Strategic Planning

Strategic planning works on two levels: short-term actions and long-term direction. Short-term plans focus on quick wins, campaign cycles, and immediate goals. Long-term planning focuses on vision, positioning, and future-readiness. Both are important, and both benefit from AI integration. AI adds structure, precision, and responsiveness across timelines. It helps teams work with clarity in short bursts and prepare for broader shifts in market dynamics.

In a short-term strategy, AI supports speed and flexibility. Campaigns adjust in real time. Algorithms track performance, test variables, and guide decisions within hours. Marketing teams act faster because data supports every move. Audience preferences change quickly. AI reads those signals and adapts. Short-term planning becomes sharper, more accurate, and less wasteful. Decisions shift from assumption to evidence.

Long-term planning demands deeper analysis. Businesses need to track trends, predict shifts, and plan for upcoming demands. AI studies customer behavior over time, recognizes patterns, and highlights slow-moving changes. These insights help companies set stronger goals. AI also supports competitive research, risk assessment, and performance forecasting. Long-term strategy gets built on a stronger foundation of insight, not speculation.

Eneco, a Dutch energy company, uses AI for both timeframes. An AI-powered customer service agent handles over 24,000 chats each month. That data feeds short-term decisions on communication patterns and service delivery. At the same time, the company uses those insights to guide long-term planning around customer experience and automation. AI becomes a shared resource across both planning levels.

Porter's Five Forces Model with AI

Porter's Five Forces model helps businesses understand market dynamics and assess competitive pressure. The framework focuses on five areas: competitive rivalry, the threat of new entrants, the threat of substitutes, the bargaining power of buyers, and the bargaining power of suppliers. Traditionally, companies relied on manual research and industry reports to apply the model. Now, AI improves the speed, scope, and accuracy of analysis across all five forces.

Competitive rivalry requires constant tracking of competitors' actions. AI tools monitor digital footprints, ad spending, product launches, and customer feedback. Real-time analysis reveals shifts in pricing, positioning, or targeting.

New market entrants bring fresh challenges. AI helps detect early signals of disruption. Platforms track emerging startups, patent filings, domain registrations, and funding news. Businesses identify potential threats before they grow. That early awareness allows timely adjustments to product design, pricing, or distribution. Market readiness improves. Risk management becomes proactive, not reactive.

Substitute products impact demand patterns. AI tracks customer preferences, reviews, and search patterns across platforms. Shifts in behavior reveal growing interest in alternatives. Companies gain visibility into why users switch or explore other options. AI links customer sentiment with usage trends. That insight supports better positioning and retention strategies.

Buyer power reflects how much influence customers have over prices and offerings. AI maps consumer preferences, feedback loops, and purchasing trends. Predictive models estimate how price changes or new offers may impact demand. Businesses respond with smarter pricing, bundling, or service plans. AI adds depth to customer insight and supports better value delivery.

Supplier power includes availability, costs, and reliability. AI scans supply chain performance, raw material trends, and vendor ratings. It flags risk points and helps with vendor selection. AI tools also forecast cost fluctuations based on global trends. Planning becomes more agile. Businesses build stronger relationships with key suppliers while managing costs and disruptions better.

Addaxis, a UK-based AI/machine learning (ML) consulting firm, integrates AI into Porter's Five Forces for high-growth sectors like generative AI. Their systems track real-time data across industry forces. This enables clients to run competitive analysis with up-to-date, dynamic inputs. Traditional models used static assumptions. AI-powered models update automatically, offering smarter, sharper, and more timely results.

AI & STP

Segmentation, Targeting, and Positioning (STP) develops the core of every marketing strategy. These three steps guide how brands identify audience groups, select who to focus on, and shape brand perception. AI strengthens each of these steps through faster processing, richer insights, and real-time adjustments. Marketers no longer rely only on demographics or fixed surveys. AI brings behavior, intent, and interaction into the analysis.

Segmentation becomes sharper with AI. Algorithms study browsing patterns, purchase history, and engagement data to identify micro-groups. The process moves beyond age or income brackets. AI captures user signals in real time and adapts to new behaviors. Data shows that AI-driven audience segmentation can raise search ad conversions by 39%. Businesses connect with smaller, more relevant groups and achieve better returns on marketing efforts. ASOS, a fashion e-commerce brand, uses AI to group users into micro-segments like streetwear shoppers, sustainable buyers, or event-based shoppers and delivers personalized outfits, ads, and discounts accordingly. This has helped ASOS improve conversion rates, reduce returns, and increase customer loyalty—demonstrating how AI-driven segmentation outperforms traditional models.

Targeting also benefits from precision. AI tracks which messages, platforms, and formats work best for each segment. Predictive analytics forecasts user responses and suggests where to invest next. Studies reveal a 32% drop in cost-per-click when using AI-powered targeting tools. Marketers reach the right audience at the right time, without overspending. Personalization becomes scalable and effective. The dating app Bumble uses AI to target users with personalized in-app campaigns and subscription offers.

Positioning gains strength through AI-generated content and visual elements. Marketers use AI to build content that aligns with each segment's expectations. Around 76% of personalization leaders automate content assembly, while 69% use AI to create lifelike images. Brands present themselves with consistency and clarity. AI helps craft the message and control how it appears across platforms. Gucci uses AI to strengthen its brand positioning by creating personalized visuals and content that align with different luxury consumer segments.

STP remains a foundational model. AI makes it faster, deeper, and more responsive. From dividing audiences to personalizing content, AI supports decisions that drive engagement and improve performance. Strategy shifts from static planning to live interaction. Brands get closer to customer needs. Results become easier to track and improve.

AI in Segmentation

Segmentation helps marketers divide audiences into smaller, defined groups based on shared traits. Traditionally, this meant using demographics, geography, or purchase history. That method had limitations. Consumer behavior often changes faster than such segments. AI changes the approach. Algorithms now process large volumes of data to identify patterns that go beyond surface-level traits. Segmentation becomes more accurate, real-time, and behavior-driven.

AI looks at multiple data points at once. Browsing history, click activity, purchase frequency, and session time all contribute to segmentation. The system learns continuously. As new data arrives, segments get updated. That dynamic response supports campaign timing, message relevance, and budget use. Marketers no longer work with static audience sets. They target based on live signals.

AI also supports predictive segmentation. The system anticipates what a user may do next based on past actions. Segments now include potential buyers, churn risks, or repeat customers. Messages match future behavior, not just past trends. That shift raises response rates. Campaigns become more proactive and less reactive.

HubSpot uses AI to automate this entire process. The platform segments customers across behavior, demographics, and interaction levels. Marketers create campaigns that reach the right segment with minimal effort. Campaign optimization becomes easier. AI tracks who engages, who drops off, and who converts. Adjustments happen mid-campaign, not after failure.

AI also reduces time spent on manual grouping. Traditional segmentation takes hours of analysis. AI handles that within minutes. Teams can focus on planning, creativity, and content. Efficiency improves. Accuracy rises. Relevance becomes measurable. More marketers recognize segmentation as one of AI's most effective applications.

Segmentation has always supported marketing strategy. AI now makes it faster, smarter, and more impactful. From automation to prediction, AI refines how businesses understand and group their audiences. Better segments mean better campaigns. Better campaigns mean stronger results. In a data-driven environment, AI-led segmentation sets a new standard for performance marketing.

AI in Targeting

Targeting turns segmented groups into focused marketing actions. Once businesses identify audience segments, the next step is choosing where, when, and how to reach them. Traditional targeting relied on broad assumptions and fixed content delivery. AI changes that. Now, systems predict the most responsive channels, optimal timing, and preferred content type. Marketers shift from generalized outreach to data-led precision.

AI uses real-time behavior data to guide targeting. Algorithms process search history, purchase patterns, clicks, and responses. The insight shows which users are more likely to act and which platforms they use the most. Campaigns have become sharper, and messages reach audiences where engagement is highest, which reduces irrelevance and improves relevance.

Channel optimization plays a key role. AI systems assess where different users spend time, such as email, mobile apps, search engines, or social feeds. Content gets delivered on the right platform for each segment. Engagement improves. Conversion rates increase. According to recent data, AI-powered predictive targeting can reduce cost-per-click by up to 32%. Efficiency becomes measurable.

Adobe Marketo applies AI to deliver targeting at scale. The platform monitors cross-channel user behavior and creates adaptive campaigns. Each customer receives content aligned with their interest, timing, and device. That creates a consistent, personalized experience across platforms. Brand recall increases. Customer relationships strengthen.

AI transforms targeting into a faster, more accurate, and responsive activity. Businesses benefit from better allocation, stronger personalization, and measurable outcomes. In fast-moving markets, AI-guided targeting sets the pace for modern marketing performance.

AI in Positioning

Positioning defines how a brand wants its audience to perceive its product or service. A clear position highlights benefits, values, and relevance. Traditional methods used focus groups and historical data to decide brand tone and messaging. Those methods often lacked flexibility and missed real-time insights. AI now plays a key role in shaping, refining, and adapting brand positioning based on continuous user interaction and behavioral signals.

Brands use AI to test content variations. Different headlines, visuals, or call-to-actions are shown to segmented users. AI tracks which combinations perform better. Positioning shifts from one fixed message to multiple targeted messages, which increases relevance, leading to higher engagement. Over 71% of marketers see AI as useful for content creation and personalization, which directly supports brand positioning.

AI tools also monitor conversations around the brand. Reviews, comments, search trends, and social media posts reveal how customers describe a product. That insight shows gaps between brand intent and user perception. Marketing teams use those signals to adjust their messaging. The goal becomes alignment, and the result is clarity.

Virgin Holidays uses AI-enhanced STP to position its offerings across six distinct audience segments. Each group receives messaging that matches its travel style, budget, and motivation. Families see safety and comfort. Young travelers see adventure and discovery. AI handles the differentiation. Positioning adapts to audience needs in real time. The result is better relevance and improved conversion.

AI helps achieve both by making each interaction relevant. From website banners to email subject lines, every element aligns with how the brand wants to be seen. AI redefines positioning from a fixed label to a flexible, data-led strategy. Brands control how they are viewed across segments, channels, and contexts. In fast-paced markets, AI enables brands to speak with precision and stay aligned with shifting audience expectations (Figure 8.2).

Personalized Content Generation & Delivery

Content plays a central role in every stage of the marketing funnel. From awareness to conversion, the right message shapes customer response. AI brings a shift in how content gets created and delivered. Generative models now support everything from email writing to ad copy and social captions. Brands use AI to save time, reduce workload, and deliver content at scale with consistent relevance.

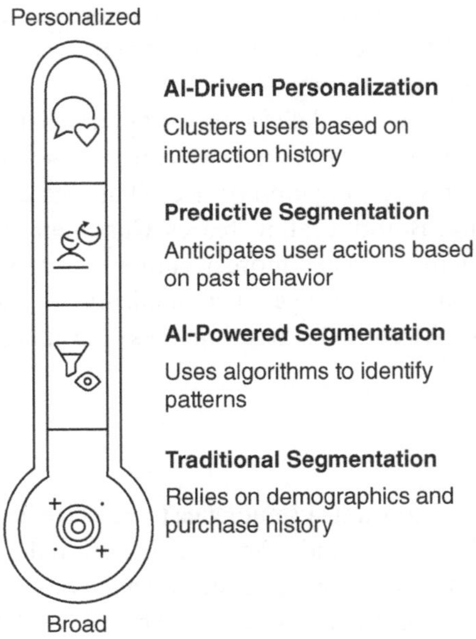

FIGURE 8.2 AI's impact on marketing: from broad to personalized strategies.

Generative AI transforms content production. Teams no longer rely only on manual drafts or templated responses. AI generates content based on tone, audience type, and performance data. Around 71% of marketers believe generative AI helps remove repetitive tasks and shift focus to strategic goals. Campaigns move faster. Personalization reaches more users. Impact increases with less effort. AI redefines content as a dynamic, data-driven tool. From creation to delivery, systems adjust based on real-time behavior and campaign goals. Brands move faster, connect deeper, and perform smarter. Estee Lauder uses generative AI to create personalized skincare and makeup content across emails, websites, and social media tailored to each user's skin needs and beauty preferences.

Use of Generative AI in Content Creation

Generative AI is changing how brands produce marketing content. Instead of relying entirely on manual creation, businesses now use AI to generate written, visual, and audio content on a scale. Tools support marketers in producing high-quality outputs faster and more efficiently. As digital demands rise, speed and consistency matter more than ever. AI helps close the gap between content need and content delivery.

Text generation is one of the most widely adopted use cases. Marketers use generative AI for email subject lines, ad copy, product descriptions, blog outlines, and social media content. Each piece is based on tone, intent, and past performance data. Content becomes sharper and more aligned with user expectations. Campaigns stay fresh across platforms. Time saved allows teams to focus on planning and performance review.

Visual content creation has also gained momentum. AI models now generate images, banners, and graphics with minimal manual input. Brands adjust size, color, and tone using prompts and presets. Klarna, a financial services company from Sweden, created over 1,000 images using generative AI in 2024. The company reduced its design cycle from six weeks to just seven days. Results arrived faster without sacrificing quality. Brands that adopt generative AI gain an edge in speed, quality, and consistency. Content reaches audiences faster, speaks more directly, and performs better across touchpoints. Generative AI supports not only production but also adaptability, ensuring that content stays aligned with changing customer expectations.

Real-Time Content Customization

Real-time content customization allows brands to respond to user behavior instantly. Instead of serving static messages, marketers now deliver content that updates in response to clicks, scrolls, or past actions. AI enables this process by analyzing data at speed and scale. Brands no longer wait for reports to optimize content. Adjustments happen while the user is still engaged.

AI maps each user's journey and predicts the next best content to show. Visitors receive targeted banners, recommendations, or messages that match their behavior. The approach supports deeper engagement and faster conversions. Around 95% of senior marketers now consider their personalization strategies successful. Timely content makes users stay longer and act quicker.

Maybelline offers a strong example. The brand launched an AI-powered app that provides real-time haircare and makeup recommendations. The system analyzes skin tone, hair condition, and user preferences. Based on this input, it suggests products customized to each individual. The app guides users step-by-step through personalized solutions. Brand value improves. User trust grows.

Performance metrics validate the impact. Personalized content, delivered in real time, increases open rates, click-throughs, and purchase intent. Enhanced personalization scores 42% among impactful AI outcomes. Brands now track micro-level behavior to refine macro-level results. Every session contributes to the next strategy cycle. Modern users expect instant response and personal relevance. Real-time content customization meets both. AI systems handle the scale, precision, and adaptation required to keep pace. From product pages to mobile apps, brands now deliver content that listens, responds, and evolves.

AI in Email Marketing, Website Content, & Push Notification

AI transforms how brands communicate across digital channels. Email marketing, website content, and push notifications once followed static templates and fixed schedules. Today, AI turns these channels into dynamic, responsive tools. Messages shift based on behavior. Timing adjusts based on intent. Content matches personal interest. The result is higher engagement, better campaign performance, and smarter resource use.

Email marketing remains one of the most effective direct channels. AI enhances its potential by automating copy generation, subject line testing, and send-time optimization. Systems analyze past open rates, clicks, and engagement trends to guide message structure. Users receive emails that reflect their preferences and timing. The shift leads to increased open rates and reduced subscriptions. Grammarly uses AI to generate tailored weekly performance emails that reflect writing habits, tone improvements, and productivity, increasing user engagement and subscription renewals.

Insider, a customer experience platform from Turkey, uses AI to power its email marketing features. The platform personalizes content and automates testing, while optimizing send times for each segment. As a result, clients improve campaign performance without increasing content volume. Efficiency rises. Relevance deepens. Teams work smarter, not harder.

Customer expectations now demand personalized communication across all digital points. AI meets that demand through faster content creation, smarter targeting, and real-time optimization. Each message becomes part of a connected experience, not a standalone push. Channels work together. Engagement becomes consistent. Brands gain control, scale, and improved outcomes.

Digital Advertising & AI

Digital advertising has evolved from manual bidding and broad targeting to automated, data-led systems. AI now drives the most critical parts of ad planning, placement, and performance optimization. Marketers use AI to segment audiences, generate content, predict user behavior, and improve return on ad spending. As digital noise increases, precision and relevance become essential. AI helps achieve both with greater speed and control. Epic Games uses AI-driven dynamic targeting to customize ads and in-game promotions based on player behavior.

Programmatic Advertising & Real-Time Bidding

Programmatic advertising uses AI to automate the process of buying and placing digital ads. Instead of manual negotiation, systems now decide when and where to serve ads based on live data. Real-time bidding (RTB) plays a key role in this system. It allows advertisers to bid for impressions in real time, based on user profiles, behavior, and contextual signals. The result is faster transactions, higher efficiency, and smarter audience reach.

AI develops the entire programmatic cycle. From audience identification to budget allocation, the system reacts instantly to changes in behavior and intent. Bidding happens in milliseconds. The algorithm evaluates thousands of variables, device, time of day, content type, geography, before placing an ad. That level of responsiveness ensures ad placements stay relevant and cost-effective.

OVO Energy, a UK-based energy provider, introduced a unique approach. The company used an AI-powered programmatic bidding to display ads only when the national grid was powered by greener energy. The system tracked real-time energy data and activated ads during low-emission periods. That initiative helped launch the world's first sustainable digital ad campaign. Performance and ethics are aligned through AI.

Efficiency goes beyond cost. AI also optimizes timing and frequency. Systems cap exposure to avoid ad fatigue. They track engagement and adjust placements based on past behavior. Advertisers use that feedback to refine messaging and reach the user at the right moment. Strategies evolve in real time, and relevance remains high. AI turns programmatic and RTB into a continuous learning system. Each impression adds data. Each click improves the model. Results improve over time. Programmatic no longer means basic automation; it represents precision, speed, and intelligence. In a dynamic advertising space, AI ensures every ad counts.

AI for AD Copy Generation & Visual Optimization

Ad copy and visuals play a direct role in driving attention, clicks, and conversions. Messaging must be clear. Visuals must be appealing. Both must match the audience's expectations. AI now helps marketers create and refine these elements using data, testing, and automation. From headlines to banners, every creative asset benefits from AI-powered improvements in speed, precision, and relevance.

AdCreative.ai, a US-based AI advertising platform, provides tools for generating conversion-focused ad creatives and product photoshoots. The platform uses competitor insights, performance trends, and audience signals to generate personalized visuals and copy. Each ad combines market intelligence with brand identity. That improves differentiation and response.

AI transforms ad copy and visual development into a responsive, data-guided process. Brands communicate with clarity, relevance, and consistency. Every ad becomes a product of insight, not just design. That shift builds stronger connections and delivers better outcomes.

Dynamic Targeting & Retargeting Strategies Using AI

Dynamic targeting uses real-time data to deliver relevant ads to the right users at the right moment. AI makes this possible by analyzing user behavior, segment profiles, and intent signals. Unlike fixed targeting, dynamic targeting updates as user actions change. AI refines audience selection, improves timing, and increases campaign precision. Brands reach users when interest is highest, not just based on static traits.

Geolocation data enhances dynamic targeting. AI tracks movement patterns and footfall data to serve hyper-localized ads. Timing and relevance improve as users receive ads based on nearby stores or their current location. On, a Switzerland-based sportswear company uses AI-powered footfall analysis to monitor user proximity and optimize campaign delivery. Ads adjust in real time, leading to improved efficiency through digital and physical channels.

Retargeting also becomes sharper through AI. Users who viewed a product but didn't buy receive follow-up ads customized to their activity. AI personalizes these messages based on viewed items, time spent, or cart abandonment signals. Messaging stays focused and timely. Dynamic creatives adjust automatically to match the exact product or category. Retargeting efforts feel personal, not repetitive.

Cross-platform coordination adds more value. AI connects user journeys across the web, mobile apps, and social platforms. Retargeting campaigns follow users as they switch devices. Ads remain consistent, yet personalized. The experience becomes seamless. AI keeps track of every step and guides message delivery without duplication, for improved engagement and reduced drop-offs.

AI gives brands control over how, when, and to whom messages appear. Dynamic targeting and retargeting become smarter with each campaign. Results improve without increasing manual work. Personalization reaches new levels of precision. Brands stay present at every key moment in the user journey, without overstepping (Table 8.1).

TABLE 8.1 AI Usage across Brands

Concept	*Brand Example*	*How AI Is Used*	*Benefits*	*Disadvantages/Challenges*
Programmatic advertising & real-time bidding (RTB)	OVO energy (UK)	Used AI-powered bidding to display ads only when the national grid ran on renewable energy.	- Improves cost-efficiency and precision. - Enables sustainability-driven ad timing. - Automates large-scale media buying.	- Risk of algorithm bias or over-automation. - Limited human control over ad placements. - Data privacy concerns.
AI for Ad copy generation & visual optimization	AdCreative.AI (USA)	Uses AI to generate ad copy, visuals, and layouts customized for each platform and audience.	- Faster ad creation cycle. - Improves engagement and visual quality. - Enhances relevance through A/B testing.	- May lack creative originality. - Overreliance on data can lead to generic tone. - Requires careful human review.
Dynamic targeting & retargeting	On (Switzerland-based sportswear brand)	Uses AI-based footfall and location data to target users near stores and retarget online visitors.	- Increases conversion through timely, relevant ads. - Cross-platform personalization. - Reduces ad spend wastage.	- Privacy concerns due to behavioral tracking. - Potential ad fatigue from overexposure. - Requires continuous data updates.

Market Research & AI

Market research drives informed decision-making across product development, communication, and positioning. AI adds speed, depth, and flexibility to this process. Traditional methods relied on surveys, focus groups, and slow data aggregation. AI now processes large datasets instantly, identifies emerging trends, and presents insights through real-time dashboards. Businesses act faster. Strategies align with current signals, not outdated reports. Emirates uses AI tools for market research to analyze real-time data from bookings, trends, social media conversations, pricing, and global events. AI moves market research from static observation to continuous insight.

Trend Prediction Using Machine Learning, Automating Surveys, & Focus Groups

Trend prediction supports businesses in staying ahead of market shifts. ML strengthens this process by analyzing vast datasets to uncover patterns and emerging preferences. Traditional methods like surveys and focus groups once required weeks of manual analysis. AI now enhances these efforts with predictive models that scan behavior, feedback, and performance signals in real time. Businesses act sooner, and decisions become more confident and relevant.

Focus group automation also gains value through AI. Voice and facial recognition tools analyze emotional responses. Systems summarize video content, highlight key feedback, and organize opinions into themes. Participants no longer need to attend in person. Virtual groups operate on a scale. AI compares responses across sessions, locations, and demographics to highlight shared drivers or concerns. Insights become more actionable.

Quantilope, a Germany-based market research platform, uses AI to combine automated surveys with trend prediction. The platform processes feedback across product categories and customer segments. Results appear in real time through visual dashboards. Marketers no longer wait for static reports. They monitor patterns live, test assumptions, and adjust messaging or offerings as needed. The speed of insight becomes a competitive edge.

AI reduces human bias in research. Results rely on behavior and pattern recognition, not opinions or assumptions. Reports focus on what users do, not just what they say. That shift improves the objectivity of market research. Strategies move from belief to proof. ML transforms trend prediction from static analysis to dynamic intelligence. Businesses understand market movement as it happens. Automated tools replace slow processes. Research becomes continuous, scalable, and aligned with current consumer behavior.

AI Tools for Collecting Data

Data collection forms the foundation of market research and campaign planning. Traditional methods involved spreadsheets, surveys, and manual aggregation. AI tools now automate these processes by pulling structured and unstructured data from multiple sources. Businesses access faster, deeper, and more diverse insights. Volume no longer limits action. AI filters and organizes incoming data in real time, enabling teams to focus on strategy instead of sorting.

AI tools monitor activity across web pages, search engines, e-commerce sites, and social platforms. Systems scan reviews, comments, product pages, and engagement rates. They track what users read, click, save, or ignore. Information becomes accessible without waiting for scheduled reports. Patterns emerge from live behavior. Strategy shifts from assumption to observation. Action becomes timely and accurate.

Social media plays a major role in AI-driven data collection. Platforms offer raw, real-time interaction. AI tools analyze posts, hashtags, comments, and shares across regions, languages, and segments. Brands understand what audiences talk about and how sentiment changes. Sprout Social, a US-based platform, uses AI to monitor social engagement and collect insights across multiple channels. Teams gain instant visibility into trends, feedback, and audience preferences.

The services segment led the AI data market in 2024 with a 59% revenue share. Demand grows as more companies look to automate and scale insight generation. AI data collection tools support industries including retail, finance, healthcare, and entertainment. AI transforms data collection into a live, intelligent process. Businesses no longer work with existing data; they operate on current insights, delivered by tools that learn, adapt, and improve continuously.

Sentiment & Competitive Analysis

Sentiment and competitive analysis help businesses understand public opinion and market positioning. AI upgrades these tasks by scanning millions of data points from social media, forums, reviews, and news sources. Text, images, and video content get analyzed for tone, patterns, and emerging signals. Decisions rely on actual feedback and competitor moves, tracked and sorted in real time. Strategy gains clarity, speed, and direction.

Visualization tools help simplify output. Dashboards display sentiment scores, brand mentions, engagement ratios, and share of voice. AI filters what matters most. Teams stay focused on the right signals. Resources get directed to areas of opportunity or concern. AI turns sentiment and competitor tracking into continuous inputs, not one-off reports. Brands listen smarter, act faster, and respond with purpose. Feedback leads to better communication, stronger products, and sharper positioning. Expedia uses an AI tracker and monitors competitor pricing and offers, allowing Expedia to adjust promotions and destination marketing quickly and strategically.

Social Listening & Feedback Mechanisms

Social listening understands what customers say about brands, products, and experiences across digital platforms. AI improves this process by scanning millions of posts, reviews, and conversations in real time. Feedback becomes measurable. Trends surface quickly. Businesses no longer rely only on formal surveys. They access live, unsolicited opinions and behavior cues from actual users. Strategy becomes more responsive and aligns with audience expectations.

AI tools analyze mentions, hashtags, comments, and keywords across platforms like Instagram, X, Reddit, and TikTok. The system identifies tone, volume, frequency, and themes within the conversations. Brands learn what customers like, dislike, or expect, without directly asking. Conversations reveal preferences, complaints, and questions that help refine campaigns, product features, or content formats. Timing matters, and AI delivers insights when they are still actionable.

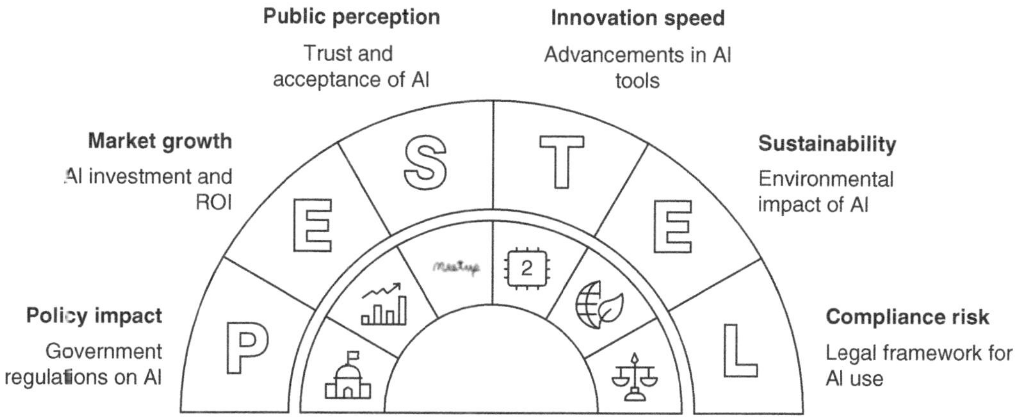

FIGURE 8.3 AI-powered market research analysis.

Social listening goes beyond brand monitoring. AI identifies rising topics, influencers, and micro-trends within a category. Businesses spot emerging opportunities and prepare responses in advance. Platforms also track competitors to benchmark visibility, engagement, and perception. Decision-makers understand their market position through public voice, not internal reports. The feedback loop becomes direct and continuous.

Talk walker, a consumer intelligence platform based in Luxembourg, uses AI for real-time brand tracking and competitor engagement analysis. Their system monitors emotional tones, brand sentiment, and trending topics across regions and categories. Marketers use this information to guide messaging, adjust media strategies, and respond to customer needs faster, which improves visibility and engagement to stay relevant.

AI-powered tools also integrate feedback across reviews, support chats, and chatbot logs. Around 55% of marketing firms use AI chatbots for engagement and data gathering. Every query, complaint, or compliment becomes structured feedback. Brands receive clear data showing what works and what doesn't; this actionable data replaces guesswork.

Feedback systems support campaign testing. AI tracks user reactions to new launches, promotions, or content in real time. Reactions help shape future versions. Campaigns no longer wait for end-phase evaluations. Teams iterate while the campaign is live. Small adjustments based on live input lead to bigger gains in performance and perception.

AI reshapes how brands engage with consumer voices. Social listening and feedback systems no longer operate in the background. They lead real-time adjustments, inform creative choices, and improve product alignment. Brands stay aware, responsive, and connected across every digital touchpoint (Figure 8.3).

CLOSING CASE: ZARA—FAST FASHION

Zara, a global leader in fast fashion, has built its brand on speed, customer insight, and trend responsiveness. The company operates on a unique model, design, production, and distribution move faster than most competitors. Product rotation happens quickly, keeping collections fresh and demand high. AI now strengthens this model by adding precision, data-backed decisions, and deeper customer understanding across marketing touchpoints.

Zara uses AI to analyze consumer behavior in real time. Systems track in-store movements, online browsing patterns, purchase history, and social media engagement. Insights from these sources shape product displays, promotions, and digital content. Marketing messages align with what customers currently explore, not what brands assume. Relevance increases. Inventory responds to demand, not just forecasting models.

AI supports Zara in personalizing communication across channels. Emails, website banners, and app notifications reflect individual browsing and buying habits. AI selects content based on user history and product interest. Messaging changes dynamically. Customers receive fashion suggestions that reflect their style and timing. Marketing becomes a dialogue, not just a broadcast.

Trend detection also plays a key role. AI tools scan global fashion content, blogs, posts, and visuals, to identify emerging styles. Zara uses this data to align its product development and marketing messages. Speed remains an advantage, but now it is supported by predictive analysis. Decisions move faster with fewer errors. Campaigns stay in sync with what customers want today.

AI enhances Zara's pricing and promotion strategies. Algorithms evaluate pricing sensitivity, competitor moves, and inventory levels. Discounts appear when most effective, not just when stock remains. Zara manages full-price sales more effectively. Profit margins stay protected while customer satisfaction improves through timely offers and new arrivals.

Zara applies AI to visual merchandising as well. Store layouts adjust based on foot traffic and purchase data. Product placement changes to improve flow and conversion. Window displays reflect top-performing items in each location. AI supports marketing inside the store, not just outside it. Every element reinforces brand appeal.

Campaign performance tracking also improves with AI. Zara monitors clicks, engagement, and conversion in real time. The system evaluates which creative assets perform best. Future campaigns build on proven ideas. Poor results get flagged early. Adjustments happen mid-cycle. Campaigns no longer run on instinct; they follow evidence.

In the fast-paced fashion sector, delays reduce relevance. Zara uses AI to reduce those delays. Marketing aligns with product, customer behavior, and channel performance. Every action connects with a goal. Every signal feeds the system. Marketing evolves continuously. AI turns Zara's speed into strategy, not just execution.

Zara's success with AI highlights the value of real-time insight, adaptive messaging, and predictive planning. The brand remains responsive without losing control. Marketing becomes faster, smarter, and more aligned with customer behavior. That approach supports Zara's position as a fast fashion leader in a data-driven world.

Discussion Questions

1. In what ways has AI reshaped traditional marketing strategy frameworks?
2. Can AI ever replace human intuition in strategic marketing decisions?
3. How does AI strengthen or challenge traditional models like Porter's Five Forces and STP?
4. How do ethical considerations arise when using AI for customer targeting and personalization?

Assignment Questions

1 Using the Amazon case from the chapter, identify and explain the specific ways it contributes to customer engagement and retention.
2 Select any one traditional marketing model. Redesign it for an AI-driven business environment, explaining each change.
3 Compare the use of AI in marketing strategy between Amazon and Zara. What key similarities and differences can be observed in their AI integration approaches?
4 Propose an AI-based marketing strategy for a new brand. Include segmentation, targeting, content personalization, and advertising components supported by AI tools.

MINI CASE: STARBUCKS

Starbucks has reimagined the interaction with its customers and employed AI throughout the marketing plan. Its millions of transactions each day around the globe push the brand to utilize its data in its app, loyalty program, and in the store to provide highly personalized experiences. The core of this strategy is the Deep Brew, the AI-driven platform of Starbucks, which examines the behavior of customers, their history of purchases, and the context. It suggests tailor-made drinks, deals, and discounts on the spot. Probably, a customer who frequently orders cold brews might get a timely notification about a new flavor on summer afternoons, which will raise the chances of buying it. AI is also used in operational and strategic planning. Predictive analytics can predict the demand for products and optimize inventory within the outlets. This guarantees efficiency in resources and minimizes wastage, as well as enlightens decisions concerning the menu design and regional tastes in the long run.

A in digital marketing is the force behind automated and dynamic advertising. Email, mobile, and social media campaigns also vary the content and timing of their activity based on the level of individual engagement. Sentiment analysis is also used by Starbucks in the process of tracking online chats, reviews, and feedback so that the brand can adjust its message to keep customers loyal. The combination of AI-driven insights and human creativity will allow Starbucks to provide experiences that seem personalized but remain the same across all the channels. This is the automation and authenticity well balanced so that the brand remains on top of the highly competitive food and beverage industry.

HBR Case Links:

- https://hbsp.harvard.edu/product/H08NRD-PDF-ENG?itemFindingMethod=search
- https://hbsp.harvard.edu/product/BEP741-PDF-ENG?itemFindingMethod=search
- https://hbsp.harvard.edu/product/H08ULX-PDF-ENG?itemFindingMethod=search

Application of Concepts

Concept (Kotler Link)	*Application in Practice*	*In-Class Activity*
AI in strategic planning (Long-term & Short-term)	AI tools forecast demand, track performance, and adjust campaigns in real time for both quick wins and long-term positioning.	**Strategy Map**: Teams design a short-term and long-term plan for a mock brand using AI dashboards (metrics, goals, and adaptations).
Porter's five forces with AI	AI monitors competitors, substitutes, and market trends dynamically—turning static analysis into real-time intelligence.	**Live Scan**: Students analyze a brand using AI data sources (e.g., social trends, pricing, or reviews) to update each of Porter's five forces.
STP & Personalization	AI segments micro-audiences, predicts intent, and tailors offers/content to each segment automatically.	**Persona Match**: Teams receive 5 AI-generated customer profiles and craft unique positioning lines or ad messages for each.
AI-driven content & advertising	Generative AI creates ad copies, visuals, and email content; programmatic tools auto-bid and optimize ad spend.	**Ad Lab**: Pairs use ChatGPT or any AI tool to generate ad copy variations, vote for the "most likely to convert," and justify the choice.
Market research & insights with AI	AI automates surveys, sentiment analysis, and social listening for faster and deeper consumer insights.	**Trend Tracker**: Each group uses recent social data or simulated feedback to identify one "emerging trend" and present how a brand should respond.

Key Terms

- Artificial intelligence (AI)
- Marketing strategy
- Strategic planning
- Porter's five forces
- Segmentation, targeting, and positioning (STP)
- Personalization
- Generative AI
- Programmatic advertising
- Real-time bidding (RTB)
- Dynamic targeting & retargeting
- Predictive analytics
- Market research automation
- Sentiment analysis
- Social listening
- Customer experience optimization

Bibliography

Beyari, H., & Hashem, T. (2024). The role of artificial intelligence in personalizing social media marketing strategies. *Frontiers in Artificial Intelligence*, *7*, 12109579. https://pmc.ncbi.nlm.nih.gov/articles/PMC12109579/

Forbes Technology Council. (2024, March 21). How AI is transforming the marketing industry. *Forbes*. https://www.forbes.com/councils/forbestechcouncil/2024/03/21/how-ai-is-transforming-the-marketing-industry/

Jarraya, B., & Foroudi, P. (2024). Artificial intelligence in marketing: Two decades review. *Vision: The Journal of Business Perspective*, *28*(3), 1–12. https://doi.org/10.1177/09711023241272308

Mustak, M., Kaartemo, V., & Jaakkola, E. (2025). Impact of artificial intelligence on branding: A bibliometric review and future research agenda. *Humanities and Social Sciences Communications*, *12*, 654. https://doi.org/10.1057/s41599-025-04488-6

Nadkarni, S., & Prügl, R. (2024). Artificial intelligence in marketing: Exploring current and future trends. *Cogent Business & Management*, *11*(1), 2348728. https://doi.org/10.1080/23311975.2024.2348728

Rust, R. T., & Huang, M.-H. (2024). Generative AI in marketing: Promises, perils, and public policy. *Journal of Current Issues & Research in Advertising*, *45*(2), 165–182. https://doi.org/10.1177/07439156241286499

de Ruyter, K., Keeling, D. I., & Ngo, L. V. (2024). AI-powered marketing: What, where, and how? *Information Systems Frontiers*, *26*(2), 389–401. https://doi.org/10.1016/j.ijinfomgt.2024.102783

Sheth, J. (2024). The use of artificial intelligence in marketing strategies: Automation, personalization, and forecasting. *Journal of Marketing Analytics*, *12*(3), 220–234. https://www.researchgate.net/publication/380423097

Wamba-Taguimdje, S. F., Fosso Wamba, S., Kala Kamdjoug, J. R., & Tchatchouang Wanko, C. (2020). Artificial intelligence in marketing: A systematic review. *Journal of Business Research*, *116*, 316–335. https://doi.org/10.1016/j.jbusres.2020.05.001

Wirtz, J., Zeithaml, V. A., & Goh, C. (2024). Artificial intelligence in marketing, consumer research, and psychology: A systematic review. *Psychology & Marketing*, *41*(5), 921–938. https://doi.org/10.1002/mar.21619

9

AI IN B2B, SERVICES AND RETAIL

Learning Objectives

1. Explain how AI transforms B2B, services, and retail marketing strategies.
2. Analyze the role of AI in enhancing personalization, automation, and predictive decision-making across sectors.
3. Evaluate ethical and privacy challenges associated with AI adoption in B2B, services, and retail contexts.
4. Apply AI-driven frameworks to improve operational efficiency, lead generation, and customer engagement.

OPENING CASE: PEPSICO

PepsiCo has remained unwavering in AI as regards retail business with an aim of enhancing efficiency, consumer understanding, and easier decision-making. The company does not merely experiment with new technologies, but uses AI on an endeavor whose outcomes are quantifiable. It can be inventory management optimization, predictive analytics, or both, but PepsiCo relies on AI and knows that it can be used to seal any loopholes that can be found in the supply chain and its retail strategy in general. Consequently, the time taken to respond to the market changes is minimized, and the execution becomes more acute at the retail level.

The company has officially introduced Pepviz, an AI-based data intelligence platform, which is based on AI models and analytics. Pepviz is a combination of internal and external retail data, producing knowledge with ample lead time of what products are performing, how consumers are shopping, and demand. PepsiCo pursues its analytics in real time so that it is able to notice trends early enough to make amends to retail approaches across a unit of stores. This is a superior analytics solution that enhances merchandising, in sales promotions and stock-out prevention, and provides retailers with more applicable recommendations, and the company, in turn, with superior retailer relationships.

DOI: 10.4324/9781003501862-9

Computer Vision is another product of the AI of PepsiCo. The retail industry can also apply AI-driven shelf monitoring sensors that assist the company in scanning the thousands of retail displays to identify efficiencies. These shelf products systematically scan the planograms or ascertain shelf availability/capacity, and a host of other questions of consumer behavior, such as the existence of competition. Field reps do not need to check themselves any longer. The AI observation can be received by them through mobile applications, which serve to guide them faster and more precisely. The company will have better visibility into the conditions in the store without wasting time.

PepsiCo can also use artificial intelligence in promotion. Algorithms can determine both the campaign that is performing and that which is not performing, including its location, consumer category, and its past performance. The AI suggestions will allow PepsiCo to create more deliberate retail campaigns. In the market where products are performing well, AI models can suggest raising their inventories, as well as in the market where they are underperforming, they can recommend changing strategies or changing positions. The goal is quite simple: sell every retailing channel what it needs, no more, no less.

Retail business is a dynamic and fast-moving atmosphere where time, accuracy, and flexibility count. PepsiCo does not apply AI to make the outputs faster, but to make them more fruitful. Machine learning portrays customer preferences that were not possible using manual output. Through this intelligence, the company is able to stock the appropriate selection on shelves in anticipation of little wastage, and at a competitive price level. It is data-related and fast change; to act smart and respond quickly.

The PepsiCo experience with AI is in a dynamic direction between the reactive retail operations and the proactive retail planning. The company does not wait to have a monthly report in order to modify media strategies. The change of behaviors or the most significant actions can be based on real-time inputs to change them within days or even hours. The kind of agility is very useful in commodified high-speed industries. The agility also further compares with collaborating with the retail partners; partners are more inclined to depend on PepsiCo's data-driven input.

Retailers such as PepsiCo do not merely use AI as a trend, but they need it as a business need. The consumers demand speed, accuracy, and knowledgeable personal experiences. The retailers demand high performance, as well as mutual knowledge brought about by collaboration. All these expectations are united as a result of smarter applications, more well-informed decision making, and creating the fastest paths to better, all via AI. The emphasis on consciously applying AI in PepsiCo can bring more success in retail performance and the addition of value to every chain in the retail network.

Introduction

Artificial intelligence (AI) is no longer limited to back-end systems or research labs. Businesses across industries now treat AI as a practical tool for solving problems, driving performance, and improving engagement. The shift is clear in sectors like B2B, services, and retail, where companies use AI not just for automation but also for better decisions, faster response times, and sharper insights. The focus is moving from experimentation to structured implementation. Siemens uses AI in its industrial operations to improve predictive maintenance, enhance production efficiency, and support smarter decision-making across global manufacturing systems.

Retail leads the way in visible adoption. Around 87% of retailers already use AI in at least one area of their operations. From checkout optimization to product recommendations, AI touches customer journeys at multiple points. Shoppers expect brands to know their preferences and respond instantly. About 81% of customers now prefer personalized experiences, and companies that fail to deliver risk falling behind. The demand for relevance and speed continues to grow.

B2B and service-based industries follow a slightly different path. Adoption is slower but steadily gaining ground. Only 21% of commercial leaders report full-scale AI deployment across their business, while 22% are still in the pilot phase. However, momentum is building. AI allows B2B players to process complex buying behavior, forecast demand, and personalize outreach at scale. AI helps shift away from bulk messaging toward smarter, need-based engagement. HubSpot uses AI in its customer relationship management (CRM) and marketing automation.

Overview of AI's Role across B2B, Services, & Retail

AI has different roles across B2B, services, and retail, depending on the nature of customer interaction, decision cycles, and operational needs. Despite these variations, the main purpose remains the same: using data and algorithms to simplify decisions, improve speed, and increase relevance. AI is no longer confined to back-office support. It now directly influences how businesses attract, engage, and retain customers in a competitive market.

In the B2B space, AI focuses on lead generation, predictive scoring, and workflow automation. Long sales cycles and complex decision-making make B2B a natural fit for AI tools that handle large volumes of information. AI helps businesses identify the right prospects, prioritize leads, and personalize communication. Platforms like B2B Rocket in the United States show this in action. The company offers AI agents that automate outreach, score leads, and set workflows based on specific business goals.

AI in retail works more on customer-facing activities. Personalization, inventory management, pricing, and in-store experience form the important focus areas. Around 87% of retailers have adopted AI in some form. Retailers use AI to analyze purchase history, browsing behavior, and local trends. Based on these insights, they adjust product placement, send personalized offers, and optimize stock. Customers now expect brands to know what they want, even before they ask. Ocado, a UK-based grocery retailer using AI and robotics for demand forecasting and warehouse operations.

As AI tools become more accessible, the gap between early adopters and late movers will widen. Companies already using AI across functions gain a sharper edge. They respond faster, market better, and retain more customers. B2B, services, and retail each show how AI can adapt to unique needs while delivering measurable impact. Salesforce enables a unified B2B customer experience through connected CRM and real-time service tools.

Shifts in Customer Expectations & Digital Capabilities

Customer expectations have changed sharply in recent years. Traditional service models no longer meet the demand for speed, personalization, and consistency. Buyers across B2B,

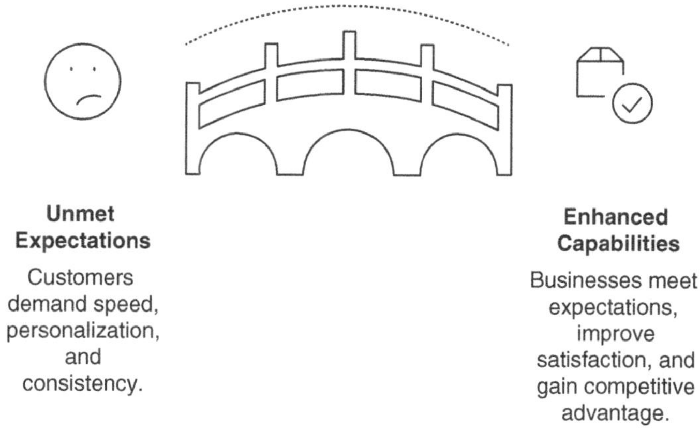

FIGURE 9.1 AI-adoption bridging the gap between customer expectations and business capabilities.

services, and retail now expect seamless experiences, regardless of channel or industry. Companies that fail to adapt risk losing relevance. The shift places pressure on organizations to match these expectations through stronger digital capabilities and faster technology adoption.

Customers also expect a consistent tone and approach across all channels. AI supports this by standardizing language, capturing important details, and learning from previous conversations. Businesses now use AI to sync responses across email, chat, social media, and web portals. Every interaction leaves behind data. AI turns that data into insights, which then guide the next move.

Digital tools evolve quickly, but expectations evolve faster. Businesses must track both. AI enables that alignment. Firms that understand how to apply AI to meet customer needs stay ahead. Those that lag in digital readiness fall behind, even if their main offering remains strong. Customer satisfaction depends less on intent and more on experience, something AI helps refine and scale. UPI uses AI route optimization to ensure faster, more reliable deliveries, directly improving customer satisfaction (Figure 9.1).

AI in B2B

AI has taken on a primary role in reshaping B2B operations. Sales cycles in B2B often run long, involve multiple stakeholders, and require high levels of precision. AI addresses these challenges with smart automation, predictive insights, and content generation at scale. Businesses use AI to save time, reduce guesswork, and increase lead quality, without losing the human touch where it matters most.

Content creation now runs faster and more targeted. Around 85% of B2B marketers report using AI-driven content strategies in 2024. AI tools generate blogs, emails, product briefs, and presentations, customized to different buyer personas. By 2025, B2B teams across industries have made AI a standard tool to boost content output and maintain consistency. The goal remains simple: say the right thing, at the right time, to the right audience.

AI transforms lead generation through smarter filters and deeper data analysis. Tools like Sales Mind AI and Salesforce's Einstein scan customer profiles, past interactions, and behavior patterns to identify high-potential leads. AI then ranks these leads by intent, urgency, and fit. Sales teams no longer waste time chasing cold prospects. They focus on qualified leads with higher chances of conversion.

AI in B2B doesn't just streamline work. It improves decision-making and increases Return on Investment (ROI) across the funnel. From prospecting to pitch, businesses gain more control and clarity. As competition grows and buyer expectations rise, AI gives B2B firms the tools to move faster, plan better, and connect smarter. Hewlett Packard Enterprise (HPE) uses AI co-pilot for customer onboarding and support, showing how AI moves beyond automation into decision-making.

Characteristics of B2B Marketing

The pace of B2B marketing is different than marketer-to-consumer marketing. Where the B2B buying process is slow, involves systems of indecision, and is driven largely by logic because of the business case, consumers are looking for value, trust, and forward engagement and not the glitz and glamour. AI can help with these expectations through accuracy, personalization, and automation throughout the marketing journey. International Business Machines (IBM) uses AI in sales enablement, such as predicting which customers are upsell candidates and automating outreach via their stack.

Another compelling aspect of B2B marketing is the multi-channel engagement. There are multiple emails, websites, webinars, etc., and all point to a social site, where the buyer will get knowledgeable prior to whatever action they will take next. IBM's Watson at Work campaign combines webinars, email nurturing, white papers, social media thought leadership, and dedicated microsites to guide enterprise buyers through every stage of their decision journey.

Considering a B2B business with complexity and diversity, the scale of the business creates another level of complexity. In a global sense, there also may be differentiated outreach simply due to the language, culture, and time zone of the company you're reaching out to. Transfer Go, a UK-based company, is currently employing AI-powered virtual agents to provide B2B financial customer support in 11 languages! Providing customer support in another language reduces friction/pain points, improves efficiency, and allows for seamless global monetization without the complications of the language.

AI Applications in B2B

The AI has created opportunities in the new B2B, particularly in the Marketing, Sales, and Support functions. Now, companies do not just save money through the use of AI; they also strive to give better results to the journey at each touch point. Starting with lead capture and opportunity close to relationship management, the AI will offer the form, speed, and volume of work to make sure the intricacy of workflow can be managed in the immediate future. The decision makers are seeking AI-based bundled tools to be included in every contemporary B2B toolkit.

The concept of lead generation has become more precise due to the implementation of AI-powered insights. Systems like Sales Mind AI look at the intent signal, online activity, and firmographic data tags of a user and provide the sellers with the best lead types of the company. The other way AI is useful is in improving organizational data analysis capabilities that can be applied to an infinite number of processes. As an example, predictive analytics models may evaluate the data of customers during a variety of promotional actions and channels to propose improvements in the customer experience and the best subsequent steps. B2B companies take advantage of this practice by relying on intelligence to improve their go-to-market strategy over time; AI has the radar that is able to quickly identify patterns that the human eye does not recognize with the help of manual means or traditional tracking methods. These involve the detection of churn, possible upselling, and the accounts that have been silent. The organizational response time and participation in the behaviors of customers are more focused and can target the strategic interactions.

AI is indeed changing and making B2B open value at quantifiable scales. Organizations can access more personalization, smarter automation, and every application alters the manner in which businesses conduct operations and communicate about commencing engagements to the conclusion of the relationship. Businesses that adopt AI technology now will operate faster, get closer, and exploit the value of every interaction they have.

Benefits of AI in B2B

AI generates measurable value for B2B by improving productivity, targeting, and relieving administrative headaches. Many businesses still have longer cycles, complex workflows, and high-dollar targets, and are having difficulty automating topics around decision-making and increasing the level of engagement. In this, AI is helping businesses make the leap. Is this only cost-reducing? No, there are benefits beyond cost savings. AI is being used to improve speed, accuracy, and engagement at every point of interaction along the buyer journey.

Speed is, overall, perhaps the biggest benefit of AI for marketing and sales teams. AI will replace the same work each day, take the place of every automated email, lead scoring, calendar fills, remind about tasks, and complete follow-ups. AI tools can repo lead activity and alert the team when action is taken, which lessens time spent on manual activities, while freeing human teams to think more strategically. It becomes productive without adding to head count; AI fills the void that slows down sales and marketing performance.

Sales processes benefit from AI by becoming more organized and timely. Predictive models help teams understand when a lead is ready to move forward. Recommendations show what content to send, when to follow up, and how to close faster. Automation reduces human error and ensures consistency. Every stage becomes more connected and informed.

Customer service improves with AI-powered support systems. Tools manage tickets, answer queries, and offer self-help options. Ushur, a US-based cloud automation platform, automates both backend workflows and conversational interfaces for enterprise clients. Their system handles inquiries, updates records, and sends alerts with minimal human input. Clients experience faster service, and companies cut service delays.

Accuracy is also another critical consideration. AI definitely eliminates mistakes in terms of information and content, pricing, prediction, and control of customer information. Predictive tools remove the issues of mismatch between the problems of timing or opportunity. There is timeliness in the information and uniformity in the responses. Clean data gives greater inputs and hence output and decision-making. The importance of AI in transforming the B2B performance is constantly being shown. The benefits may be achieved at each step of the funnel, from the first click to the final contract. Dell Technologies uses AI for demand forecasting, marketing copy optimization, and decision-making across its B2B operations.

Ethics in B2B

B2B AI has ethics in the form of checklists, compliance assessments, and compliance frameworks. Compliance, however, is not the end. Companies have to be devoted to the principles of fairness, transparency, and accountability in all their activities with AI. The buyers have expected companies that are involved in any type of automation to act ethically in terms of data, automated interactions, and decisions that are made. With AI technologies penetrating every aspect of B2B operations, they are going to be as ethical as performance. Engaging in responsible AI is no longer a bonus; it is a driving force for trust and long-term relationships with clients. Deloitte have AI Risk management framework to ensure their AI systems.

At the core of ethical challenges lies data. Many AI systems are fed information about customers and firmographics. Therefore, from a business perspective, data collection, processing, and usage should be done transparently and ethically. Disclosure allows customers to feel safe, thus allowing companies to build trust. When companies violate those standards, they run the risk of classification, risk liability, and loss of reputation. Ethics creates boundaries and helps a company avoid purposeful or unintentional abuse of data.

A second ethical challenge is bias. If an algorithm is trained on thematically incorrect or insufficient datasets, the model will create a misconception that ends up biasing a population or group. In B2B, this can be very damaging to selling in, supporting customers, hiring tools, lead scoring, customer engagement tools, etc. Ethically, companies should perform audits on a routine basis, maintain balanced datasets, provide quota limits to review samples in the data collection phase, and have a pathway for model reviews and validations. Businesses must identify and locate hidden biases before it perpetuates.

One company from India, Yellow Messenger, illustrates how ethics and AI coexist. They provide an enterprise, conversational platform where they build ethics into the platform as part of the solution. Clients implement the platform for customer engagement, and ethical AI allows them to do it transparently and with privacy and automation respect. This way, the company is reflecting the demand in the industry for ethical AI systems that do not compromise on performance.

AI in Service Marketing

The rise of AI has blurred the lines in Service Marketing. Companies are now leveraging AI not only to manage customer contact but also to improve service quality, enhance employee productivity, and elevate customer experience. AI enables service providers to respond faster, solve customers' issues more accurately, and provide consistent service across all channels. As service delivery continues to evolve and grow in adoption, AI will become the backbone of the service, instead of being considered as an option for service delivery. Comcast uses large language models to assist its service agents in real-time, improving accuracy and consistency across multiple channels.

When it comes to Field service operations, they have already established their operations, service delivery, client interaction, and oftentimes even workforce, both reliant on AI to manage, track, and optimize workflows. Take note that approximately 80% of the high-performing field service companies are already reliant on AI to manage their work tasks and to improve their efficiency. Today's AI tools manage many aspects of service jobs;

scheduling the jobs, forecasting service issues, and even managing technicians through step-by-step procedures. AI will assist with predictive analytics to minimize any downtime, and service processes are automated to execute the service at speed.

AI improves personalization by analyzing data at scale. Over 60% of service agents say they could improve their performance with better access to data. AI provides those insights. Agents receive real-time suggestions based on customer history, preferences, and sentiment. Faster answers and smarter engagement follow. Customer feedback gets analyzed instantly, helping managers adjust service strategies on the go.

Nature of Service Marketing

Service marketing focuses on delivering experiences, not just transactions. Unlike physical goods, services are intangible, variable, and time-bound. Customers judge value through delivery, interaction quality, and outcome. Businesses must manage expectations, maintain consistency, and personalize engagement across each touchpoint. AI now has an important role in helping service providers meet these demands with more precision and less delay. H&R Block, a tax consulting company, is an AI-powered tax filing assistance that provides personalized guidance, reduces human error, and speeds up the experience.

In service marketing, trust and responsiveness are crucial for customer satisfaction. Customers evaluate services by evaluating how they feel before, during, and at the conclusion of the service experience. Rapid response, the relevance of suggestions on short notice, and the success of resolving a problem will shape whether the customer is satisfied. With AI technologies, we can achieve a level of speed and responsiveness through communication and rapid response in any context that was not previously possible. This applies to everything from booking a service to providing feedback, and using AI-enabled tools will help improve or enhance each part of the journey.

Wander log, a U.S.-based travel planning app, highlights this model well. The company uses Chat GPT-powered AI to serve as a virtual travel planner. Users receive customized itineraries, activity ideas, and travel tips based on preferences. The AI assistant organizes the journey while adjusting suggestions with each input. The service becomes dynamic, personal, and efficient, qualities primary to modern service marketing.

Process of AI in Service Marketing

AI operates within service marketing through a defined and repeatable process. Each stage, data collection, analysis, automation, and feedback, supports better delivery, stronger personalization, and higher efficiency. Businesses align AI systems with service goals to guide interactions, optimize workflows, and reduce manual load. The process ensures customer experiences remain seamless, data-driven, and scalable, regardless of service type or industry. KLM Royal Dutch Airlines collects data via AI and helps in automating flight info through a chatbot.

Data collection forms the first step in the AI cycle. Service interactions produce vast amounts of structured and unstructured data. AI tools gather this through chats, emails, calls, surveys, and platform activity. Every click, keyword, and rating adds to the data pool. Clean and relevant inputs allow AI to produce useful outputs, guiding next steps in real time and improving decision accuracy.

The second stage involves analysis and pattern recognition. AI processes large datasets using natural language processing, sentiment analysis, and machine learning (ML) models. These systems detect trends, uncover service gaps, and recognize common queries. By turning raw data into insights, AI helps service managers make quick adjustments. Patterns also help predict what customers might need next based on past behaviors.

Integration also plays an important role. AI systems need to connect with CRM applications, helpdesk applications, and communications apps. A cohesive system allows for consistent and unbroken data flow and synchronized actions. AI then provides consistent service across various touchpoints, including email, chat, mobile apps, and social channels. Customer sastra clients move from channel to channel without the embarrassment of providing duplicate or redundant information.

AI Applications in Service Marketing

Automation has been surpassed by the use of AI in service marketing. The AI applications utilized by organizations are employed to handle customer engagement, to streamline the service provision speed, to tailor customer engagement, and to provide cost benefits. AI tools have the ability to monitor the entire customer experience, such as awareness, engagement, feedback, and retention. AI tools are able to calculate all the data, predict customer needs, and suggest a response within a short period of time. This is still aimed at delivering a superior, low-friction service that is consistent.

Conversational AI is clearly the most relevant of the service marketing trends embracing AI tools. Organizations are using chatbots, voice assistants, and virtual agents to generate follow-up responses to a high volume of customer requests and questions. By capturing customer inquiries and requests through chatbots, customers can receive immediate responses, experience shorter wait times before being connected to a live agent (if needed), and have complex queries quickly identified and routed to the appropriate managed agent. In banking, Kasis to has developed KAI, a conversational AI platform for use by financial services organizations. KAI is a conversational AI application with preconfigured intents for common banking inquiries and is designed to incorporate ML in its capability to allow the platform to continuously improve with each interaction.

Recommendation systems enhance the relevance of services to the customer. They use AI to evaluate the customer's history, preferences, and interaction timing to make recommendations of highly correlated products, services, and even content. For example, travel apps like MakeMyTrip, Trip it recommend itineraries, telecoms recommend certain plans, and healthcare providers recommend consultations. The power of AI is that it makes the recommendation relative to that individual and to that scenario. Relevant recommendations yield higher engagement. Customers will spend more time with such organizations, they will convert more quickly to make purchases, and will retain their loyalty over long periods.

Benefits of AI in Service Marketing

AI has already contributed substantial value to service marketing, primarily through customer engagement advancements, speedier service processes, and lower costs of service. Organizations are utilizing AI to automate service tasks while ensuring quality.

This escalation allows teams to concentrate on faster, more customized customer experience, as they have more time to staff the customer's impressions with AI through real-time data, and AI systems generate insights to make better decisions. Overall, customer expectations for speed and reliability in front-end experiences have enabled population capacity at lower costs for delivery with AI experiences. Zendesk is a customer support SaaS which has AI-driven sentiment detection and provides support across the world.

The new efficiencies represented the largest value creation for productivity. AI is helping customers/agents control and manage repetitive service-related tasks (e.g., respond to customers' questions, assign service requests to routing tickets, and update records). Automated processes save agents and allow them to focus on unique or complex service-related issues. Workflows become more constrained. More customer capacity may be assigned without hiring more service and support representatives. Approximately 95% of decision makers at AI-enabled organizations report improved time and cost efficiencies in delivering ongoing service operations.

Response quality also improves. AI tools apply natural language processing to understand customer intent and tone. In benta, a US-based company, offers conversational AI that uses this technology to improve customer engagement. The system delivers accurate, on-brand responses with minimal delay. Customers feel heard, and agents avoid repetitive typing. Communication becomes more accurate and professional.

AI enhances service consistency. Businesses often struggle with varying service quality across teams or shifts. AI-driven systems follow structured logic, predefined language, and verified content. Customers receive the same level of support, regardless of timing or agent experience. This reduces complaints and builds brand trust over time.

AI also improves accessibility. Customers reach support across channels, web, mobile, social, or voice, without a learning curve. Smart systems recognize users, pull up data, and continue conversations across devices. Every customer receives equal support, regardless of location or platform. This widens the reach and appeal of service offerings. Service marketing grows stronger with AI. The benefits compound over time, better responses, sharper insights, and leaner operations.

Privacy & Ethics in Service Marketing

When companies use the personal data of customers in their marketing, which is essentially what any AI-enabled system is doing, to maintain protection of customer rights and public understanding of AI use, we have to respect the three standards expected: ethical consent, ethical transparency, and ethical use. Ethics must be foundational to all aspects of how an organization collects, processes, stores, and uses customer data in service interactions.

AI marketing is data-driven, and in order to utilize AI as a basis for AI-serviced marketing, data collection methods must be utilized. AI systems are examining customer preferences, querying, behavior, and feedback, but if there aren't sufficient protections against misuse and overreach, not to mention what some ethical observers would classify as abuse, we have to establish ethical practices. Businesses must inform users when collecting data and why; consent should always be voluntarily given and complete. When customers would not consent if they feel they are being tricked/phished, being tracked (cryptic consent), or a policy that is too vague. The ethical aspect of service marketing begins when you generate value through transparent communication.

Data protection is a vital aspect of ethics. AI companies need to put in place appropriate security measures to protect data from misuse and breaches, including encryption, restricted access to certain data, and regular audits. Customers assume their data is protected during transference outside their control and by consent during collection. While it may have been good marketing and purpose for the brand, violating this customer expectation will harm the company's brand and perception of the AI experience, which will likely have legal ramifications. Compliance with external standard requirements, such as state, national, and global legislation, respectively, such as general data protection regulation (GDPR) and California Consumer Privacy Act (CCPA), ensures that the company is operating ethically from a data collection perspective.

Omilia, a Cyprus-based AI company, is proactively addressing such issues by launching privacy-first virtual assistants. The company designs customer care tools that use ML. These products are designed to incorporate security, privacy, and ethical considerations, according to the company's founders. The company's systems comply with privacy obligations and provide information to users, as and when requested. Ethical issues influence product design, as well as day-to-day operations (Table 9.1).

TABLE 9.1 AI Application in Service Marketing

Brand/Company	*AI Application in Service Marketing*	*Advantages*	*Disadvantages/ Limitations*
Wanderlog (U.S.)	Uses ChatGPT-powered AI as a virtual travel planner, creating personalized itineraries, recommendations, and real-time travel guidance.	- Delivers highly personalized experiences. - Enhances user engagement and satisfaction through co-created travel plans. - Adapts suggestions dynamically to user inputs.	- Over-reliance on AI can reduce human interaction. - Quality depends on data accuracy and user inputs.
Kasisto (U.S.)	Developed KAI, a conversational AI for banking that handles queries, provides financial advice, and learns from interactions.	- Provides 24/7 customer support with instant responses. - Improves operational efficiency and reduces costs. - Learns continuously to improve response accuracy.	- Data privacy and compliance challenges in financial contexts. - May lack emotional understanding of sensitive customer issues.

(*Continued*)

TABLE 9.1 (Continued)

Brand/Company	*AI Application in Service Marketing*	*Advantages*	*Disadvantages/ Limitations*
Ada (Canada)	Offers AI-powered chatbots for customer service automation and workflow management across multiple sectors.	- Reduces response time and increases agent productivity. - Ensures scalable, consistent service quality. - Frees human agents for complex cases.	- Struggles with ambiguous or emotional queries. - Risk of impersonal communication reducing empathy.
Omilia (Cyprus)	Designs privacy-first AI virtual assistants emphasizing security, ethical data use, and compliance with privacy laws.	- Builds user trust through ethical AI design and transparency. - Ensures data protection and consent-based interaction. - Aligns with GDPR and global privacy standards.	- Limited personalization due to strict privacy controls. - Higher cost and complexity of implementation.

AI in Retail

Recently, retail was also one of the three leading businesses according to the rate of AI adoption. AI helps retailers: (1) forecast demand, (2) control inventory, (3) develop applicable offers, and (4) automate customer interactions. Notably, AI has ceased to be an assistant; it is independently making decisions on behalf of businesses where products are sold both through the online and brick-and-mortar environments. The retailers are adopting AI to minimize congestion in the supply chains, to improve the shopper experience, and compete in a dynamic environment. JD.com, a Chinese company, operates fully automated AI retail stores and uses AI to manage real-time inventory and logistics performance.

The uptake rates are impressive. Approximately 87% of retailers have adopted AI in at least some fashion in their company. Some have adopted AI in 1–2 use cases, and others have adopted 3–5 use cases, ranging from inventory optimization to personalized promotions. Roughly 60% of retailers have plans to add AI investments in the near term with the intention to broaden coverage and improve utilization. Retail executives now view AI as a strategic asset. By 2025, around 80% of them expect to have adopted automation across important functions. Market forecasts back this momentum. The AI in the retail market, valued at $7.14 billion in 2023, is expected to grow to $85.07 billion by 2032. That growth confirms AI's role in shaping how retailers serve, sell, and scale.

Changing Dynamics in Retail

The retail sectors are very dynamic, and they have been evolving quickly in reaction to customer behavior, digital expansion, and escalating consumer demands. The majority of old models fail to reflect the rate or the extent of polarization that is observed through the eyes of the contemporary consumer. The consumers are demanding to have an interchannel efficient experience, quicker speed of the retailer services, and personalized offers. It is natural that retailers are taking on AI to enable them adapt to these changes in more effective, quicker, and superior ways to establish themselves in a competitive market that is becoming more and more crowded. Morrisons, a UK-based company, uses AI-powered technology and real-time order optimization to ensure faster grocery delivery across online and in-store.

Digital transformation in retail has moved beyond e-commerce. Retailers are seeking to blend digital and physical experiences, providing retailers with the ability to provide a single shopping journey for the consumer. AI can process real-time insights, track behavior, and perform predictive analytics for all the related processes of managing the physical environment and the store experience at the same time! Retailers are not "guessing" about what their customers want anymore. They are powered by advanced, sometimes automated, data analysis that drives customer behavior. AI optimizes decision-making in relation to pricing, stock and replenishment, store layout, and messaging. War by Parker in the U.S. reflects this shift clearly. The company uses an AI-powered frame recommendation system that considers face shape, preferences, and purchase history. It also applies augmented reality (AR)-based virtual try-on features, allowing users to test frames digitally. These tools combine convenience with relevance, creating a better shopping experience. Customers feel understood, and conversion rates improve.

Retailers also face pressure to speed up backend operations. AI has an important role in demand forecasting, replenishment planning, and supplier coordination. The AI in the supply chain market, already valued at $7.15 billion in 2024, is expected to grow steeply over the next decade. Smarter inventory flow prevents overstocking and out-of-stock situations. Retailers gain better margins and customer satisfaction.

AI Applications in Retail

Retailers now apply AI across the entire value chain. From customer experience to logistics, AI supports faster decisions, improved accuracy, and better personalization. The range of use cases continues to grow, including product discovery, stock management, demand forecasting, and checkout optimization. AI simplifies the complexity of retail operations by automating routine tasks and generating real-time insights across every interaction. Lululemon, a Canada-based company, uses AI for predictive inventory, product innovation insights, and automated checkout experiences.

Inventory management also benefits from AI integration. Predictive analytics helps retailers avoid both overstocking and stockouts. Systems forecast demand by location, season, and customer profile. AI tracks sell-through rates, supplier lead times, and local trends. Adjustments happen in real time. Retailers respond quickly, reduce waste, and improve overall inventory flow. Supply chain AI already holds a market size of $7.15 billion in 2024 and is growing rapidly.

AI also powers visual recognition in physical stores. Computer vision systems identify product placement, stock levels, and customer movement. Retailers improve planogram compliance and detect shelf gaps automatically. Tools notify staff before items go out of stock. Layouts adjust based on how customers interact with displays. Data improves visibility and helps teams act faster. Trigo, an Israel-based AI company, shows how this works in practice. The company enables cashierless stores using AI-powered computer vision and sensors. Shoppers enter the store, pick items, and walk out. The system records purchases automatically. Retailers reduce queue time, cut staffing costs, and improve customer convenience. Accuracy increases, and theft risk decreases due to real-time monitoring.

Benefits of AI in Retail

AI transforms retail by making operations faster, decisions sharper, and customer experiences more relevant. The benefits span across functions, personalization, supply chain, merchandising, and customer engagement. Retailers that invest in AI gain measurable improvements in both efficiency and satisfaction. The technology simplifies processes that once required heavy resources and manual effort, allowing businesses to adapt quickly and scale confidently.

Inventory management becomes more precise. AI tracks stock levels, predicts demand, and automates replenishment across locations. Retailers avoid costly overstock and missed sales due to stockouts. Nextail, a company based in Spain, uses ML to optimize merchandising decisions. The platform adjusts inventory in real time based on sell-through rates, local demand, and historical data. Stores remain well-stocked and responsive.

Supply chain optimization adds further value. AI reviews logistics data to streamline transportation, detect delays, and improve warehouse planning. The global AI in supply chain market is growing rapidly, projected to reach $192.51 billion by 2034. Retailers reduce lead times, save on storage, and maintain service levels during peak periods. Operations run smoothly, even under pressure.

Customer service gains speed and consistency. AI-powered chatbots and voice systems handle common requests instantly. Shoppers track orders, start returns, and ask questions without waiting. Agents get involved only when needed. Support teams work more efficiently. Customer satisfaction increases because help arrives fast, accurate, and on the preferred channel.

Ethics of Retail

Retail AI ethics go beyond compliance. Customers want the expectation that businesses won't abuse the trust placed in them, treat their data responsibly, remain transparent, and achieve fair outcomes. AI can affect pricing, product visibility, and where promotional targeting happens. When there are no ethical rails or guidelines provided to AI and the people working with it, retailers stand to quickly lose customer trust and face widespread backlash. Responsible AI will instill customer confidence that it remains a responsible technology that creates value, without exploiting users or unduly influencing decisions. Tesco, a UK-based company, uses AI systems for inventory, loyalty data, and pricing.

A large source of ethical concern is how data is collected. Retail AI systems learn from a variety of data, including browsing history, purchases, and location. Customers need to know what data a retailer collects and how it is put to use. Customers' consents must be continuous consents, not simply blanket agreements. Privacy notices and the ability to opt out or restrict options serve to safeguard customers' rights and reduce unintended misuse. Ethical data practices create credibility over the long-term.

Transparency is arguably the most important ethical dimension. Customers need to know when AI is recommending a product, a promotion, or when they are interacting with a service. Potentially hidden AI decisions may diminish confidence. Ethical systems should have explainability features, or ways to show customers how decisions were made. The transparency keeps customers informed, and the teams that use the technology are responsible. Among customers, trust grows when confusion is addressed.

An example is provided by RELEX Solutions in Finland. RELEX has created AI tools for utilizing algorithmic planning and performance tools for optimizing inventory and supply chain processes. RELEX's systems are ethical because the AI can trace its algorithms at any moment in time to achieve transparency.

Surveillance concerns are rapidly growing, and this includes issues with stores that capture video with computer vision systems. Customer movements are tracked, their behavior and engagements are tracked, and an analysis is determined. An ethical retail system would obfuscate the customer and preserve the footage as a safeguard, and limit who the footage is accessible to after capture. Retailers should also let customers know the circumstances concerning where their movements will be tracked, and why. Being clear leads to transparency, reduces the risk of misuse, and protects the dignity of each customer.

Pricing algorithms must also maintain standards of fairness. AI systems make pricing decisions based on dynamic inputs of demand, proximity to the location of the buyer, and the behavior of the buyer. If there are no external rules placed on the input of decisions made, it could become discriminatory in pricing, much like digital redlining. Retailers must enforce rules that limit extremes pertaining to price and routinely checks on the behavior of models. Fairness adds much more value than any short-term profit realized from manipulation or taking advantage of the consumer.

Challenges of AI

AI continues to shape how businesses engage, operate, and grow. Despite its widespread attention, implementation remains a work in progress for many. The gap between potential and performance still exists. Businesses face technical, operational, and cultural challenges in deploying AI at scale. While some have moved forward, others struggle to align AI with real-world needs, budgets, and expectations.

Scalability stands out as a major issue. Many businesses start AI projects in isolated use cases, but few reach full deployment. Around 74% of companies report difficulty in scaling AI value across their operations. Pilots may show promise, but shifting from test environments to live systems reveals unexpected obstacles. Costs rise. Data misaligns. Results vary. Internal systems fail to support wider integration. Spectrm is a company based in Germany that addresses the integration issue by simply enabling companies to use AI-powered 1:1 across communication platforms. Their solution fits into existing workflows without having to re-engineer an entire technical stack.

Adoption gaps remain visible across sectors. In B2B, only 21% of commercial leaders report enterprise-wide AI deployment. Around 79% still operate at pilot or early implementation stages. Businesses face a lack of clarity on where and how to apply AI effectively. Use cases often remain limited to marketing or customer engagement, missing broader operational improvements. The value stays stuck in narrow functions. Espressive, a

U.S.-based platform, addresses this through specialized AI tools that support employee services. Their systems manage internal support tickets and simplify responses through structured workflows. By focusing on implementation, they reduce resistance and improve usability, two of the important barriers to AI adoption.

AI carries huge potential, but the challenges of successful deployment and adoption, and the barriers to trust and bitumen realization should be present in the organization's toolbox. The businesses that are defining the future will encounter many barriers, but those who understand how to deal with the barriers will be prepared and cautious to act and deliberately pivot. Trying to use AI is not just about the tools and technology; timing, teams, and transparency contribute to the success of AI.

CLOSING CASE: HILTON

Hilton has a long way to go on its journey toward using AI as part of their service strategy. As a true global hospitality leader with thousands of properties and millions of guest touchpoints, Hilton has to do things differently. At its heart, Hilton's service experience foundation includes consistency, personalization, and speed. Hilton employs AI to help add value to these core areas of its customer experience, without automatically removing the human element. AI systems and automation are a clear path to improved service.

As mentioned, Hilton integrates AI across multiple stages of the customer journey. Not only before booking, but also engagement before check-in, during, and after their stay, with AI tools consistently providing guests the best suggestions, quickest access to service, and reduced variability in the service process with a consistent service delivery. For example, Hilton's new chatbot "Connie" is a semi-autonomous virtual assistant that answers questions, provides directions, and even recommends local attractions. Connie has been built on IBM's Watson platform and integrates directly to Hilton property systems, so guests get the best, most timely answers without needing staff action first.

Personalization is also a continued primary driver of Hilton's AI strategy. Hilton can analyze booking data, guest preference data, in-room service and activity preferences, and loyalty-based customer behavior data to make individualized suggestions and recommendations. The types of rooms, services, and offers all change based on the guest profiles collected. Communications are adapted based on language preference, timing of communication, and the preferred communication style of the guest. Guest communications fit their journey, whether they are planning a stay or checking out. Their experience has become easy, smooth, and focused, and their expectations are aligned.

AI has also made its internal work operations identity better. Hilton uses machine learning models to generate demand forecasts, develop and manage pricing levels, and optimize inventory allocations. AI tools help teams strategically prepare for busy seasons, reduce the risk of booking errors, and respond to dynamic pricing. Revenue managers have enhanced visibility, and individual properties can align their resources and tactics based on real-time demand. Guests benefit from available options and assurance of commensurate value for pricing; the business benefits by maximizing occupancy and maximizing effective guest consumption of all inventory.

Two areas where Hilton can see immediate improvement are improving their performance time and automating front-of-house tasks. Virtual assistants can check guests in, assist with digital room keys, and help fulfill many simple guest requests. By using virtual assistants, Hilton lowers wait time and the impact on the front-desk staff's workload. As AI assists the process, employees can focus on more complex needs and higher-value interactions. The combination of these two stories (AI and human customer service) creates an experience that ensures more personalization without sacrificing efficiency.

AI will also help Hilton analyze feedback from guests faster and easier. With AI tools, Hilton's service teams can mine guest feedback from surveys, social media posts, and all service ratings to identify patterns. For example, sentiment analysis identifies guests who are less engaged, and notes any concern and ranking positively in terms of comments or tabled research on a specific property. Hiltons use this sentiment analysis and structure to make action decisions to change all aspects of guest preparation. They can focus training on communication needs, allocations of resources, and identifying specific needs to resolve particular requests. With specific guest requests identified, Hilton's action can increase guest satisfaction, and they can act sooner based on real needs.

Security and trust is also forefront draw. Hilton corporate is committed to data security onto of the governance around AI. Corporate has plenty of framework control over the use, transparency, or consent around AI data use. Guests control their preferred communication methods, while still using AI systems to check in, or transaction Aurora award point transactions and status requests. Hilton has been here for a long time and expects to bring guests back to Hilton stronger than ever, with the reliability of Hilton service today, with intelligence like AI backing it all.

Hilton's investment in AI is ahead and is truly tied to the future of service. They are enhancing personalization, machine learning driven efficiency, and scalability for all guests, with quotes on their experience. AI will never replace hospitality for Hilton, but it can help. AI is the future of all news in the travel and hospitality space. Once technology has cabled itself together, formed incredibly high expectations and offers, and defined a routine foundation backed with thoughtful, natural, and functional AI to enhance expectations and hospitality in six months, the same way Hilton has elevated the customer experience with their service innovation.

Discussion Questions

1 How does AI differ in its application between B2B, service, and retail industries?
2 Discuss how AI improves personalization in retail while maintaining consumer trust and data ethics.
3 What are the key ethical considerations when using AI for customer engagement in service marketing?
4 How can AI-powered predictive analytics change the traditional B2B sales cycles?

Assignment Questions

1. Select a company from either B2B, services, or retail and analyze its adoption journey using this chapter's framework.
2. Design an AI-based lead scoring model for a B2B firm. Explain how it improves sales efficiency.
3. Compare the use of AI in customer service at Hilton and another hospitality brand.
4. Evaluate how AI-driven ethics frameworks can be integrated into retail operations to build consumer trust.

MINI CASE: SEPHORA—REDEFINING RETAIL AND SERVICE WITH AI

Sephora, one of the world's leading beauty retailers, has revolutionized its customer experience by embedding AI across both retail and service operations. With thousands of stores worldwide and millions of online customers, Sephora uses AI to personalize recommendations, optimize inventory, and create a seamless omnichannel experience. At the heart of Sephora's strategy is its AI-powered recommendation engine. Through machine learning, the system studies purchase history, browsing patterns, and preferences to suggest products that best fit each customer's needs. The "Color IQ" and "Skincare IQ" tools analyze skin tone and type to recommend foundations and treatments accurately. These systems replace guesswork with data-driven precision, enhancing satisfaction and reducing returns.

AI also supports virtual try-ons via augmented reality. Using the "Sephora Virtual Artist" app, customers can test thousands of makeup products in real time. The system uses facial recognition and deep learning to ensure lifelike results. This feature bridges the gap between online and in-store shopping, providing an interactive and engaging experience.

On the backend, AI-driven analytics forecast product demand and manage inventory across stores. Predictive tools monitor stock levels and automatically reorder fast-moving items, minimizing out-of-stock situations. Sephora also employs sentiment analysis to evaluate customer feedback from reviews and social media. These insights guide product strategy, campaign timing, and service improvements. Sephora's use of AI chatbots and voice assistants further enhances service speed and consistency. The chatbots handle common queries, track orders, and suggest complementary products. Customers enjoy 24/7 assistance, while service teams focus on complex interactions requiring human empathy.

By integrating AI into both marketing and operations, Sephora has built a data-driven ecosystem that unites efficiency, personalization, and emotional engagement. The brand demonstrates how AI can elevate retail and service marketing without losing the human element. How does Sephora balance technological automation and human interaction to ensure both personalization and emotional connection in its customer experience?

Application of Concepts

Concept (Kotler Link)	*Brand Example*	*Application of AI*	*Benefits*	*Challenges/ Limitations*
AI in B2B lead generation	Salesforce Einstein	Automates lead scoring, ranking, and personalized outreach.	Improves targeting accuracy and conversion rates.	Data dependency and risk of algorithmic bias.
AI in service personalization	Hilton Hotels	Uses chatbots and predictive models to customize guest services.	Enhances guest satisfaction, speed, and engagement.	May reduce perceived "human warmth" in hospitality.
AI in retail operations	PepsiCo ("Pepviz" platform)	Aggregates sales and retail data for predictive inventory planning.	Reduces stockouts and improves collaboration with retailers.	High implementation and integration costs.
AI in service delivery	Ada (Canada)	Automates ticket routing and chat support for service firms.	Increases resolution speed and efficiency.	Limited capacity for emotional or complex queries.
Ethical AI & transparency	Yellow Messenger (India)	Builds privacy-first conversational AI systems for enterprises.	Builds trust, compliance, and long-term relationships.	Requires ongoing auditing and governance frameworks.

Key Terms

- Artificial intelligence (AI)
- Predictive analytics
- Personalization
- Conversational AI
- Machine learning (ML)
- Lead scoring
- Recommendation engine
- Computer vision
- Sentiment analysis
- Automation
- Data ethics
- Chatbots
- Omnichannel experience
- Predictive forecasting
- Ethical AI governance

Bibliography

Davenport, T. H., & Mittal, N. (2023). *Working with AI: Real stories of human–machine collaboration*. MIT Press.

Dwivedi, Y. K., Hughes, L., & Carlson, J. (2023). *AI-enabled customer experience in retail and services*. Springer

Huang, M.-H., & Rust, R. T. (2021). Artificial intelligence in service. *Journal of Service Research*, *24*(1), 3–18. https://doi.org/10.1177/1094670520902266

Mustak, M., Kaartemo, V., & Plé, L. (2021). Artificial intelligence in business-to-business marketing: A bibliometric review. *Industrial Marketing Management*, *98*, 258–272. https://doi.org/10.1016/j.indmarman.2021.08.008

Wamba, S. F., & Akter, S. (2019). Understanding the role of artificial intelligence in service innovation. *International Journal of Information Management*, *49*, 454–464. https://doi.org/10.1016/j.ijinfomgt.2019.07.009

10

AI MARKETING FOR A BETTER WORLD

Learning Objectives

1 Explain how AI contributes to ethical, purpose-driven, and socially responsible marketing.
2 Analyze the role of AI in balancing profit-driven and purpose-driven marketing goals.
3 Evaluate ethical concerns in AI marketing, including bias, data privacy, transparency, and manipulation.
4 Identify frameworks and principles—such as fairness, accountability, transparency, and inclusivity for ethical AI use in marketing.
5 Discuss real-world applications of AI in sustainable marketing through case studies.

OPENING CASE: COCA-COLA

Coca-Cola is using machine learning and AI to achieve both business growth and social good. Doing business in more than 200 countries globally, Coca-Cola has an immense footprint that extends beyond traditional capabilities. With machine learning and AI, Coca-Cola can be more than a beverage company; it also operates at the decision-making level, resource management, and limits the organization's impact. There is a continuous loop of analytics and decision-making where AI is a tool for Coca-Cola in making operations smarter, and enables efficiencies to better reflect socially responsible action.

By leveraging AI to build an agile supply chain, Coca-Cola, at the point of sale, has included demand volatility based on region, climate, and additional emerging trends associated with locations. Reducing excess inventory and mass transport waste, AI is a way for Coca-Cola to optimally enhance resource management, which can eliminate harmful emissions and organic waste. This not only saves Coca-Cola money comparatively, but it also reduces the demand for energy and other raw materials. The reduction in the demand for

DOI: 10.4324/9781003501862-10

and use of energy and raw materials will also benefit the raw materials manufacturers' supply chains—the carbon footprint will follow the complete manufacturing systems through the logistics.

On water conservation and more productive packaging experience, Coca-Cola also uses AI. The AI systems monitor factories and water usage, diagnose water inefficiencies, and suggest fixes. The use of AI was also used in testing AI systems to reduce plastic in materials used. Coca-Cola has previously developed plastic drinks bottle characters by maintaining the same quality drinks bottled with less plastic and no diminishment of responsiveness. While Coca-Cola can promote either the tangible benefits or accountable social leaning virtues, both its capabilities and schemes are aligned with efforts. No matter when considering practical applications, there are added use benefits.—The models for AI systems can also reduce the frequency of tests and trials, lead to better compliance, and be more responsive to speed.

Product development has increasingly become more focused. AI is summarizing social media postings, market trends, and customer service ideas and opinions into suggested flavor ideas by lodging them (he means incorporate them) into better taste, thus removing guesswork and detail from customer service (CS) teams. In launching new beverage flavor's, it was along these sorts of vectors, consumers' overall preference globally associated with each area were engaged uniquely throughout the trial phase, confirming the productivity has direction, more timely & efficient in maturity, by making better decisions regarding truly providing suitable product concept wishers. AI is shortening the product cycles/physical releases to better match consumer preference. It is identifying and reducing disappointment cycles from failed developmental concepts and, thus, resource waste.

AI is also being used by Coca-Cola as a way to interact and engage with customers better, with incentives that are more precise, relevant, and usable to the customer experience expectations. For example, it uses the AI functionality in a chatbot but also exhibits AI-driven content engagement to share suggestions and promotions through AI-reliant guidance feedback (with the developmental ask to men generate surveys later from the AI). Coca-Cola also relies on its AI data modeling systems to segment all its audience in real-time, identifying relevance in marketing automation with intelligent time relevancy of communication and reducing overpaying for irrelevant marketing priced differences. Collective consideration helps convey more people being efficient & using the best resources.

At the crux of all this, the use of AI enables broader dimensions of specificity, toward Coca-Cola's operational practices, led by its commitment toward anything potentially responsible business practice. AI not only provides targeted operational efficiencies, but the compounded advantages associated with such technology assist a significant number of aims that are not even seen or captured in the revenue sheet output. It enables enhanced efficiency while wasting fewer resources. Coca-Cola's commitment toward AI is a worthy discussion for many businesses, especially larger organizations with significant operating footprints. It highlights the notion that AI can build a bridge of community trust from cost-effective business practices that are socially smart and socially responsible, offering that the two do not have to be mutually exclusive. Although the change may seem insignificant, they are currently defined as a place of what can happen in the longer term.

Using AI to enhance operational, engagement, and marketing capability is not only about automation or profit return. For businesses like Coca-Cola, it is about being smart with resources, people, and business intelligence for all types of integrated skills. The public relations (PR) added incentives for harnessing AI in supporting resources, which opens unique doors for businesses that can describe eco-efficient ways to reduce some environmental outcomes, lessen gaps in supply flow losses, and act intentionally to continuously meet their consumer feedback. Such activity is exactly how to develop a better business that is dynamic and fast, but also responsible for others and assures sustainability for the future.

Introduction

Artificial intelligence (AI) has moved beyond theory and early trials. It now drives decisions, processes, and strategies across industries. Businesses are not just exploring AI; they are actively adopting it to stay relevant and efficient. The shift is happening fast. AI has an important role in shaping how companies interact with customers, manage operations, and plan for the future. The pressure to adopt AI is no longer optional. It has become a main part of modern business.

Top businesses have already made AI a priority. Around 91% report ongoing investments in AI. That signals a long-term view, not short-term interest. The trend is not limited to big firms either. In 2022, 35% of all organizations used AI in some form, an increase from the year before. Those numbers will keep rising. As AI tools become more accessible and results more measurable, more companies are expected to follow the path.

AI in marketing goes beyond automation. It brings logic, speed, and precision to brand communication. Companies can now act on real-time feedback, test ideas quickly, and scale outreach without losing personal touch. The shift marks a new phase in business thinking, where intelligence, not just scale, drives success.

Increased Significance of AI in Marketing

AI has begun to disrupt how marketing works. Previously, marketing was often a process of analysis and guesswork to inform a marketing action. Marketing campaigns had ingrained patterns, inherently long feedback loops, and advertisers trudged through arbitrary execution timelines. AI allows marketers to anticipate what consumers will do while observing an authentic, acute understanding of real-time consumer behavior. That's powerful; being able to understand and apply real-time consumer insights to refine messaging, read patterns, and respond to evolving circumstances creates space for sharper targeting and more efficient campaigns. Marketing is foremost less about how much messaging a company can push through marketing automation and is increasingly focused on relevant timing and thoughtfulness when responding to the consumer and their needs.

The rise of digital platforms only accelerated the necessity for smarter marketing tools. Otherwise, a marketer's job is to plot how customers engage brand interactions across multiple channels—websites, apps, emails, and social media. Comprehensively mapping those interactions, let alone managing them manually, required more representative control than words provide. AI provides companies the opportunity to put order around that complexity. Ultimately, AI tools provide a clearer sense of the larger data sets companies can work from; AI will do this faster than a marketer ever could. A marketer can confidently support decisions and pull their teams around factual outcomes opposed to what may have happened in the past. It is impossible to have bad outcomes when a company can illustrate how and why favorable outcomes occur and have significantly lower costs of doing so.

The Salesforce platform also helps businesses transform their strategies. It identifies gaps, detects rising trends, and points out missed opportunities. Teams can act faster and test new ideas with confidence. The learning loop improves with each campaign. Feedback from one step helps improve the next. Over time, this builds smarter marketing systems that adapt rather than follow static rules. That brings both consistency and improvement without raising the workload.

Purpose

Currently, the purpose of AI has expanded in marketing. Companies are using AI for more than making sales. It helps companies align their effectiveness with responsible business practices. Now, the purpose is more about creating long-term positive value for customers and providers alike. The foundation will share ethical engagement, sustainable growth, and strategic communication. AI helps companies realize these objectives without operational or cost burdens. The technology enables speed, but it also keeps companies moving in the right direction.

Adobe's tools now even save time for creative teams by automating boring deliverable/repetitive activities, providing more dedicated time to focused content creation. Approaching dedicated time on meaningful ideas is possible without valuable time being wasted by tensions in the bottlenecks created by marketers having to execute plans. Purpose-driven marketing requires brands to hold themselves accountable for data usage, rather than purity. AI does help in compliance management with the new rules. AI in marketing can.

Defining "Better World" in the Context of Marketing

Marketing now carries more weight than just boosting visibility or driving sales. As customer expectations shift, brands face pressure to act with more responsibility. People want companies to add value beyond products. They look for fairness, purpose, and a sense of shared progress. In this setting, the idea of a "better world" means creating business practices that support people, communities, and the environment, all while staying commercially strong.

Customers also see the positive side of AI. Around 40% believe AI improves their lives. But they place trust only in companies that apply AI responsibly. Around 72% expect organizations to use AI in ethical and transparent ways. Meeting those expectations forms the main part of what a "better world" means in today's marketing context. Brands that balance growth with care earn loyalty, trust, and long-term support.

Societal Well-Being as a Marketing Goal

Marketing today has a larger role than just promoting products. Companies now use marketing strategies to support social goals and address real-world problems. The idea of societal well-being has entered the mainstream of many brand strategies. AI helps turn that goal into action. Companies use AI to understand needs, reach underserved communities, and offer meaningful solutions. The approach combines commercial focus with a responsibility toward people and communities.

Customers expect more than just good products. Around 80% of shoppers believe brands must use AI ethically. That includes using data for good, avoiding biased content, and targeting with care. When companies meet those expectations, they help reduce digital harm and raise the quality of engagement. That builds trust, improves reputation, and creates space for long-term relationships. Ethical use of AI directly supports broader well-being goals.

Companies also look inward when setting marketing goals. Around 95% of employees think businesses should benefit all stakeholders. That includes workers, customers, suppliers, and communities. Marketing efforts now reflect that mindset. AI tools help companies identify gaps, study social issues, and craft campaigns that respond to those concerns. In doing so, they connect more deeply with audiences and bring value beyond transactions.

Warby Parker offers a strong example of using marketing for social impact. The U.S.-based eyewear company uses AI-powered virtual try-on tools that make shopping easier. At the same time, the company runs a "Buy a Pair, Give a Pair" program. For every pair of glasses sold, another goes to someone in need. This model connects AI-driven convenience with a real, measurable contribution to global vision access.

Profit to Purpose-Driven Marketing

Marketing now moves from chasing only profits to supporting broader purpose-driven goals. Brands today focus on long-term value instead of short-term wins. Customers expect companies to contribute to environmental care, fair labor, and honest business. AI has an important role in helping companies achieve this shift. It adds clarity, efficiency, and real-time feedback, allowing marketing strategies to support both performance and purpose without losing pace.

Companies no longer treat purpose as a side goal. Around 95% of employees believe businesses should benefit all stakeholders. That view shapes how marketing functions. Brands now design campaigns that reflect social and environmental commitments. AI tools help manage the balance between customer needs and ethical standards. By using AI to predict trends and segment audiences, companies avoid waste and offer more mindful solutions.

Patagonia shows how purpose-led marketing can work in real settings. The U.S.-based outdoor brand uses AI to personalize product suggestions. The system studies customer behavior and recommends items that match needs while discouraging unnecessary purchases. This strategy supports responsible consumption. Patagonia combines AI-driven personalization with a clear message: buy only what's needed. That builds a unique brand position focused on care over excess.

Concept of Marketing for a Better World

Marketing for a better world has an even broader intent than brand or business growth. The ultimate goal of better marketing is to improve lives while building mutual relationships with customers. Organizations are increasingly using AI, not just to sell, but to inform, direct, and positively influence healthy choices. Marketing channels can be better channels for positive change. That can take the form of financial literacy, more sustainable behaviors, responsible communication, and data transparency, all with intelligent tools that can help feed strategy and impact.

Role of AI in Achieving

AI has a primary role in helping marketing evolve toward more thoughtful and purposeful outcomes. Brands now rely on AI not just for speed or cost reduction, but to improve how they connect with people. Smarter tools bring clarity to complex data, support better planning, and improve content relevance. The focus has shifted toward creating meaningful interactions. AI powers that shift by making campaigns more responsive, ethical, and efficient.

Digital platforms dominate how people consume content today. Over 3.96 billion people use social media globally. Each user interacts with multiple platforms, spending an average of 143 minutes daily. That creates constant pressure on brands to remain visible and relevant. AI supports that demand by helping marketers identify the right moments, messages, and formats. With AI, marketing becomes more in sync with attention patterns and user preferences.

Customer service also benefits from AI-driven tools. Around 24% of marketers consider AI most helpful in handling service tasks. Chatbots, voice assistants, and virtual support reduce delays and increase satisfaction. These tools solve problems faster while freeing up human teams for higher-value work. The improvement in service experience directly shapes customer trust and brand loyalty. AI handles scale without reducing quality.

Marketing now depends on AI to function with precision and purpose. From data sorting to content delivery, every step gains speed and direction. Brands that use AI well reach wider audiences, reduce waste, and support more meaningful engagement. The role of AI has moved from supportive to primary.

Overview of AI Application in Marketing

AI today plays an essential part almost everywhere in marketing. From content and campaign planning to customer-facing communication, AI platforms and tools add efficiencies and amplify results, allowing brands to leverage AI to evaluate user habits, anticipate trends, and deliver appropriate messages personalized to users' behaviors in moments of need. AI platforms mitigate the randomness from marketing messaging and enable marketing teams to adopt much faster operations and take more thoughtful actions; this results in faster execution, more relevant content, and better decisions about the resources available in a specific marketing context.

How AI Can Drive Personalization, Efficiency, & Social Value

AI offers marketing more than growth: it supports personalization, improves productivity, and creates social impact. Brands have AI available at their disposal to create personalized experiences that not only fulfill the individual needs of their customers effectively but are also more tightly aligned to less wasteful and more thoughtful business practices. These

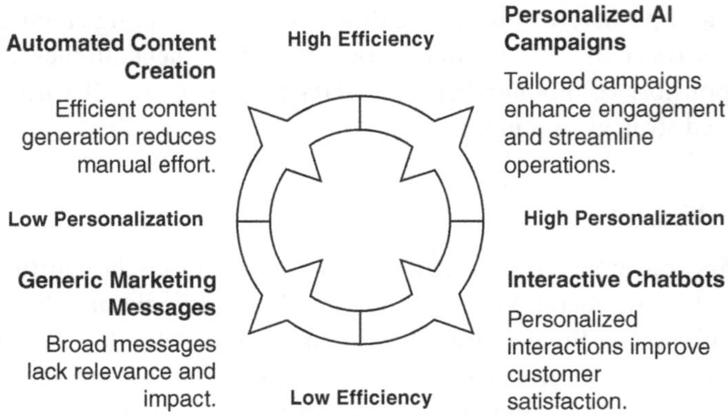

FIGURE 10.1 AI's impact on marketing.

tools are enabling brands to figure out what customers truly want and how to connect with them meaningfully, while also giving companies the opportunity to align with social causes that influence messaging, behavior, and action to create more responsible communication/activism (Figure 10.1).

Ethical Considerations in AI Marketing

AI brings major improvements to marketing, but it also introduces serious ethical concerns. Customers want brands to act responsibly with data, communication, and technology. Trust becomes harder to earn when people feel uncertain or left out of decisions. AI tools can improve speed and personalization, but without clear safeguards, they may cause damage to brand credibility. Ethical concerns now shape how AI-powered marketing must operate.

Privacy ranks among the top issues. Around 63% of consumers worry that generative AI may compromise personal data. Many users remain unsure of how their information gets used or stored. Only 56% trust retailers to protect their privacy when AI tools are involved. These numbers show the gap between customer expectations and current practices. Responsible brands must close that gap through clarity, control, and choice.

Business risks have also increased. Around 47% of organizations reported at least one AI-related consequence in 2024. Mistakes in targeting, bias in content, or breaches in privacy can harm reputation and customer loyalty. Around 92% of professionals agree that companies need to reassure users about data use. Ethical marketing now demands proactive communication, strong data policies, and internal training.

Marketing built on AI must balance innovation with responsibility. Brands that act with care, stay transparent, and protect users will gain a stronger, more lasting position. Ethics is no longer optional; it shapes the future of how AI fits into marketing.

Bias & Discrimination Algorithm

AI Systems are generally a distillation of the data they are fed to produce outputs on reality. If bias contaminates that data, you can devalue and misrepresent people. As marketing teams, you may experience brand issues when you create AI algorithms that reinforce stereotypes or ignore audiences that are not uniform. For example, any bias in AI generally destroys brand reputations, and then we all get notions about equity, worth, and worthlessness. When coding with AI tools, fairness and accuracy should be regarded in advance of and in tandem with coding, and more importantly, through a culture of fairness across marketing teams.

There are many variations to the bias that comes from marketing algorithms. Targeting might ignore an entire demographic pyramid (e.g., ethnic group), the content can overrepresent one demographic while completely ignoring others, and there are several voice and face recognition tools that "may" do worse based on skin tone, and more specifically on gendered differences. They cause reduced trust and ensuing reach into audiences. To provide legitimacy to fair and ethical protocols for marketing, teams ought to take the time to update, modify, perform a performance review, and manage the performance of the AI tools that they are utilizing.

AI systems will continue to be a reproduction of social patterns that have already entrenched themselves in the original data. If there is an endless reservoir of past marketing content that is overrepresented, the algorithm will act, often without any direction. Without a lot of mediation, AI will merely strengthen a bad habit. In this light, marketing campaigns cannot hope for DRP (Diversity, Representation, or Participation). Organizations in marker need to be engaged with the data inputs and then not simply use the output but consistently check for unintended disparity in the outputs. This legacy activity helps to eliminate some of the "extractive" bias we all have and create a better and fairer space for customers to exist in.

Gillette is a modern example of creating a systemic way to handle these issues. One of the personal-care brands scoped out an AI-supported marketing campaign system on inclusiveness. They included diversity demographics, including the transgender demographic, as part of their intent to respect everyone who recognizes an identity. The brand spent considerable leverage of AI to audit their gaps of representation and define their content. In fairness, the team aided the AI to consider their sources of diversity and not only the algorithm narrating what was most prevalent.

Gillette's campaign leverage is a solid example of decision-making enacting action, versus simply stating intent. AI will confirm bias, or it may reflect an intent not replicate bias in it; it is all in the direction. In these instances, once marketing teams find a way to educate AI based on creative intent, commitment, or moral commitments due to the value-led culture of marketing, it generates some degree of fairness, accuracy, and inclusiveness. Organizations that can square up and leverage the fight against discrimination do it so by creating algorithms, developing a better connection with the people and contributing to a better digital world.

Consumer Privacy & Data Ethics

AI in marketing depends heavily on data, making privacy and ethics a main concern. Brands collect, analyze, and act on user information to personalize content and improve engagement. Without strong privacy safeguards, this approach can lead to misuse, mistrust, or legal consequences. Ethical handling of data builds trust, strengthens brand credibility, and protects user rights. As AI grows more advanced, clear boundaries must guide how data is gathered and used.

Consumer trust in AI remains uncertain. Around 63% of users worry that generative AI may harm personal privacy. Many still doubt whether companies can protect sensitive data during AI-driven processes. Only 56% believe retailers can guarantee data safety with these tools. These concerns reflect a growing need for transparency. Users want to know what data gets collected, how it is used, and whether it remains secure at every stage.

Many users are still unaware that they are engaging with AI. While only one in three think they are using AI-backed platforms, the actual study reveals that 77% are using them. This knowledge gap increases the chance of perceived deception. Confusion arises when brands do not specifically state where AI has a role in their engagement and where the ability to manage personalization settings is located. Ultimately, ethical marketing should be driven by informed choice, not clandestine automation. Clear and concise privacy labels, consent dialogues or pop-ups, and opt-outs will help disambiguate confusion.

Unilever acknowledges issues around privacy and the ethics of data as outcomes of its retail media networks. Brand marketing relies on targeted, real-time marketing based on the customer data it uses in its campaigns, but also takes into account consumer data privacy. The company is considerate about consent protocol and data overcollection, and ensures it avoids negotiating irrelevance with the sensitive data of its customer base. Ultimately, the system is a means to ensure user data is inherently designed to support value delivery and not exploitation.

AI is powered by data, but ultimately it is driven by values, so value alignments dictate what the data can be used for and how users consent to using that data. Unilever has built a strategy to show that privacy-driven personalization can scale. These provide user options to limit exposure while still creating relevant and helpful experiences for the consumer. AI can be a force for good, advancing not just speed and profit, while marketing can move toward fairness, safety, and long-term residual value. AI becomes a tool for good, not just speed or profit. Marketing then moves toward fairness, safety, and long-term connection.

Transparency & Explainability of AI Models

AI models shape how marketing works, but they often operate behind layers of code and automation. Without transparency, these models can confuse users, mislead teams, or produce biased outcomes. Explain ability becomes essential for trust. Brands must ensure that marketing teams understand how AI systems make decisions. Customers also deserve to know how their data influences outcomes. Clear rules, visible logic, and human oversight must define the use of AI in marketing.

Lack of explain ability leads to risk. Around 47% of organizations reported at least one AI-related consequence in 2024. Errors in targeting, tone, or placement often trace back to unclear model behavior. When teams don't understand why a system works a certain way, they struggle to adjust or improve it. That creates gaps in accountability. Strong explanatory ability helps identify issues early and improves both performance and safety.

Unilever's model includes regular audits. The company checks AI outcomes for consistency, accuracy, and alignment with ethical goals. These checks detect unintended bias, content issues, or user experience problems. If a model behaves unpredictably, the team can adjust inputs or change how the system weighs factors. Explain ability supports correction. Without it, errors go unchecked and risks grow.

Responsible Use of AI to Avoid Manipulation

AI offers marketers the potential of influence at scale. With that potential comes power—a responsibility to protect users from manipulative practices. Manipulation using AI in marketing is eroding trust, and trust is essential for long-term relationship building. AI systems can exploit vulnerabilities, personalize too much, or drive impulsive behaviors. Don't forget that if consumers feel fooled, misguided, or trapped, consumer confidence dips. Brands focused only on immediate conversion could lose reputational momentum while seeing a short-term return. Practicing ethical marketing, even though AI creates clarity, balance, and honest communications—values that yield loyalty and reduce regret.

So, as an example of responsible AI marketing, we can point to Pedigree. The pet food manufacturer recently announced a set of AI campaigns organized around education rather than manipulation. There were no hard-core promotions; campaigns were driven by awareness and understanding of pet care, nutrition, and responsible ownership. While the AI campaigns would record behavior and user interests, the messages were dog-welfare-centric. The goal of these campaigns is to educate and inform, not pressure into nonessential purchases.

Pedigree's AI directive advances content in a personalized format but only where ethical lines are not crossed. Users receive tailored articles focusing on things like care and products based on their actual needs and recognize that there is no pressure or persuasive messaging in the tactics. Pedigree avoids urgency creators, triggering fear, or overlooking the experience of both the pet and the pet owner. Pedigree is earning user attention, user engagement, and recognition through helpfulness, not through manipulation.

Presenting guard rails keeps brands responsible. All AI tools must apply administrative restrictions that convert and limit targeting related to sensitive characteristics. Marketers are also responsible for testing messaging with regard to tone and intent. Companies are encouraged to implement feedback loops as well, for users to identify problems or opt out altogether. They would be sporting ideas of safer marketing, and losses can be mitigated over time if planning a full-scale campaign.

Frameworks & Principles for Ethical AI

Brands create systems with stability by considering an ethical framework. Their practices adhere to it, monitor consumers' perspectives, and adjust, iterate, and continuously experiment to avoid unintended consequences. Auditing becomes a part of the workflow. If issues arise, they relate to intent, not operating based on established data patterns. These are the practices that minimize risk and build consumer trust. Ethics move from abstract consideration to concrete practice when they are in a workflow; they emphasize being modeled by their leadership every day.

AI for Good—UNSDGs & Alignment with Societal Values

AI applied to marketing can support wider social objectives. AI can promote equity, justice, education, care for the environment, and health when aligned with the classic United Nations Sustainable Development Goals (UNSDGs). For brands, it provided a framework for generating value that lies beyond financial profit. AI tools facilitate this through enabling more empowered, accurate, targeted, and values-driven marketing. Brand and purpose are linked through commitment, and AI aligns itself with societal goals and objectives.

Aligning with brand and societal values strengthens relationships and connections. Many consumers expect brands and companies to stand for something and create leading brands as social catalysts. AI can be used to listen to what consumers, critics, and culture demand from marketers; AI is adaptive and responsive. Real-time, relevant content timed with social currency creates greater and more trusted engagement. When values align with messages, and messages align with actions, consumers respond. AI's data insights strengthen this connection through the use of volume, velocity, and analytical pull-through.

A notable example is Ben & Jerry's, which demonstrates this alignment in practice. The U.S. ice cream brand embraces AI to power many of its marketing campaigns that champion social justice; examples include racial equity, climate action, and economic fairness. The brand strives to ensure that AI is augmenting and not the arbiter or decision maker for their campaigns. The brand's human teams make decisions on content and course of direction, while AI is used to optimize timing, placement, and personalization.

Human Centered AI

Human-centered AI makes people the leading decision maker technology. In marketing, this simply means that AI is only used as AI, with the purpose, to express human values, support well-being, and create trust. Essentially, a brand shifts its perception of the user from being data to being a person with rights, needs, and expectations. Human-centered toward representation and enabling fairness, transparency, equity, and inclusion, and meeting business key performance indicators and intersectional social responsibility.

Human-centered AI and design requirements start with intention. Businesses must be clear as to how technology will be used to meet human needs. For example, how to create informed choice minimize harm and avoid unjust bias? To the best of our knowledge? AI must enhance human well-being, not manipulate it. In marketing, this translates to no intrusive personalized messaging, exploitative content, or selective profiling. Everything that it does should be filtered through the purpose lens.

Human-centered AI implementation will also require strong feedback loops. Users must have areas to report into, to provide sense-making, interrogation, and influence their relationship with AI. A brand benefitted in listening and establishing clear channels. What has become more significant is explainability and the user's ability to manipulate, monitor, and interact. The marketing team creates relevance and also acknowledges autonomy, which enables shorter and better relationships.

Human-centered AI lines up with what is becoming increasingly expected by the public. Users want organizations that care about their needs, not just the speed of response. Similarly, their expectations and preferences are constructed by the same four constructs of transparency, fairness, and empathy, which also balance against quality and cost. AI has allowed companies to see pathways, as long as they are committed, consistent, and intentional. Ethical systems promote trust, reduce risk, and provide meaning for users across their lived experience.

Principles: Fairness, Accountability, Transparency, & Inclusivity

Fairness is about unbiased systems. AI systems are built on their data. If AI systems are trained on data that excludes certain groups of people or normalizes undesirable stereotypes, then the system will continue that practice. Brands will need to monitor and make adjustments to their advertising campaigns. Fairness requires data sets that are inclusive, targeting that is balanced, and content that represents the diversity of consumer identities, voices, and expression. All users are worthy of equal respect, equal visibility, equal access to appropriate messaging—regardless of their background, identity, or preferences.

Inclusivity means that the campaigns represent the diversity within the target audience. Many AI systems work better on their dominant groups, if they work at all, unless the teams take care to correct for that. Inclusive design includes the training of the systems to see, recognize, and support all identities, voices, and expressions. Inclusive content connects with users in ways that are much deeper and representative of modern life and expectations. Marketing becomes the mirror of the world in which we live (it is not filtered or limited).

Google uses "fairness," "accountability," "transparency," and "inclusivity" through the AI-powered marketing tools they create and deploy. Google works on building systems that promote representation/diversity, avoid discriminatory patterns, and maintain some level of fairness. Despite any algorithmic balance that must be respected, Google's marketing campaigns celebrate people from various backgrounds. Internal policies establish accuracy for training, testing, and monitoring the AI models team members use. Inclusion will be a result of a functioning system, as opposed to an effort intended to correct the issues of greenwashing and/or equity washing.

AI marketing should have an ethical structure. Fairness, accountability, transparency, and inclusivity are processes within that ethical structure. When companies embed fairness, accountability, transparency, and inclusive processes into their systems, all marketing will be respected, accurate, and centered on humanity. Google's example shows that scale and ethics can grow together when backed by clear commitment and thoughtful design (Table 10.1).

Challenges & Barriers

AI adoption in marketing promises value but brings significant challenges. Many companies struggle to move from pilot projects to scalable solutions. Around 74% report difficulties in realizing consistent value from AI. Barriers range from unclear strategy to a lack of skilled talent. While the technology advances quickly, many organizations lag in readiness. Success requires more than tools; it demands alignment across people, processes, and mindset.

Most effective AI leaders follow the 10–20–70 rule. They invest 10% in algorithms, 20% in data and infrastructure, and 70% in people and processes. That breakdown highlights an important issue, technical solutions alone can't deliver results. Cultural resistance, unclear ownership, and weak workflows often block progress. Teams must rethink how they work, not just what they use. AI adoption must sit within a larger operational and leadership framework.

Comfort levels also vary across teams. Around 65% of C-suite executives feel confident with AI adoption. That number drops to 53% for engaged employees and just 30% for

TABLE 10.1 Ethical AI applied by Brands

Brand Example	*Ethical AI Strategy/Framework Applied*	*Key Principles Reflected*	*Success Example*	*Limitations*
Ben & Jerry's (U.S.)	AI for Good—Alignment with UNSDGs & Societal Values: Uses AI to design and time campaigns promoting racial equity, climate action, and social justice.	Fairness, accountability, social responsibility, transparency	Successfully aligned marketing with UN Sustainable Development Goals (SDGs), creating authentic and values-driven campaigns. Maintained human oversight to ensure messages remained ethical and socially conscious.	Risks of data over-reliance and message fatigue when advocacy messaging dominates; maintaining balance between brand purpose and commercial goals can be difficult.
Patagonia (U.S.)	Human-Centered AI: Applies AI for education-based personalization while prioritizing ethics, transparency, and environmental values.	Transparency, Empathy, Human Oversight, Sustainability	Built consumer trust and loyalty by using AI to inform and empower, not manipulate. Created consistent, purpose-driven communication aligned with environmental ethics.	Limited personalization flexibility due to strict consent policies and data minimalism; slower campaign scalability compared to competitors using aggressive targeting.
Google (U.S.)	Fairness, Accountability, Transparency & Inclusivity (FATI Framework): Promotes explainable and bias-tested AI marketing tools like "Why This Ad?" and Transparency Reports.	Fairness, accountability, transparency, inclusivity	Set global benchmarks for AI ethics and explainability. Empowered users with control over ad personalization and visibility into algorithmic decisions.	Faces ongoing scrutiny over algorithmic bias and representation gaps in AI systems, highlighting the need for continued auditing and human oversight.
Microsoft (Global)	Responsible AI governance framework: Embeds fairness, inclusivity, and compliance across all marketing and product AI systems.	Governance, accountability, fairness, data privacy	Developed a strong Responsible AI Standard ensuring compliance with global regulations (e.g., GDPR). Enhanced stakeholder trust through transparent reporting and ethical deployment.	Implementation complexity across global markets; high operational cost for continuous governance, auditing, and cross-regional adaptation.

disengaged ones. Managers show only 46% comfort. These gaps in understanding and trust reduce momentum. Without shared confidence, adoption slows, resistance grows, and results weaken. Clear communication, training, and support are needed at every level.

Sector-specific differences add another layer of complexity. Industries like manufacturing, healthcare, and information services show higher AI use, around 12%. In contrast, construction and retail report lower adoption, closer to 4%. These differences stem from digital maturity, data readiness, and operational flexibility. Marketing teams in slower-adopting sectors often face legacy systems, fragmented data, and budget limits.

AI in marketing works best when the foundation is strong. Organizations need clear goals, ethical guidelines, and flexible systems. Technology only delivers value when teams know how to apply it, monitor it, and improve it. Challenges remain real, but structure and culture can turn them into progress.

Data Quality & Availability

Data quality is one of the most important components for results from AI-driven marketing. If the data is not clean, consistent, and complete, even the best systems will not be able to produce useful results. Data is paramount to help an AI system produce good outputs from its models. If data gaps are happening because an AI system cannot access the right data sources for many different reasons, then brand targeting will fail, brand personalization will be weak, and brand performance measurement and/or reporting will likely be ineffective. Often, brands are simply unable to get their data under control to collect, consolidate, and maintain their data through the process of scaling reliably.

Data availability will also be a part of how AI actually functions. In many cases, companies as well as industries do not have structured datasets available for use, or more realistically, companies may have datasets that are not integrated. Inconsistent format/s, outdated data, or missing values are likely to hamper the potential of AI systems to work. One of the downsides of using an AI (at least a proof of concept, is the cost of the insight) is they become cheap based on the number of insights they deliver. If we are spending more time cleaning the data than we do analyzing it, we are not completely saving time. AI systems lose their ability to learn by developing patterns when they have no patterns or have incomplete patterns. Marketers are missing their targets because the AI system cannot ingest the complete context, nor find various links among various datasets.

Commercial real estate is a classic example of data quality. JLL is one major firm in the U.S. and identified these data issues and particular barriers, due to the variable nature and reliance on working with different commercial real estate businesses, decided to work on the data draw before moving on to the AI data-driven marketing systems. JLL needed to properly collect and analyze data for these systems to work. With the nature of the real estate category, they managed, recorded, and handed over numerous unstructured documents. JLL system could not scale beyond a base commitment, without developing and integrating proper data collection protocols, standardizing and integrating—before applying AI tool functionality at whatever mass scale it desired.

The company unified its data across locations, client interactions, and property types. AI systems could then analyze customer needs, market trends, and deal timelines more accurately. Marketing teams used these insights to build targeted campaigns, segment audiences, and automate outreach. JLL turned data clarity into a competitive advantage. AI performance improved because the foundation became stronger.

Many sectors face similar data issues. Lower adoption rates in industries like construction and retail reflect weak digital systems and uneven record-keeping. AI tools need complete customer journeys, transaction histories, and feedback loops to create value. Without those elements, systems produce weak signals. Marketing loses its sharpness, and personalization fails to connect.

Improving data quality also requires clear ownership. Teams need defined roles for data management, maintenance, and auditing. Automated tools help, but human judgment remains essential. Frequent updates, accurate tagging, and strong data policies build lasting structure. Marketing then benefits from faster feedback, stronger insights, and scalable content.

Trust also connects to data quality. Poor data leads to wrong assumptions and mismatched content. Customers lose confidence when messaging feels off. Clean data allows AI to maintain relevance and respect user context. That improves satisfaction and reduces opt-outs. Marketing success grows from consistent accuracy across every touchpoint.

JLL's approach shows that solving data quality issues is not optional; it's foundational. AI can only amplify what exists. Brands must strengthen the base before scaling smart tools. With reliable data, systems respond better, decisions improve, and campaigns become more meaningful. Data is not just a technical asset; it's the backbone of ethical, effective AI in marketing.

Governance & Regulatory Issues

The use of AI in marketing will lead to new requirements for governance and regulation. As newly crafted tools become increasingly sophisticated, the potential for misuse, bias, and privacy violations also increases. Therefore, it is the responsibility of organizations to set out a clear framework that directs the way AI targets. Governance includes establishing boundaries, assigning accountability, and ensuring that AI remains compliant with laws and values. Without sufficient governance, any AI deployment can create ethical gaps, legal challenges, and, ultimately, erosion of trust with the public.

AI regulations, if they exist, are somewhat inconsistent and often vary by jurisdiction and industry. Countries are beginning to develop rules that govern privacy, consent, accountability, transparency, and algorithmic fairness. Organizations that leverage marketing systems that violate these regulations risk fines, lawsuits, or reputational damage that cannot be valuable to anyone. Governance will help organizations develop sustainable systems that both comply with the law and evolve with the developing legislation. Governance also establishes internal norms that provide accountability and uniformity in thinking and behavior across multiple delivery teams.

Good governance is more than just checklists for knowing the legal items. Organizations need to establish frameworks that create distinct structures to provide monitoring of the marketing related to AI, and also to assess the possible intended and unintended impacts. These organizational systems will thrive when provided with leadership support systems, management attention, and integrated into daily operations. Guidelines will be good if they are simple enough to follow, but detailed enough to develop an understanding of the nuance and to address edge cases. Marketing-related teams require a support system that describes how the ethical principles apply to campaigns in the real world.

Microsoft provides an exceptional example of the governance of AI. Microsoft created a situated structure with formal ethics that guides its thought processes and AI. It creates a structure with principles for transparency, fairness, reliability, and privacy of the AI. Microsoft applies these principles to the abilities of the technical systems, as they apply to business operations. In the context of marketing, Microsoft wants to ensure that it is using the AI captured in the data at scale appropriately, while respecting consent, not coercing terms of use, and achieving consistency in its brand commitments.

This structured framework also requires a built automated approach to regularly evaluate and review policies involving AI processes. Microsoft will check its AI tools regularly to evaluate drift, bias, or intended and unintended impact. The human oversight is always primary. Teams will have been provided with training and tools, with assigned roles and accountability in relation to the management of Microsoft AI. This framework creates internal confidence and provides assurance to external users that the AI works under control, rather than in a fully automated phase.

Marketing campaigns are delighted to be aligned with this clarity. AI tools can recommend content, share formats, adapt audiences, and facilitate personalization, but only within framed acceptable bounds. This allows risk to diminish, and in some cases improve relevance. Microsoft accepts that it will only react to changes by consistently applying standards. Microsoft also publishes standards and reports on how it approaches the use of AI for reporting transparency.

Other brands are identifying that demands are also increasing to have similar applied practices. Governments seem to be applying regulations by the minute, therefore public expectations rise with technical implementation capability. Marketing gets the frontline of the user-facing aspect of AI. It naturally brings a higher sense of responsibility to the delivery of relevant, safe, and ethical conditions. Users expect an AI system to work fairly, keep their data secure, and treat people with respect. It is governance can forget about addressing these conditions.

Microsoft's practice shows you that structured frameworks are also reducing risk and improving consistency. Microsoft's brand is using the policies developed to its advantage, rather than restricting them. If governance holds up innovation, marketing is able to scale with confidence and control. Responsible use of AI relies on developments that provide structure, leadership, and clarity. In our quickly paced field, strong governance means your marketing can remain authentic to increase trust.

Organizational Readiness & Mindset

AI adoption in marketing depends heavily on organizational readiness. Tools alone cannot drive change. Success comes from mindset, structure, and internal alignment. Companies must prepare teams to understand, trust, and apply AI responsibly. That requires training, cultural shifts, and leadership commitment. Without these elements, even advanced systems struggle to show value. AI becomes effective only when people and processes evolve alongside the technology.

Readiness varies across roles and engagement levels. Around 65% of C-suite executives feel confident about adopting AI. That number drops to 53% for engaged employees and only 30% for disengaged ones. Managers fall in between at 46%. These gaps create friction.

Some teams move forward while others hesitate. Consistent adoption requires shared comfort and clarity at all levels. Leaders must set direction, but employees must drive day-to-day execution.

Mindset has a defining role in adoption. Teams that view AI as a threat resist change. Others who see AI as a tool for improvement act faster and with more purpose. Building this mindset takes time. Companies must communicate clearly, show real examples, and invite open discussion. The shift requires not just skill-building, but also belief in the value of transformation. Trust and participation grow when people feel involved and prepared.

The transition was driven by strong communication. The leadership team communicated a purpose for AI adoption. The leadership team communicated progress as it occurred, sharing the progress with the teams and celebrating progress once milestones were achieved. This helped maintain momentum and engagement throughout the process. More than a technical change, it was a systemic shift toward how the organization approached customers, growth, and new ideas. Toys "R" Us not only looked to integrate AI and digital technology into their retail business but also to engage and develop as a digital-first brand.

Being ready for change also means being prepared to fail well. AI systems perform to greater and lesser degrees of effectiveness and impact; if their performance isn't what a team expected, teams must see this opportunity to learn rather than consider it a failure. To look at failure as an established point of learning contributes to a growth mindset that uses experimentation, feedback, and incremental improvements to further develop ideas. Organizations that value experimentation, learning, and feedback develop teams that become flexible and capable as they coalesce around new and better behavior over time.

Toys "R" Us illustrates that organizational transformation is about a mindset and structure; after investing in the people and aligning organizational systems and processes, the company was able to move forward. Support for their change effort came in the form of AI; readiness was a critical part of that process. Lasting change is not just about buying or implementing new software; it's about changing beliefs around ownership and continuous learning. Organizational readiness turns ambition into action and enables businesses to make AI deliver on what matters most.

Balancing Commercial Goals & Social Impact

The use of AI in marketing needs to balance commercial gain and social value. Typically, companies want to grow revenue, expand reach, and retain customers, without facilitating negative social impact. Meanwhile, companies face increasing expectations to behave responsively. At a minimum, customers are looking for transparency, ethics, and consideration of social causes. AI can facilitate both objectives, but it needs to be designed and deployed with wow and care. Misalignment represents friction, and purposeful adoption can produce value in both forms.

Warby Parker illustrates how this can successfully work together in marketing. The eyewear brand balances social mission and AI-driven tools, continuously evolving new processes and services. For example, Warby Parker's AI allows their team to communicate transparently about their pricing, with clear messaging of their offers, and personalized user experiences, while positively feeding the inequities of affected communities through their Buy a Pair, Give a Pair mission. In this complex marketing environment, the AI dimensions allow Warby Parker to extend communications and reach, while the social mission allows them to influence all aspects of the content and intent.

Warby Parker is not predatory; they are adding value proportionate to the target audience, allowing their social mission to unleash marketing potential. Their systems utilize AI effectively to suggest frames that meet the user's style and fit, while also giving accurate representations of what the user receives in terms of product quality and care, which is of actual value to the customers. When the customer feels transparency, they value the invitation to make their own purposeful decisions. The customer feels acknowledged and respected as a person and not a sales opportunity. Their social impact initiative is part of the experience, rather than "added value."

Warby Parker has also ensured consistency in values between the company's current digital systems and the company's values. Their marketing teams are coached on annual guidelines around tone, intent, and ethical considerations of marketing data, etc. The AI systems operate under a range of rules defined by the company. Their systems will not do sensitive or predatory targeting. The company undertakes internal checks and priorities as teams review their equilibrium with ongoing user feedback in real time, and actual value for the users. The company will make changes and augmentations to its systems so they stay relevant to their users, according to a complex market landscape and ever-evolving social norms.

Balancing goals also means managing internal expectations. Leadership teams must align on how to measure success. Metrics like engagement, loyalty, and brand sentiment matter as much as sales. AI dashboards can track both commercial and social impact. Teams then get a full view of how their campaigns perform, beyond basic numbers. This approach supports smarter, more holistic decisions.

Warby Parker shows that AI can scale both purpose and profit. The brand uses intelligent tools not just to grow, but to grow right. Clear pricing, strong storytelling, and real social contribution create a model others can follow. Balancing goals does not mean choosing one over the other. It means building systems that support both, and letting values guide every step (Figure 10.2).

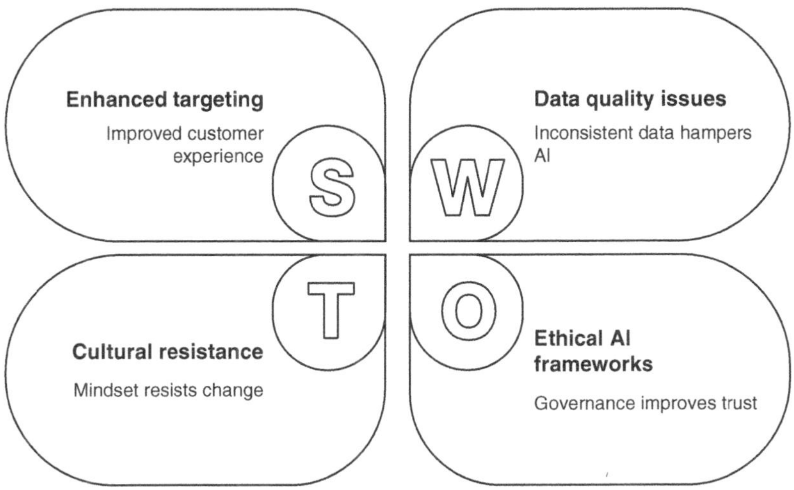

FIGURE 10.2 AI adoption in marketing: challenges and solutions.

Future Outlook

AI will continue to shape the future of marketing across industries. As systems grow smarter and more accessible, businesses will explore new ways to connect, create, and deliver value. Personalization, automation, and ethical practices will evolve together. Companies that align technology with responsibility will lead the way. Purpose-driven marketing, supported by AI, will gain more traction as customer expectations continue to rise.

Emerging channels will see rapid growth. The digital audio advertising market is projected to reach $12.16 billion in 2025 and $14.84 billion in 2029. AI will play a major role in shaping personalized audio content and targeting. At the same time, social media advertising will continue to expand, from $228 billion in 2024 to $256.5 billion in 2025. AI will help brands respond in real time, create custom content, and manage engagement at scale.

Generative AI will become more primary to innovation. Around 67% of top-performing companies already report strong value from using these tools. Brands will use AI to generate visuals, text, and campaigns with greater speed and control. Creative teams will focus more on direction and less on execution. AI will take over repetitive tasks, allowing more time for strategy and improvement.

Ethical marketing will also see stronger integration. Purpose-driven campaigns are expected to keep growing throughout 2024 and beyond. Consumers will demand transparency, respect, and relevance. Brands that meet those expectations with smart, respectful AI tools will gain stronger loyalty. The future of marketing will blend performance with principles, where intelligent tools support not only growth, but also meaningful impact.

Evolving Role of AI in Marketing for Social Goods

The evolving capability of AI is also helping with accessibility. Brands are now able to offer deeper, tailored experiences than differences in formats, such as language or visual design. The advancements within and from AI will eventually usher in the inclusion of users previously excluded. Through leveraging more deeply inclusive experiences, marketing has become more accessible, functional, and aligned with broader social values. Most importantly, AI adds reach without undermining empathy.

Purpose-driven marketing continues to rise in importance. Consumers expect brands to take a stand and, more significantly, act responsibly. Similarly, AI systems help companies deliver on that promise in ways that are scalable and decisive. When AI experience is used in personalization, it mostly entails the content of the messaging created in sales, which was considered going out to reflect value in the story. Data will assist users in anticipating what is important for consumers, but it does not tell them how to respond to issues. Agendas and values will ultimately shape outcomes over automation.

Emergence of Purpose-Driven Marketing

Marketing traditionally focused on features of products, along with promotions, discounts, and other incentives to capture consumer attention. Today, there must be a connection to global issues or causes that relate to some consumer aspect or, more importantly, something that it stands for. Purposeful marketing increases the value of a company to a consumer, moving beyond specific phrases or slogan statements. The intersection of marketing with authenticity, consistency, and alignment with values should not be treated lightly. Incorporating AI allows brands to identify significance in audience segments and build campaigns that resonate with audience motives and intentions. As relevance increases, so too does trust.

Brands are also using AI to support representation. As consumers become more aware and care more about diversity, inclusive marketing becomes more critical. AI systems identify under-representation and help target sectors and audiences so that businesses are communicating in ways that reflect the diversity of modern audiences. The inclusive approach not only connects to more audiences, but it also strengthens emotional connections. Effective purpose-driven campaigns become personal, informed by data, and driven by values.

There are brands that demonstrate how AI can support purpose-led strategies. Amazon has made purposeful marketing a focus across each of its selling channels. Amazon's marketing teams use AI-enabled platforms and processes, as well as some of Amazon's personalized engines, to deliver inclusive marketing across a diversity of communities. The personalization engines have the capacity to leverage significantly more targeting-outcome combinations while, at the same time, being relevant and respectful. The marketing teams, in addition to considering general consumer behavior or preferences, think about the context of the cultures and audiences. To them, AI is a strategy to deliver personalized content that communicates local relevance, timeliness, and significance while maintaining the scale benefits of a large organization.

Amazon has long embraced trust as a principle within its marketing strategy. While AI has assisted in being clear with recommendations and advertising, as well as in obtaining product reviews, trust is defined by a free account of how the recommendations and ads are targeted, and why consumers should believe the reviews without misleading them. An account that is ethical, bias-reduced, and freed from manipulation and exploitation develops trust through organizational accountability and honesty. These tools can balance managing the pace of constant environmental changes while providing clear accountability for brands.

Interpretation of AI Ethics

United Nations Educational, Scientific and Cultural Organization (UNESCO)'s concentrated consideration of flexibility and practice has a critical collaborative dimension. Organizations that partner with UNESCO receive additional resource knowledge, current and developing case studies, and updates on policy and practices. The umbrella framework aligns and demystifies ethical interpretations across continents and industries, including helping marketers consider what the identification of cultural sensitivities requires, how to facilitate algorithmic fairness, and sustain continued public engagement with dialogue. The overall value is a practice of ethics has a consistent aspect, and is justified by both policy and practice engagements.

Additionally, the practice of interpretation creates a form of internal consistency within organizations. All teams are working to the same ethical guidelines for a campaign, region, and media format. The Field leader sets a shared expectation and normalizes compliance with tools. Over time, as the marketing function matures, it is less reactive. Ethical alignment is not obstructive to performance but part of performance. The result is teams being able to make better decisions, support to reduce confusion, risk, and operate with integrity.

As AI systems develop and algorithms become more powerful, organizations need to remain agile in their interpretation of their ethical frameworks. Static outside of simple linear timeline restrictions, the dynamic nature of the tools and public expectations will never balance the expectations of the current ethical duties regime. Therefore, as a guideline, organizations should have frequent but regular reviews, let's say once a year, of their ethical operating framework. Similar to consultation with relevant regulators, and other appropriate professional my users and modern era experts in their industry. The review feedback loop will provide marketers the opportunity to frame their policies, and illuminate their ethical understandings, creating clearer direction (of practice), easier to achieve if the ethical guidelines are integrated into integrated planning and action (IPA) plans, purpose of ethical powers, improved reputation management, and censorship of backlash with lower risk.

Emerging Future Trends

AI in marketing continues to evolve, with several trends set to shape the future. As technology matures, new tools and methods will influence how brands engage audiences. Businesses will move toward systems that offer deeper personalization, greater transparency, and more interactive experiences. These trends will not only improve performance but also redefine how users experience digital marketing. Forward-thinking companies already explore these shifts and build readiness into their strategies.

Conversational AI is gaining strong momentum. Users prefer fast, direct interactions with brands. AI-powered chatbots and voice assistants offer 24/7 support and human-like communication. These tools help answer queries, recommend products, and guide users through purchases. As models improve, responses will become more context-aware, accurate, and intuitive. Brands that adopt conversational AI will offer smoother journeys and stronger customer satisfaction.

Voice search optimization is also becoming an important trend. More users now search using voice, especially on mobile and smart devices. AI helps brands understand natural language patterns and adjust content accordingly. Marketing teams optimize for tone, length, and phrasing, ensuring their content aligns with how users speak. Voice search strategies will expand reach and increase visibility in emerging customer segments.

Transparency remains critical as AI tools grow in capability. Customers demand to know how AI systems work, what data they collect, and how decisions are made. Ethical AI will focus on explain ability, consent, and fairness. Companies must provide clear answers about personalization engines, targeting methods, and content algorithms. Transparency builds trust and prevents backlash, making it a long-term advantage.

HubSpot demonstrates how to respond to these trends. The U.S.-based marketing and sales software platform integrates conversational AI and voice search tools into its system. Marketers use these features to create seamless, real-time engagement with users. HubSpot also emphasizes transparency by offering features that explain how AI works within its tools. That helps businesses stay informed while building trust with their audiences.

Ethical frameworks will become part of daily operations. Marketing platforms will offer built-in guardrails to ensure fairness, avoid over-targeting, and prevent misuse of data. Teams will receive automated suggestions on how to improve ethical alignment. These steps reduce risk and build more balanced strategies. AI then supports both performance and values without compromise.

AI integration will also reach deeper into content creation. Generative tools will produce text, video, and graphics faster. Marketers will shift toward directing strategy while AI handles execution. Personalization will become more dynamic, driven by behavior, context, and even emotion. As systems learn and improve, messaging will adapt in real time.

HubSpot's platform highlights how AI will continue to guide the next wave of marketing. Brands will focus on conversation, transparency, and speed, supported by systems that adjust instantly. The future points toward smarter, more interactive, and more human-centered marketing. Companies that prepare early will gain the edge. AI will no longer serve just as a tool; it will become a partner in shaping meaningful, measurable, and responsible engagement (Figure 10.3).

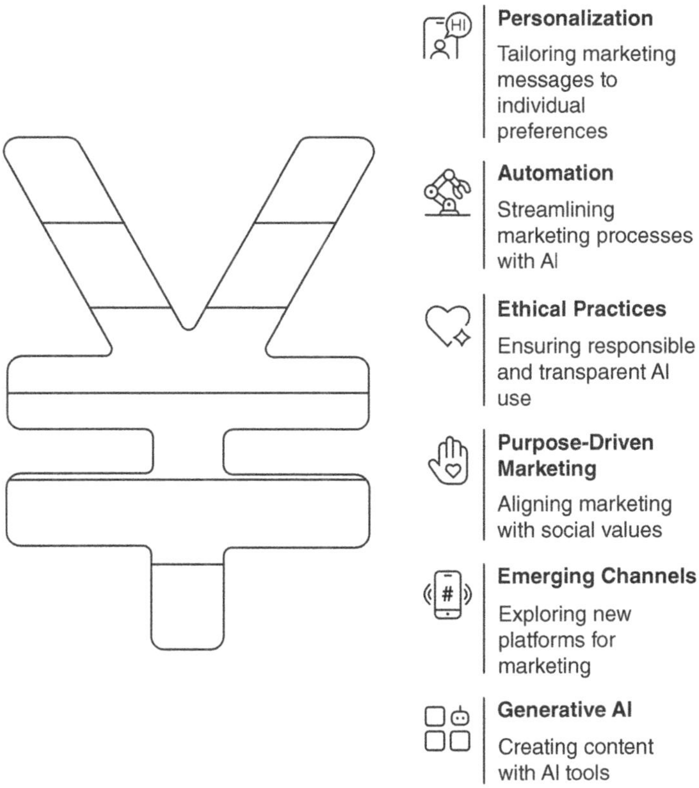

FIGURE 10.3 The future of AI in marketing.

CLOSING CASE: UNILEVER

Unilever stands as one of the most globally recognized consumer goods companies, operating across food, personal care, and household products. The brand reaches over 3.4 billion people daily through its wide portfolio. With a long-standing commitment to sustainability and social impact, Unilever has redefined how large companies approach responsible growth. That vision now includes the strategic use of AI to create both business efficiency and social value.

The company embeds purpose into every part of its operations. From ethical sourcing to climate action, Unilever builds its marketing and product strategies around values. Consumers expect brands to act responsibly, and Unilever responds by making that expectation part of its identity. AI now supports this shift by helping the company make better decisions, reduce waste, and create personalized, responsible customer experiences across markets.

AI is a great asset to Unilever in areas where there has previously been a limit to scale and complexity when precision of meaning is the goal. Unilever processes an enormous amount of consumer information in different countries, and AI tools analyze the information in real time to identify needs, anticipate behavior, and recommend content. Campaigns become relevant, targeted, and timely. Rather than broad strokes or one-size-fits-all strategies, AI recommends how Unilever can speak to people in ways that correspond to their preferences and values.

Unilever also incorporates AI in its retail media networks. These networks deliver real-time digital advertisements tailored to real consumers through partner platforms, while respecting data privacy regulations. Unilever designs these tools with ethical boundaries built into them. Consent, control, and transparency are the foundation of its digital advertising model. When customers receive personalized content, their data is secure. That structure creates performance and trust.

Unilever applies AI to lessen its environmental impact as well. It monitors energy use and supply chain emissions and recommends improvements with its tools. Its marketing campaigns also promote responsible consumption. AI helps Unilever to see trends around sustainable choices and allows the brand to elevate its eco-friendly product offering. Personalization enhances the narrative show consumers their options align with their lifestyle and environmental concerns.

The company conducts ethical audits on its AI systems across functions. Internal teams scan for bias, assess whether tools are fair, and use monitoring to evaluate content tone. They routinely audit AI systems to ensure they continue serving performance and values. AI exists in a framework governed by humanity and principles. The brand builds accountability into every aspect of decision-making, from campaign design to audience.

Unilever also emphasizes upskilling its teams to execute AI in a responsible and safe manner. Employees receive training on data ethics and privacy rules, and on AI tools. Employees develop the right skills to balance creativity and vision with responsibility. Marketing gets faster, and at the same time, more thoughtful and relevant. Every decision process is filtered by purpose, and this is supported by intelligent systems that have a ruleset to follow.

Unilever is an example of how to embody real change through the use of AI when it follows its values. Unilever combines global opportunity with local relevance, commercial growth with social consciousness. AI supports Unilever to work smarter, engage deeper, and act faster, while always remembering what matters most. That balance models a marketing design inspired by innovation that creates sustainability for people, planet, and progress.

Discussion Questions

1 How does AI shift marketing's traditional focus from profit to purpose?
2 In what ways can AI help brands like Coca-Cola and Unilever promote sustainability and social responsibility?
3 What are the major ethical risks associated with AI-driven marketing, and how can organizations mitigate them?
4 Should AI decision-making in marketing always require human oversight? Why or why not?

Assignment Questions

1 Select a global brand and critically assess how it uses AI for marketing and social good. Identify both opportunities and ethical challenges.
2 Develop a short AI-powered marketing campaign concept that aligns with at least one of the UNSDGs.
3 Compare "AI for Good" initiatives by two companies and analyze how each aligns with fairness, transparency, and inclusivity.
4 Evaluate the concept of "human-centered AI" in marketing using examples from Patagonia.

MINI CASE: SUSTAINABILITY AT IKEA DRIVEN BY AI

IKEA, which is a furniture retailer based in the world, has incorporated AI marketing and operations to facilitate sustainability and increased social impact. The AI-based programs in the company aim at optimizing resources, engaging customers, and being circular economy-oriented. The use of AI tools assists IKEA in making decisions based on the demand for a product and avoiding overproduction and waste. Machine learning algorithms are used to analyze logistics to reduce carbon emissions during shipping and warehousing, resulting in a quantifiable decrease in energy consumption.

Regarding marketing, the AI-based recommendation systems used by IKEA offer a product selection depending on the sustainability preferences of a customer. As an example, environmentally-friendly customers are given customized offers on recycled or eco-friendly products. Such individualization also encourages customer satisfaction, but also responsible consumption. AI chatbots also inform customers on the practice of recycling and sustainability, reinforcing the image of the brand as a purpose-driven brand at IKEA. IKEA is doing all it can to make sure that ethical practice is upheld through the use of strict data privacy and transparency provisions. Customers are able to see the use of their data and select an option to stop at any point. The marketing AI systems of the company are also continually audited in terms of prejudice and inclusivity, and communication is always respectful and representative of cultures.

The outcomes have been notable—the use of AI in sustainability marketing has resulted in increased levels of customer loyalty, better brand trust, and minimized operational waste. The success of IKEA shows that AI can contribute to both environmental objectives and business development. It gives an example of AI marketing to a better world, in which ethical innovation and customer interaction align with each other to produce a good social and ecological impact. The case of IKEA shows how the integration of AI can be human-centered, transparent, and sustainable to make marketing an environmental and social good.

Application of Concepts	*Brand Example*	*Application of AI*	*Benefits*	*Challenges/ Limitations*
AI for sustainable marketing	Unilever	Uses AI to analyze supply chain and consumer data to reduce waste and support sustainable production.	Promotes eco-efficiency, reduces environmental footprint, and aligns brand purpose with sustainability.	Requires strong data infrastructure and ongoing monitoring for accuracy.
Ethical & transparent AI use	Microsoft	Implements Responsible AI Framework to ensure fairness, accountability, and transparency in marketing applications.	Builds consumer trust and strengthens brand integrity.	High governance costs and complexity in ensuring compliance across markets.
AI-driven purpose marketing	Patagonia	Uses AI tools to tailor campaigns promoting environmental protection and conscious consumption.	Strengthens brand purpose and customer loyalty through authenticity.	Limited scalability due to niche, purpose-focused audience.
AI in social impact campaigns	Ben & Jerry's	Employs AI-driven sentiment analysis to align social justice campaigns with consumer values.	Enhances message relevance and engagement while promoting inclusivity.	Risks of misinterpretation or bias in sentiment data analysis.
Transparency & data ethics in AI marketing	Google	Publishes AI Transparency Reports and provides users with "Why This Ad" explanations.	Promotes responsible AI marketing and user empowerment through transparency.	Continuous challenge to balance personalization with privacy expectations.

Key Terms

- AI marketing
- Purpose-driven marketing
- Ethical AI
- Human-centered AI
- Transparency
- Accountability
- Fairness
- Inclusivity
- Data ethics
- Bias & discrimination algorithm
- AI for good
- UN Sustainable Development Goals (UNSDGs)
- Responsible consumption
- Explainability
- Societal well-being

Bibliography

Ben & Jerry's. (2024). *Using AI to promote social justice and sustainability*. https://www.benjerry.com
Coca-Cola. (2023). *AI and machine learning for sustainability and marketing efficiency*. Coca-Cola Company Reports.
Gillette. (2024). *Inclusive marketing and AI ethics in practice*. Procter & Gamble Communications.
Google. (2024). *AI transparency and fairness reports*. Google AI Ethics Portal.
IKEA. (2024). *AI for circular economy and sustainability in marketing*. IKEA Global Impact Report.
Microsoft. (2024). *Responsible AI principles and governance framework*. Microsoft Corporate Blog.
Patagonia. (2023). *Human-centered AI for sustainable marketing*. https://www.patagonia.com
Unilever. (2024). *Transparency and ethical data practices in AI-driven marketing*. Unilever Sustainability Reports.
United Nations. (2015). *Transforming our world: The 2030 Agenda for Sustainable Development*. United Nations.
Warby Parker. (2023). *AI-driven personalization with social purpose*. Company Impact Report.

INDEX

Pages in *italics* refer to figures, pages in ***bold-italics*** refer to boxes and pages in **bold** refer to tables.